NEW Junior Cycle Religion

A Question of Faith

The Educational Company of Ireland

Lori Whelan • Niamh McDermott

First published 2019

The Educational Company of Ireland

Ballymount Road

Walkinstown

Dublin 12

www.edco.ie

A member of the Smurfit Kappa Group plc

The paper used in this book comes from Managed Forests For every tree felled at least one new tree is planted

Editor: Deirdre O'Neill

Design and Layout: emc design

Proofreader: Kristin Jensen

Cover Design: Rochelle Lazaro & emc design

Cover Photography: Shutterstock: 13_Phunkod

Illustrations: Shirley Chiang

Photos: See pages 327–328 for list of all photo credits

Copyright acknowledgements

Page 58, 'Why Non-believers Need Rituals Too', *The Guardian*, 27 December 2013; page 52, Reverend Chris Bennett; page 69, Jewish Prayer, the Office of the Chief Rabbi of Ireland; page 238, 'Over 14,000 drivers caught on their phones in 2017 – and some were posing for selfies', Christina Finn, TheJournal.ie, 8 August 2017; page 297, 'Irish Muslims Condemn Ramadan Terrorist Attacks', Michael Sheils McNamee, 28 June 2015, TheJournal.ie; page 313, adapted from 'Bucket Puppies Just Two of Many', 4 January 2019, *Limerick Post*, used by permission *Limerick Post* and Limerick Animal Welfare; page 221, 'Where Do Your Values Come From?', Eric D. Brown; page 88, 'Enniskillen Bombing' adapted extract from *Revolutionary Christians who Live the Gospel* by Clare Richards, © 2000 Kevin Mayhew Ltd. Reproduced by permission of Kevin Mayhew Ltd. (www.kevinmayhew.com). Licence No KMCL210219/02; page 68, Cian Lynch, adapted from 'I Say a Few Prayers or Go to Mass and it Brings me to Level Ground', Marisa Kennedy, 8 October 2018, Pundit Arena.

06J21

This one is for my son, Conor, and my daughter, Holly, who bring a smile to my face each and every day. And, of course, Kieran. – *Niamh.*

Thank you, Donogh, for your continued love and support. Many thanks also to my parents, Margaret and Paddy, and my in-laws, Margaret and Denis. I appreciate and cherish all that you do for me. This book is for you all. – *Lori.*

Note from the Authors

The authors would like to sincerely thank all at Edco, particularly Martina Harford, Julie Glennon and Declan Dempsey.

Thank you to our editor, Deirdre O'Neill, for her hard work, patience and advice – we couldn't have done it without you.

The Authors

Lori Whelan and Niamh McDermott are both graduates of Mater Dei Institute of Education and are teachers of religion at Manor House School, Dublin, and Coláiste Choilm, Tullamore. They have worked as Associate Trainers with the Religious Education Support Service. They have also worked in the role of Chief Advising Examiners with the State Examination Commission at both Higher and Ordinary Levels. They devised and delivered a series of lectures in Dublin City University as part of the postgraduate diploma course in Religious Education.

CONTENTS

Introduction

Welcome to *A Question of Faith*.

This book will guide you on your journey through your three years of Junior Cycle Religious Education. Religious Education aims to help you develop as a person and will encourage you to think about, reflect on, question and find answers to some of life's biggest questions.

The Religious Education Specification has been designed in such a way that people of all religious faiths and people with a non-religious outlook on life can learn and grow as individuals. As we live in a multicultural society, it is important to have an awareness of our own beliefs and those of others.

It is also important to recognise the contribution that history and the Christian religion have made to the Ireland we live in today.

We all have to make decisions and choices around moral issues. Religious Education can help you to understand what your own values are and how they can help you in the decision-making process.

Most importantly, Religious Education will encourage you to be respectful and understanding of different beliefs and ways of living, both religious and non-religious.

Extra Resources

As well as this textbook, you will also have the support of *A Question of Faith Student Activity Book* and digital resources, which you will find on **www.edcolearning.ie**. There is also a *Teacher's Resource Book* that will help your teacher and provide extra activities for them to use. The activities will let you see if you have understood what you have learned and encourage you to think about how you feel about it.

The Religious Education Specification

There are three strands of learning on your course. They are:

Strand 1: Expressing Beliefs

Strand 2: Exploring Questions

Strand 3: Living Our Values

Each of these strands will be explained in more detail as you meet them in the textbook.

Three Elements that Support the Strands

You will also see the terms **Enquiry**, **Exploration** and **Reflection and Action**. These are elements that describe a set of skills and an approach to learning that are important to Religious Education.

These elements will help you to become more engaged with a topic you are learning about. They also encourage you to have dialogue and discussion about the topic. They will also allow you to think about how what you are learning can relate to your own life and to the lives of others.

Learning Outcomes

Each of the three strands has between nine and twelve learning outcomes. These are statements that describe the knowledge, understanding, skills and values you should be able to demonstrate after a certain period of learning. Each chapter in the book relates to one or more of these learning outcomes.

Learning Intentions

Every chapter has a set of learning intentions at the beginning. They will allow you to see what your teacher wants you to know, understand and be able to do as a result of the learning and teaching activities in that chapter.

Icons Used in this Text

⬡ Individual work activity

⬡ Pair work activity

⬡ Group work activity

⬡ Class discussion activity

⬡ Placemat

∞ Denotes a link between chapters and themes

❋ Weblink reference

⚬ Research activity

📖 Write the Answer

Digital Resources

The digital resources for *A Question of Faith* will enhance classroom learning by encouraging student participation and engagement.

To provide guidance for the integration of digital resources in the classroom and to aid lesson planning, they are **referenced throughout the textbook** using the following icons:

PowerPoint presentations summarise key themes and encourage class discussion.

A series of stimulating **videos** that allow students to observe religion in action.

A comprehensive list of **weblinks** as resource recommendations.

Song Sheet documents that explore the links between music and religion.

Teachers can access the *A Question of Faith* **interactive e-book** and additional resources at **www.edcolearning.ie**.

Wellbeing Indicators

The wellbeing of students is a very important element of the Framework for Junior Cycle. Wellbeing is about feeling well mentally, physically, emotionally and socially. When you have a strong sense of wellbeing, you can cope better with difficulties you may face and interact with others more positively.

At the start of each chapter you will see the wellbeing indicators that are relevant to the teaching and learning in that chapter.

ACTIVE

- Am I a confident and skilled participant in physical activity?
- How physically active am I?

RESPONSIBLE

- Do I take action to protect and promote my wellbeing and that of others?
- Do I make healthy eating choices?
- Do I know where my safety is at risk and do I make right choices?

CONNECTED

- Do I feel connected to my school, my friends, my community and the wider world?
- Do I appreciate that my actions and interactions impact on my own wellbeing and that of others, in local and global contexts?

RESILIENT

- Do I believe that I have the coping skills to deal with life's challenges?
- Do I know where I can go for help?
- Do I believe that with effort I can achieve?

RESPECTED

- Do I feel that I am listened to and valued?
- Do I have positive relationships with my friends, my peers and my teachers?
- Do I show care and respect for others?

AWARE

- Am I aware of my thoughts, feelings and behaviours and can I make sense of them?
- Am I aware of what my personal values are and do I think through my decisions?
- Do I understand what helps me to learn and how I can improve?

Key Skills

There are eight key skills that are part of the Framework for Junior Cycle. Using these skills will help you to develop the knowledge, skills and attitudes to face many challenges in today's world. They will also help you to take responsibility for your own learning. You will see some of the following key skills listed at the start of each chapter.

 **KEY SKILLS YOU WILL USE IN THIS CHAPTER**	• Being literate • Communicating • Managing myself • Being creative • Working with others • Managing information and thinking • Staying well • Being numerate

Literacy Library

As with other subjects, you may come across some challenging words and terms in your Religious Education course. Any difficult words or terms are clearly explained in Literacy Library boxes.

Classroom-based Assessments (CBAs)

CBAs are classroom-based assessments. Throughout your textbook and activity you will see the CBA paperclip icon beside some activities. This icon tells you that the skills you are using in these activities are similar to the ones you might use when doing your CBA and so could be very helpful. You will have one CBA in second year and one in third year.

1 : A Person of Commitment

2 : The Human Search for Meaning

The CBAs will provide an opportunity for you to:

- Research a topic of personal interest
- Use digital technology to learn and present your learning
- Analyse information and draw personal conclusions and insights
- Engage in learning beyond the classroom
- Make plans, set goals and evaluate your progress in achieving your goals
- Communicate clearly and effectively
- Collaborate with others on tasks
- Reflect on your learning.

STRAND 1
EXPRESSING BELIEFS

To have a belief means that you accept something exists or that it is true. It can also mean to have trust or faith in something or someone you cannot always see or prove.

In order to live a happy and meaningful life, people have always used their beliefs as a guide or a pathway. This is still the case today. Some people's beliefs are very strong and play an important role in their everyday life. Others may struggle to explain their beliefs.

Like our personalities, our beliefs may be similar to other people's but they are unique too. Some beliefs are based in or come from religions, while others have nothing to do with God/gods.

In this strand we will explore some common beliefs held by people throughout the world. To allow everyone to express or show what their beliefs are, it is important that we respect the beliefs of others, even if they are different from our own. We will look at how people express their beliefs through their culture or way of life.

Why, do you think, is it important to respect the beliefs of others?

LITERACY LIBRARY

Belief:
Core or central ideas of a religion, which give it its identity and often affect the lives of the believers.

Unique:
One of a kind, unlike anything else.

Respect:
Having a high regard for something and thus treating it with consideration.

Culture:
Ideas and customs of a particular people or society.

CHAPTER 1
The Five Major World Religions

SOL: 6, 8
LO: 1.1, 2.4, 2.5, 3.3

LEARNING OUTCOME

Present the key religious beliefs of the five major world religions found in Ireland today.

KEY SKILLS YOU WILL USE IN THIS CHAPTER

- Being literate
- Working with others
- Communicating
- Being creative
- Managing information and thinking

WELLBEING INDICATORS IN THIS CHAPTER

LEARNING INTENTIONS

At the end of this chapter, I will

1 Have learned about how Buddhism began and have an understanding of some of the key religious beliefs of Buddhism

2 Be aware of the person of Jesus Christ and be able to present a group presentation on some of the key religious beliefs of Christianity

3 Have worked in groups to design a quiz on some of the key religious beliefs of Hinduism

4 Understand some of the key religious beliefs of Islam

5 Have learned about the founding story of Judaism and be able to see similarities between the key beliefs of Judaism and the other major world religions.

Religion is what people believe about God or gods, and how they worship. There are many different religions found all over the world today. In the past Christianity was the main religion in Ireland. However, times have changed and today Ireland is home to people of many different religions and cultures.

As people of different beliefs live and work side by side, it is important that we all have some understanding of the main religious beliefs found in Ireland today.

Having an understanding of the key religious beliefs of others helps us to respect the role religion plays in their lives. Even if we don't have a religious belief ourselves, we can still learn about other's beliefs. For example, I may not play the game of hurling, but I can learn what the rules are and appreciate why other people enjoy playing it.

While there are many different religions found in Ireland today, we are going to look at five of the major ones.

Key Religious Beliefs

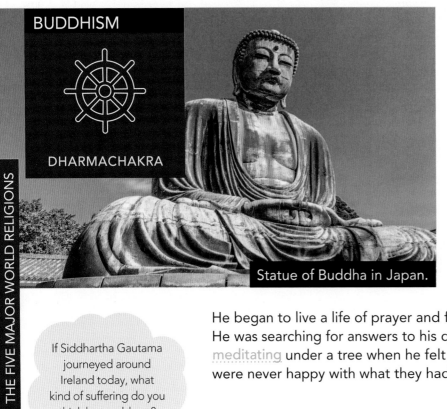

BUDDHISM

DHARMACHAKRA

Statue of Buddha in Japan.

Buddhism began in the north of India around the fifth century BCE.

It was founded by a man named Siddhartha Gautama, who later became known as the Buddha. He was the son of a rich king and queen.

He left the palace to see what the real world was all about. On his journey he saw an old man, a sick man and a dead man.

He realised that life was full of suffering. Then he met a monk who owned nothing but was happy and content.

If Siddhartha Gautama journeyed around Ireland today, what kind of suffering do you think he would see?

He began to live a life of prayer and fasting with some monks. He was searching for answers to his questions about life. One day he was meditating under a tree when he felt enlightened. He believed that people were never happy with what they had and this caused them suffering.

THE FIVE MAJOR WORLD RELIGIONS

1

LITERACY LIBRARY

Compassionate:
To be kind and show an understanding for others.

Gossip:
Talking about someone else's private business.

Look at your school's code of behaviour. Can you see anything in it that links with the guides from the Eightfold Path?

- **Middle Way:** The Middle Way means finding happiness between extreme luxury and extreme hardship. It is about living a balanced life.

- **Nirvana:** Nirvana is being in a state of perfect happiness and peace. It is a feeling of freedom. Nirvana can be reached by following the Four Noble Truths, the Eightfold Path and the Five Precepts.

- **The Four Noble Truths:**
  1 Life is full of suffering. People cannot always be happy.
  2 The main cause of suffering is desire and greed.
  3 People can reach nirvana by not being greedy and selfish towards others.
  4 The Middle Way is the path to true happiness.

- **The Eightfold Path:** The eight guides for following the Middle Way.
  1 Right understanding (think about what we are doing with our lives).
  2 Right thought/attitude (be compassionate rather than selfish).
  3 Right speech (speak the truth and avoid gossip).
  4 Right action (help others, don't harm living things or the environment).
  5 Right work/livelihood (do something useful, avoid jobs that harm others).
  6 Right effort (be positive and honest in our thoughts).
  7 Right mindfulness (be aware of what you feel, think and do).
  8 Right concentration (calm your mind by practising meditation and focus on the present moment).

- **The Five Precepts:** This is a moral code that contains the basic rules for living a good life for Buddhists.
  1 Do not harm or kill living things.
  2 Do not take things unless they are given freely.
  3 Be content with a simple way of life.
  4 Do not speak unkindly or tell lies.
  5 Do not abuse drugs or drink alcohol.

- **Rebirth:** Individuals go through many cycles of birth, living, death and rebirth (reincarnation). After many cycles a person may reach nirvana if they practise the Eightfold Path and the Five Precepts.

THINK, PAIR, SHARE

In **pairs**, think about which three steps of the Eightfold Path are the most important.

Why do you **think** this?

Share your thoughts with the class.

WRITE THE ANSWERS Enquiry

1 What did Siddhartha Gautama become known as?

2 Finding happiness between extreme luxury and extreme hardship is known as _____.

3 Nirvana means _____.

4 What are the basic rules that Buddhists follow for living a good life called?

5 The _____ is a guide for following the Middle Way.

THINK, PAIR, SHARE

Write down two things you **think** would be difficult about following a Buddhist way of life and explain why.

Write down two things about the main religious beliefs of Buddhism that you think could make the world a better place to live in and give reasons for your opinion.

Discuss your ideas in **pairs**.

Now **share** those thoughts with the rest of the class.

 Novice Monks

RESEARCH Exploration

In small groups research the following things you have learned about in this chapter:

• Nirvana
• The Eightfold Path
• The Four Noble Truths
• The Middle Way.

Try to find out more detail about them.

You can look up websites, see if you can find images related to the topic and present your findings on a poster for the rest of the class.

 Search online to find more information about Buddhism in Ireland.

CHRISTIANITY

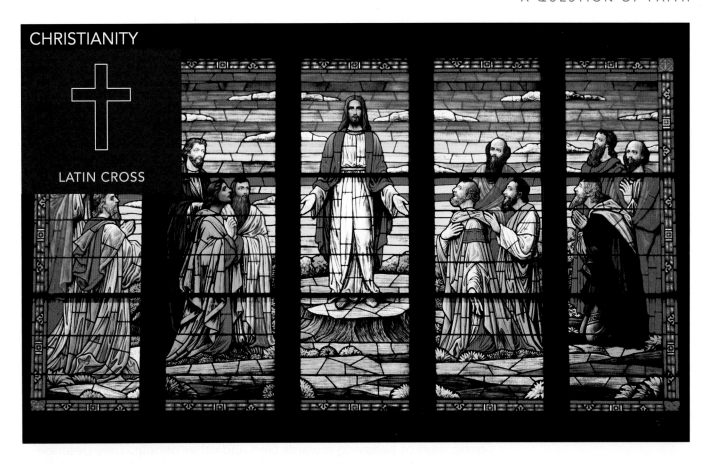

LATIN CROSS

LITERACY
LIBRARY

Province:
A large section of
a country or region.

Crucify:
To kill by tying or
nailing to a cross.

See also Chapter 15

Christianity is a **monotheistic** religion, which means its followers believe in one God only. The religion has its roots in Judaism. (You will learn about Judaism later in this chapter.) Christians believe God is the creator of all life.

Christianity was founded by Jesus Christ, who was born to a couple named Joseph and Mary in a town called Bethlehem. Christians believe he is the Son of God.

Jesus grew up in Nazareth in the province of Galilee, which was ruled by the Romans. He went on to travel through Palestine, preaching and teaching, with a group of followers known as the twelve apostles.

He told stories, performed miracles and showed people a new way of living.

After coming into conflict with different groups, he was sentenced to death and was crucified.

THE FIVE MAJOR WORLD RELIGIONS

1

LITERACY LIBRARY

Justice:
Fair and reasonable behaviour towards others.

Inspired:
When someone or something gives you new ideas that you feel positive about.

Can you think of any people or organisations in Ireland today that work to bring about the Kingdom of God on earth?

- Christianity began in Palestine in 33 CE.

- **Kingdom of God:** The Kingdom of God is not a place. It is a way of living based on Jesus's message of truth, justice, peace and love.

- **The Crucifixion:** Jesus died on the cross so that those who believe in him will be forgiven their sins.

- **The Resurrection:** Jesus rose from the dead and appeared to witnesses. Christians believe that this shows God's power over life and death.

- **The Ascension:** Forty days after his resurrection, Jesus was taken up into heaven – body and soul.

- **The Holy Spirit:** Jesus promised that he would stay with his followers, so after he went to heaven he sent the Holy Spirit to guide them.

- **Baptism:** Baptism is a ceremony performed by most Christian churches. Water is used as a symbol to show the person has become a follower of Jesus.

- **Eucharist:** A thanksgiving meal of bread and wine, which is celebrated by Christians. It remembers the Last Supper Jesus had with his apostles.

- **The Bible:** The Bible is the sacred text or book that Christians believe is the word of God, written by men who were inspired by the Holy Spirit.

- **The Beatitudes:** A moral code given to Christians by Jesus. They are good ways of behaving towards God and other people. They describe qualities followers must have in order to be part of the Kingdom of God. The central message from the Beatitudes is simple: people should love God and their neighbour as they love themselves. Followers of Jesus need to be prayerful and gentle and repent when they do wrong. They need to be fair to everyone and forgive those who do wrong to them. They must try to be respectful, peaceful and have integrity. Look at Matthew 5:1–12 in the New Testament to see what the Beatitudes said.

THE BEATITUDES   Matthew 5:1–12

Now when he saw the crowds, he went up on a mountainside and sat down. His disciples came to him, and he began to teach them, saying:

Blessed are the poor in spirit, for theirs is the kingdom of heaven.
Blessed are those who mourn, for they will be comforted.
Blessed are the meek, for they will inherit the earth.
Blessed are those who hunger and thirst for righteousness, for they will be filled.
Blessed are the merciful, for they will be shown mercy.
Blessed are the pure in heart, for they will see God.
Blessed are the peacemakers, for they will be called sons of God.
Blessed are those who are persecuted because of righteousness, for theirs is the kingdom of heaven.
Blessed are you when people insult you, persecute you and falsely say all kinds of evil against you because of me.
Rejoice and be glad, because great is your reward in heaven, for in the same way they persecuted the prophets who were before you.

- **The Church:** People who belong to Christianity are seen as 'the Church'. They are God's body on earth, a community of believers.

LITERACY LIBRARY

Repent:
To say sorry when you have done something wrong.

Integrity:
Honesty; doing the right thing.

Righteousness:
Being morally right or good.

Persecuted:
Punished or treated badly.

WRITE THE ANSWERS — Enquiry

1 The Kingdom of God is _____.
2 The Ascension is when Jesus rose from the dead. True or false?
3 Name the moral code followed by Christians.
4 Where did Christianity begin?
5 The _____ is a thanksgiving meal celebrated by Christians.

GROUP ACTIVITY — Exploration

In groups of four or five, design and produce a PowerPoint presentation on the key religious beliefs of Christianity.

Share your finished presentation with the rest of the class or with another class group in your year.

RESEARCH — Exploration

Pick one of the following topics you would like to know more about:
- The Kingdom of God
- The Crucifixion
- The Resurrection
- The Holy Spirit.

Use the Gospels, which are found in the second half of the Bible, The New Testament, to help you.

Write a report on your findings.

A baby being baptised into the Christian faith.

THE FIVE MAJOR WORLD RELIGIONS 1

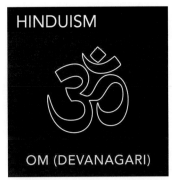

HINDUISM

OM (DEVANAGARI)

Hinduism was founded in India in 2000 BCE.

- **Brahman:** Brahman is a <u>supreme</u> soul or spirit that has no shape or form. Hindus believe that everything in the universe flows from Brahman.

- **Polytheistic:** There are many Hindu gods and goddesses, so Hinduism is an example of polytheism, which means believing in more than one god. The gods and goddesses represent different parts of Brahman's power and character.

- The three most important gods are:

Brahma

The god who created the world. Identified with four faces and four arms. His four arms face different directions, showing he is everywhere.

Vishnu

The god who protects people from evil and wrongdoing. He is an avatar, which means he has taken on both human and animal forms.

Shiva

The god who destroys and rebuilds. He has three eyes, symbolising the moon, sun and fire.

- **Dharma:** Hindus believe that they must always do what is right and correct for themselves. Every form of life and every group of people has its own dharma.

- **Samsara:** Samsara is the belief that when you die your soul is reborn in another body as an animal or as a person. You are reborn over and over until you become perfect.

- **Karma:** Karma means that when you do good, good will come your way; if you do bad, bad will follow you.

- **The Vedas:** The Vedas are Hindu sacred texts that teach and guide Hindus on how they should live their lives.

LITERACY LIBRARY

Supreme:
Higher being, God.

Incense:
A substance that is burned for its sweet smell. Often used in religious ceremonies.

- **Shrine:** Most Hindus have a shrine or small altar in their home to their favourite god. They pray and meditate at it and often burn incense and light candles.

- **Vegetarians:** Most Hindus are vegetarians because of their belief in reincarnation. Cows are considered to be very special, as their milk gives nourishment.

WRITE THE ANSWERS — Enquiry

1 Why is Hinduism described as a polytheistic religion?

2 Brahman is _____.

3 Name the three most important Hindu gods.

4 Explain what samsara is.

5 Karma is _____.

GROUP ACTIVITY — Reflection and Action

In small groups design a quiz on the religious beliefs of Hinduism.

Write out the questions and correct answers.

Test how much the other groups have learned on this topic by using your quiz on another group.

RESEARCH — Enquiry

Pick one of the following three Hindu gods:

- Brahma
- Vishnu
- Shiva.

See what you can find out about your chosen god using the internet.
Present your findings and draw an image of this god on a poster.

A Hindu woman praying at a shrine in her home.

 Search online to find more information on Hindusim.

ISLAM

CRESCENT & STAR

LITERACY LIBRARY

Prophet:
A person called by God to receive an important message and to preach it to the people.

Revelation:
A vision, dream or voice through which God makes himself known to a person and reveals or presents information to them.

The followers of Islam are called **Muslims**.

Islam is a **monotheistic** religion, which means its followers believe in one God only. The God of Islam is called Allah.

Islam has strong roots in Judaism. (You will study Judaism later in this chapter.)

- **Muhammad:** Muhammad was the last and greatest prophet sent by Allah to guide his people on the right path. He was born in Mecca. After seeing greed and fighting all around him, he went to a cave to pray. He received a revelation from God when the Angel Gabriel appeared to him.

- **Kaaba:** The Kaaba in Mecca is a big building covered in black. It was initially built by the Prophet Adam. Later on the building was raised up by the Prophet Abraham. The Kaaba is Islam's holiest shrine. Muslims face towards it when they pray.

- **Qur'an:** The Qu'ran is the sacred text of Islam. Muslims believe it is the word of Allah. It contains their beliefs and moral codes.

- **Six Articles of Faith:** The Six Articles of Faith are things Muslims must believe in:

  1. One God
  2. Angels
  3. Prophets
  4. Holy Scriptures
  5. Day of Judgement or the afterlife
  6. God's will or fate.

The Kaaba surrounded by pilgrims.

The Kaaba in Mecca, Saudi Arabia.

THE FIVE MAJOR WORLD RELIGIONS

1

Search online to find more information on Islam.

- **The Five Pillars of Islam:** The Five Pillars of Islam are the moral code containing practices Muslims must perform in order to live a proper life.

1	2	3	4	5
A statement of belief. There is only one God and Muhammad is his messenger.	Muslims should pray five times a day, facing Mecca. Before praying, Muslims clean themselves in a practice known as wudu. They use prayer mats to kneel on and recite parts of the Qur'an while performing a set of movements. This is know as a ra'ka.	Muslims should share the wealth Allah has blessed them with by giving 2.5% of their yearly savings to charity.	During the month of Ramadan Muslims don't eat or drink between sunrise and sunset. They pray more and focus on their faith.	The Hajj is a pilgrimage to Mecca that every Muslim should make once in their lifetime. Different stages of the Hajj are linked to Muhammad and Abraham.
CREED	PRAYER	CHARITY	FASTING	PILGRIMAGE

- **Halal:** Things that are allowed in Islam. For example halal meat comes from an animal that has been slaughtered in a certain way.
- **Haram:** Things that are forbidden in Islam. Pork and alcohol are examples of things that are haram in Islam.

WRITE THE ANSWERS   Enquiry

1 What is the name Muslims give to their God?

2 Name the last and greatest prophet in Islam.

3 The Kaaba is the sacred text of Islam. True or false?

4 The Five Pillars of Islam are:

   a _____   c _____   e _____

   b _____   d _____

5 What is the name of the time when Muslims fast?

GROUP ACTIVITY   Reflection and Action

Find out if there is a Muslim student in your school or area.

Discuss with your teacher the possibility of inviting them to speak to your class about their religious beliefs.

Prepare some questions you might ask them.

RESEARCH   Exploration

Go online and find a video of the following:

1 A Muslim performing their prayers.

2 A Muslim speaking about their experience of Ramadan.

3 A video about the Hajj.

THE FIVE MAJOR WORLD RELIGIONS

1

JUDAISM

STAR OF DAVID

Jewish people believe in one God only. This is known as **monotheism**.

Judaism was founded in Israel by Abraham and later Moses.

- **Covenant:** God made a covenant, or promise, with Abraham. If Abraham was faithful to his God, he would become the father of many.

  He was to travel to a land called Canaan. This became known as the Promised Land.

  Abraham remained faithful to God and was even willing to sacrifice his own son, Isaac, to show his obedience.

  Abraham's people were known as the Israelites. They suffered greatly over the years and were made slaves by the Egyptians.

- **Moses:** A shepherd called Moses saw a burning bush one day that was not actually on fire. God's voice spoke to him telling him to help the Jewish people.

  Moses was frightened, but went to see the pharaoh, the Egyptian ruler. The pharaoh refused to set the Jews free, so God sent ten plagues on Egypt.

  Finally God sent the last and most terrible plague. An angel of death passed over each house in Egypt, killing the first-born son. The Jews were told to sacrifice a lamb and to rub the blood on their front doors. The angel would know they were Jews and pass over their houses.

  After this the pharaoh agreed to let the Jews go, but once they had set off he changed his mind and sent his army after them.

  When the Jews reached the Red Sea, God parted the waters, allowing them through. This event is called the **Exodus**.

See also Chapter 18

Moses receiving the Ten Commandments.

THE FIVE MAJOR WORLD RELIGIONS

1

Plague:
A large number of terrible things that happen at the same time.

Covenant:
A promise or agreement made between God and his people.

Sabbath:
A day or time set aside for rest and worship.

- **Torah:** God gave Moses the Torah, which means 'teaching'. It gave details about how God wanted his people to live.

- **The Ten Commandments:** The second covenant God made with his chosen people, the Jews. They were to follow these commandments and remain faithful to Him. It is the Jewish people's moral code.

- **Prophets:** As time passed the people began to forget their covenant with God, so God sent prophets to help them. A prophet is a person called by God to receive an important message and preach it to the people. Jeremiah and Isaiah are two examples of prophets.

- **Kosher:** Kosher means 'clean and pure'. For meat to be kosher an animal must be killed in a certain way. Pork and shellfish are not kosher.

- **Shabbat:** The Jewish Sabbath begins on a Friday evening at sunset and ends at the same time the following day. It is celebrated because in the Torah God told his people to keep the Sabbath day holy and to use this day to rest and remember God. It is a family event.

WRITE THE ANSWERS Enquiry

1 Where was Judaism founded?

2 What is a covenant?

3 A prophet is _____.

4 Name the Jewish moral code.

5 What does kosher mean?

CLASS DISCUSSION Exploration

Look at the key religious beliefs of the other four major world religions.

What similarities can you see between them and the main religious beliefs of Judaism?

Report the findings of your discussion on the class board.

RESEARCH Reflection and Action

Use the internet to find information on what happens during the Sabbath.

Role-play what is said and done in your class.

REFLECTIVE ANSWER

Think about your own attitude to the key religious beliefs of the five major world religions found in Ireland today and answer the following questions:

1 What are your own most important religious beliefs?

2 Which major world religion did you find most interesting to learn about and why?

3 Which religion's key beliefs do you feel you know the most about?

PowerPoint summary

Weblinks

 Search online to find more information on Judaism.

CHAPTER 2
Communities of Faith

SOL: 6
LO: 1.2, 1.3, 1.10

LEARNING OUTCOMES

Investigate two communities of faith with a real and important presence in the areas where they are found.

Explore communities of faith from two of the five major world religions.

Engage with members of a community of faith and appreciate how their religious beliefs have an effect on their day-to-day life.

KEY SKILLS YOU WILL USE IN THIS CHAPTER

- Working with others
- Managing information and thinking
- Communicating
- Being creative
- Managing myself

WELLBEING INDICATORS IN THIS CHAPTER

LEARNING INTENTIONS

At the end of this chapter, I will

1   Be aware of the communities of faith found in my own area
2   Understand how the Islamic Foundation of Ireland has a vibrant presence in its community
3   Have learned how one community of faith in the Christian religion has an influence on the people who live in the locality
4   Understand how the religious beliefs of a young Muslim person affect their life.

Within the five major world religions that you will investigate in your Junior Cycle Religious Education course, there are a number of communities of faith who have their own specific identity or vision.

A community of faith is a group of people who share similar religious beliefs or ideas.

CLASS DISCUSSION Enquiry

What communities of faith are you aware of in your own locality or area?

How do you know about them?

How would someone who is not from your area know these communities of faith are present?

WRITE THE ANSWER Enquiry

Write a report of the discussion above and what you learned from it into your copybook.

We will now look at two examples of communities of faith who have a real presence in their locality. Alternatively you might like to investigate a community of faith and its presence in your own area.

COMMUNITIES OF FAITH 2

17

The Islamic Foundation of Ireland

LITERACY LIBRARY

Mosque:
A place of worship for Muslim people.

Vibrant:
Full of energy and life.

The Islamic Foundation of Ireland (IFI) mosque on the South Circular Road in Dublin acts as a place of worship and a focal point for Muslims in the south city centre. The mosque also doubles as the IFI's headquarters, which looks after the religious, social and cultural needs of Irish Muslims.

Until 1983 Muslims in the area had worshipped at a house, but as the number of members grew, they needed a larger premises. They purchased a building that had previously been a Presbyterian church and turned it into their own place of worship.

The mosque is not just a place to pray for the Muslims who live in the area. It is also a community centre for Muslims and has a shop that sells halal meat. The building also houses a canteen and offices. As well as running the mosque, the IFI also runs Muslim primary schools in Clonskeagh and Cabra in Dublin.

The presence of this community of faith can really be felt in the local area on a Friday, which is their day of weekly congregational prayer, when up to 800 Muslims gather together to pray. Muslims in Dublin also travel to the mosque for funerals and marriages. The Muslim community of faith has a real and vibrant presence in the locality of South Dublin.

This presence can be felt in the wider community twice a year when the mosque holds an open day to allow members of other faiths and the community at large to explore Muslim faith and Islamic culture. It is a great opportunity for Muslims to integrate with their locality and for non-Muslims to understand and appreciate what their Muslim neighbours believe and how they practise their faith.

Dublin Mosque, South Circular Road.

Muslims celebrating Eid at the mosque in Clonskeagh, Dublin.

WRITE THE ANSWERS Enquiry

1 What is a community of faith?

2 Why did the Islamic community purchase an old Presbyterian church?

3 As well as the mosque, what else would you find at the IFI on the South Circular Road in Dublin?

4 When would large numbers of Muslims gather at the mosque and why would they be there?

5 Why are the open days, which are held twice a year, important events?

What difference would having the Islamic Foundation of Ireland make to the life of a Muslim person living in Dublin?

COMMUNITIES OF FAITH

2

Search online for more information on Islam in Ireland.

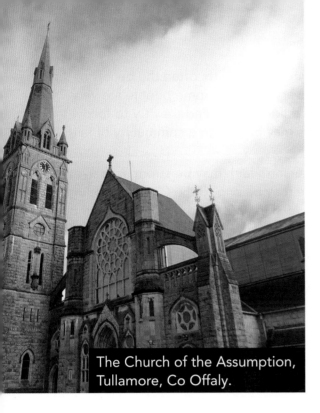

Tullamore Parish

Another community of faith that has a significant presence in its locality is Tullamore parish in Co. Offaly.

A parish is an area made up of a church or churches belonging to the Christian community. There is normally a parish in every town or village in Ireland.

Tullamore parish is a very active community that reaches out to people in the area in many different ways. The work the members of the community do has a very positive effect on the people who live there.

In order to investigate how important this community of faith is to the people in the locality, watch the link to the video showing an interview between a second year student and a priest, or leader, from the Christian community of faith. You can then answer the questions below.

The Church of the Assumption, Tullamore, Co Offaly.

Ben from Cross and Passion College in Kilcullen, Co. Kildare.

WRITE THE ANSWERS   Enquiry

1 How big is Tullamore parish?

2 Explain how the parish helps to serves people's religious faith.

3 Give two examples of how people are involved in the parish.

4 Do you think Tullamore parish is a very active one? Give reasons for you answer.

5 Describe a positive effect the parish has on the people who live in the area.

RESEARCH   Exploration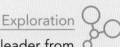

Discuss with your teacher the possibility of inviting a leader from a community of faith in your area to your school.

Before they arrive, plan what questions you will ask them about how their community of faith reaches out to people in the locality. Arrange to email the questions to them in advance so they can be prepared.

When a person belongs to a community of faith, often the beliefs of their religion or faith can affect their everyday lives. Some people are very dedicated or committed to their religious faith and they try to follow the rules and guidelines daily. Others may belong to a community of faith but don't follow all the rules exactly.

At different times in their life a person's faith may be stronger than at other times. For example, some people may belong to the Christian community of faith, but they may not go to worship on a Sunday, which is their holy day or Sabbath.

In order to fully understand how the religious beliefs of a community affect or influence the daily life of its members, log on to edcolearning.ie and watch the interview between a Muslim student and one of his non-Muslim classmates.

See also Chapter 7, p.70.

Eoin and Waseq from Coláiste Choilm in Tullamore.

CLASS DISCUSSION   Reflection and Action

1 In what ways is Waseq's daily life affected by his religious beliefs?
2 How is Waseq's life affected by his religious beliefs during Ramadan?
3 Do you think it is easy or difficult for him to live by his religious beliefs? Why do you think this?

WRITE THE ANSWER   Enquiry

Write your own personal response to what you learned from the video into your copybook.

REFLECTIVE ACTIVITY

Think about your own attitude to how communities of faith have an important presence in your community and how religious beliefs can affect people's lives and answer the following questions:

1 Do you have personal or religious beliefs that affect your everyday life?
2 If you could visit any community of faith in your area and learn about them, which community of faith would it be and why?

 PowerPoint summary

Weblinks

CHAPTER 3
The Contribution of Christianity to Irish Culture and Heritage

SOL: 8
LO: 1.2, 1.4

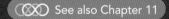 See also Chapter 11

LEARNING OUTCOME

Investigate how Christianity has contributed to Irish culture and heritage.

KEY SKILLS YOU WILL USE IN THIS CHAPTER

- Communicating
- Being creative
- Working with others
- Managing information and thinking

WELLBEING INDICATORS IN THIS CHAPTER

LEARNING INTENTIONS

At the end of this chapter, I will

1 Understand the meaning of culture and heritage

2 Be able to tell the story of St Patrick

3 Be able to explain what Ireland was like when Christianity came to the island

4 Be able to tell the story of St Brigid

5 Be able to show how the Dominican Order continued to spread Christianity.

LITERACY LIBRARY

Culture:
A way of life for people. It is how they do things, for example in music, arts or sport.

Heritage:
Something that is passed down from one generation to the next.

THINK, PAIR, SHARE

Imagine for a moment that you are an American citizen thinking of coming to Ireland on holiday to experience its culture and heritage. **Think** about the questions below.

What would you believe Irish culture and heritage to be?

What springs to your mind?

What, do you think, would they associate with Ireland?

In **pairs**, make a list. **Share** your thoughts with the rest of the class.

Before we begin to look at how Christianity has contributed to Irish culture and heritage, it is important for us to go back in time and discover how Christianity came to Ireland in the first place. You might be discussing this in History class also, so before you read on think about what you can remember.

THE CONTRIBUTION OF CHRISTIANITY TO IRISH CULTURE AND HERITAGE

3

The Arrival of Christianity to Ireland

Before Christianity came to Ireland, Ireland was a pagan country that believed in many gods. The country was dominated by the Celts for about 900 years.

Around the fifth century there were some Christians living in Ireland. Missionaries had been sent to Ireland by the pope to spread the word of God. One such missionary was Palladius, but the missionary we most associate with Ireland is St Patrick.

ST PATRICK

Patrick was born in Roman Britain (Roman Britain was the area of the island of Great Britain that was governed by the Roman Empire from 43 AD – 410 AD).

He became a priest and bishop and arrived in Ireland as a missionary.

By the beginning of the sixth century, Ireland was mainly a Christian country due to the missionary work that was being carried out in the country.

Christianity replaced the pagan religion, and the Celtic festivals of Bealtaine, Meitheamh, Lughnasadh and Imbolc became Christian festivals instead. The coming of Christianity brought significant changes to Irish culture and heritage.

Circle stones, Belmullet, Co Mayo.

THE CONTRIBUTION OF CHRISTIANITY TO IRISH CULTURE AND HERITAGE

3

LITERACY LIBRARY

Holy Trinity:
The Father, Son and Holy Spirit – three persons of the Christian Godhead.

Every year Irish people celebrate St Patrick's Day on 17 March. It is a cultural and religious celebration in Ireland, but it is also a global celebration of Irish culture.

This day is a public holiday in the Republic of Ireland. Celebrations involve public parades, festivals, Irish traditional music and the wearing of green shamrock. St Patrick is said to have used the shamrock, a three-leaved plant, to explain the Holy Trinity to the pagan Irish.

WRITE THE ANSWERS   Enquiry

1 What kind of country was Ireland before Christianity became the main religion?

2 Who brought Christianity to Ireland?

3 Name the four pagan Irish festivals.

4 In the grid below, link the pagan festival with the changing of the season. Research information on the festivals online if you need help with the answers.

Bealtaine	Summer
Meitheamh	Autumn
Lughnasadh	Spring
Imbolc	Winter

Culture and Heritage

Now that you know how Christianity came to Ireland, let's look more closely at how this world religion has contributed to Irish culture and heritage. But what do we mean by culture and heritage?

Culture can be defined as our customs and traditions, our music, our art, our literature, our sports and our folklore that we associate with Ireland.

The cultural **heritage** of Ireland includes a wide range of monuments, objects, landscapes and structures that were shaped by Irish people over thousands of years.

Have you been to see the Book of Kells?

LITERACY LIBRARY

Stonemason:
Person who has a skill working with stone, for example someone who can make stone crosses.

The Monasteries

Today you can find the Book of Kells in Trinity College, Dublin. About half a million people visit it annually. The Book of Kells is Ireland's greatest cultural treasure and the world's most famous illuminated manuscript. It contains a richly decorated copy of the four Gospels (Mathew, Mark, Luke and John) in Latin.

As well as being scribes, some monks were stonemasons and they carved high stone crosses.

Glendalough, Co. Wicklow.

THE CONTRIBUTION OF CHRISTIANITY TO IRISH CULTURE AND HERITAGE

3

Manuscript:
Handwritten document.

Crozier:
A hooked staff carried by a bishop.

Chalice:
A large cup or goblet.

The Book of Kells

Many new monasteries were built in Ireland when Christianity became rooted into the country. Holy men and women built monasteries as places to pray and honour God.

These monasteries were places of learning. The Bible was studied in the monasteries by the monks. They wrote manuscripts in the scriptorium of the monastery. These monks were called scribes. One example of a manuscript is the Book of Kells.

High Stone Crosses

The carvings on the high cross were used to teach monks about the story of Christianity.

Other monks made croziers, chalices and brooches from metal and adorned them with gold and amber. One famous example of their work is the Ardagh Chalice. This period was known as the Golden Age (400–800 AD).

The monks were skilled craftsmen and have taught us a lot about their lives through the beautiful pieces of work they left behind for us to study.

The Ardagh Chalice.

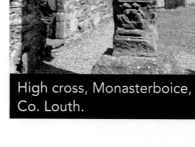

High cross, Monasterboice, Co. Louth.

Copy the 3-2-1 box below into your copybook and fill it in.

3-2-1		
3	**2**	**1**
things I have learned	things I found interesting	thing I want to learn more about

Read the following story about St Enda, who came to live in Ireland to set up a monastery on the Aran Islands.

St Enda

Enda was born during the fifth century AD. His feast day is celebrated on 21 March, which is four days after we celebrate the feast day of our patron saint, St Patrick. He set up a monastic settlement (monastery) on the Aran Islands, which is truly a beautiful place off the west coast of Ireland. At first about 150 people joined him on the monastery site.

These men lived simple lives. They lived in stone cells and slept on the ground. They ate their meals together but in silence. They were self-sufficient because they grew their own vegetables, fished for their food and made their own clothes. They prayed many times during the day and read from scripture.

St Enda's monastery became an important place of pilgrimage. St Enda died in old age around 530 AD. An early chronicler of his life acknowledged that it would 'never be known until the day of judgement, the number of saints whose bodies lie in the soil of Aran' due to the work that St Enda did on the island in setting up a monastery so rich in culture.

WRITE THE ANSWERS Enquiry

1. Where did St Enda set up his monastery?
2. What is a missionary?
3. What happened at the monastery?
4. What does 'self-sufficient' mean?
5. What did the writer mean when he said, '[It would] never be known until the day of judgement, the number of saints whose bodies lie in the soil of Aran'?

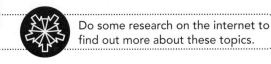
Do some research on the internet to find out more about these topics.

Read the following story of St Brigid of Kildare, who, along with St Patrick, is one of Ireland's patron saints.

St Brigid of Kildare

Brigid was born near Dundalk in Co. Louth in 450 AD. Brigid's father named her after one of the most powerful goddesses of the pagan religion – the goddess of fire.

Brigid was inspired by the preaching of St Patrick and she became a Christian. She wanted to devote her life to working for God and to looking after poor, sick and elderly people. She eventually entered a convent and made her vows to dedicate her life to God.

News of her good works spread far and wide and other young girls joined the convent to work beside her. She founded many convents in Ireland, but the most famous one is in Co. Kildare. Many say that this convent was founded beside the oak tree where the town of Kildare now stands.

Brigid also founded a school of art, including metalwork and illumination, and in the scriptorium of the monastery the famous illuminated manuscript, the Book of Kildare, was created.

One thing we most associate with this saint is the St Brigid's cross. Making the cross is one of the traditional rituals in Ireland to celebrate the beginning of spring. The cross is made from rushes that have been pulled rather than cut.

St Brigid died in 525 AD. She is the female patron saint of Ireland. She is also known as Muire na nGael, or Mary of the Gael, which translates into Our Lady of the Irish. Her feast day is 1 February.

WRITE THE ANSWERS   Enquiry

1 Brigid was born near _____ in Co. Louth in
   _____ AD.

2 She founded many convents in Ireland, but the most famous one is in
   Co. _____.

3 One thing we most associate with this lady is the _____
   _____.

4 St Brigid's feast day is on _____.

Christianity has contributed in many ways to Irish culture and heritage.
We owe a lot to the men and women who dedicated their lives to God
from the fifth century onwards. They taught us how to build round
towers and high crosses, how to make illuminated manuscripts and
how to live self-sufficient lives.

Our culture and heritage stem from men and women like Patrick,
Brigid and Enda who dedicated their lives to God.

St Patrick sowed the seed of what Christianity could bring to the
people of Ireland and St Brigid and St Enda cultivated his ideas and set
up teaching monasteries in Ireland.

GROUP ACTIVITY   Reflection and Action

Imagine you are living in fifth-century Ireland.
What would you like to teach the people around you?
Write a blog post outlining what you would like to tell them.

Round tower in Clondalkin, Dublin.

THE CONTRIBUTION OF CHRISTIANITY TO IRISH CULTURE AND HERITAGE

3

The Dominican Order

In 1206 a Spaniard, Saint Dominic de Guzman, founded the first community of Dominican women in France. In 1224 the Dominican friars arrived on Irish soil. The Dominican Sisters in Cabra, Dublin trace their origin to the foundation of the Dominican nuns in Galway in 1644. Sr Mary Lynch and Sr Julian Nolan, on their return from exile in Spain, re-founded the community in Galway. This congregation is just one section of the worldwide Dominican family. It is a family of priests, brothers, sisters and laity. Their mission is education in the broadest sense and schools are one aspect of this mission.

St Dominic's vision was to bring the word and works of God into an active engagement with the main culture of the day. The network of Dominican schools and colleges in Ireland has inherited a rich tradition in education, with each new generation finding new ways of passing on Christian values. This involves the constant effort to create a faith and culture so that intellectual change and growth as a Christian go hand in hand. The Dominican education is developed in a spirit of trust and freedom, linked with responsibility. It looks for the co-operation of everyone and is mindful of justice issues. It offers a multifaceted or complex curriculum and is opposed to unhealthy competition or academic cramming.

Their motto, *veritas* (truth), symbolises the aim of Dominican schools and colleges, which is to pursue truth in all its forms. It acknowledges the unique giftedness of each individual and their journey in discovering the truth about themselves, others, the universe they share and the creator of all. They strive to be communities that are centred on Christ and on Gospel values. Everyone works together and learns to make informed judgements while praying together and forgiving each other for any wrongdoing.

LITERACY LIBRARY

Multifaceted:
With many sides.

Complex:
With many parts.

What do you think St Dominic would say about Ireland today?

PowerPoint summary

Weblinks

Search online to find the short film *A Day in the Life of the Dominican Studium*, Saint Saviour's Priory, Dublin.

WRITE THE ANSWERS Enquiry

1 Who set up the Dominican Order?

2 What was St Dominic's vision?

3 What is the Dominican Order's motto? What do you think of this motto?

4 Research another religious order, for example Holy Faith, Poor Servants of the Mother of God or De La Salle. Share their stories with your class group.

5 Write a blog post on a religious organisation today that contributes to Irish culture and heritage.

REFLECTIVE ACTIVITY

Think about your own attitude to the contribution of Christianity to Irish culture and heritage and answer the following questions:

1 What did you find most interesting about this chapter?

2 Do you think culture and heritage are important? Why/why not?

3 Compare and contrast the lives of St Patrick, St Brigid and St Enda. Which story do you prefer?

Grotto in the grounds of St Mary's Dominican Church, Galway.

THE CONTRIBUTION OF CHRISTIANITY TO IRISH CULTURE AND HERITAGE 3

CHAPTER 4
Religious Themes in Music

SOL: 4, 6
LO: 1.5, 2.1

LEARNING OUTCOME

Explore how religious themes can be found in today's world in music.

KEY SKILLS YOU WILL USE IN THIS CHAPTER

- Staying well
- Communicating
- Working with others
- Managing information and thinking
- Being creative

WELLBEING INDICATORS IN THIS CHAPTER

LEARNING INTENTIONS

At the end of this chapter, I will

1 Understand how music plays an important part in people's lives

2 Be able to explain why people use music to express their religious faith

3 Give an example of how music is used in a Christian ceremony

4 Give an example of how a contemporary song may have religious meaning for people.

Sigrid

The presence of religion in our society can be seen very clearly in some places, such as holy buildings, churches, mosques or synagogues. However, if we look around us closely we may be surprised to see references to religion in unexpected places. They can be found in what people call 'the arts'. The arts means areas in which people can be creative and express themselves. Examples of the arts would be art, music, literature and film.

Music

Music plays an important part in all our lives. It is difficult to imagine a world without music. We can choose to listen to whatever kind of music we like: rap, pop, R&B, folk, jazz or opera, to name just a few. We are also surrounded by background music in lots of places, such as shops and restaurants.

People respond in different ways to music, depending on their beliefs and experiences. A song can have huge meaning for one person, but not strike a chord with the person sitting beside them.

'When you hear a certain piece of music, your mind is often transported very vividly to a place or a memory that means something to you. Like the sense of smell, songs are highly evocative and can bring back memories of significant times, places and people.'
Stephen Fischbacher

'Music can name the unnameable and communicate the unknowable.'
Leonard Bernstein, conductor

People often turn to the medium of music when they are trying to express their emotions. Some of the most famous songs ever written have been about themes or ideas such as love, relationships, loneliness and happiness. Music is often added to an event or celebration.

CLASS DISCUSSION Exploration
What kind of events or celebrations have music as part of them?
How does having music at the event make a difference?

Century:
One hundred years.

Contemporary:
Modern or relating to the present day.

Inspire:
To influence or guide someone.

For centuries people have used music to explore or share what they feel about religion and faith. It can be difficult to put into words the beliefs or questions we have about something as big and mysterious as God.

Different world religions also use music during their celebrations to help them create an atmosphere or to speak to their God/gods. For example, the Christian religion uses religious songs called hymns and the Buddhist religion uses chanting, which is the singing of words or sounds.

An example of a Christian ceremony where music can be very important is a funeral. A funeral is the ceremony that takes place after someone has died. It allows people to say goodbye to their loved ones and to remember and celebrate their lives. For Christians, a funeral has an even deeper meaning. It reminds them that through their baptism, a person is a follower of Jesus Christ and in death, they are beginning a new life with God. Christians believe that after death a person will enter into ever-lasting life with their God. This belief gives Christians comfort and hope.

One hymn often sung at funerals is 'Be Not Afraid':

> Be not afraid, I go before you always,
> Come, follow me, and I will give you rest.

What, do you think, are the words of this hymn saying to Christian believers? How would it give them comfort and hope?

Religious themes are also present in music in what we call contemporary culture. Sometimes the person writing the music deliberately gives it a religious theme. At other times someone listening to the music may find something in it that reminds them of their religious faith or helps them to understand religion more clearly.

One example of a song that was not deliberately given a religious meaning is the Beatles song 'Let It Be'.

The Beatles were a British rock band who became world famous in the 1960s and 1970s. One of their members, Paul McCartney, wrote 'Let It Be'. He said it was inspired by a dream he had of his mother, who had died when he was fourteen.

However, many people have found a religious meaning or theme in the song. McCartney has said that fans of the song should feel free to find whatever meaning they want in it.

RELIGIOUS THEMES IN MUSIC

Have you ever been to a religious event that had music as part of it? What difference did it make to the celebration?

GROUP ACTIVITY   Enquiry

See if you can find a version of the song 'Let It Be' online and listen to it as a class.

In your groups, discuss what religious themes people might find in the lyrics and why.

Share the results of your discussion with the rest of the class.

 Song Sheet

Let's look at a more contemporary song that has a religious theme clearly present in it.

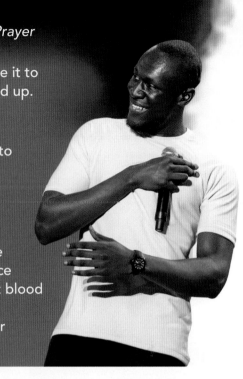

Stormzy is an English rapper who was born in 1993. He released an album in 2017 called *Gang Signs and Prayer* and has always been very open about his faith.

In an interview he once said, 'If it doesn't add up, I give it to God. Me getting that No. 1 on the last day doesn't add up. I give it to God.'

When he won two Brit Awards in 2018 he said in his acceptance speech, 'Firstly, I always give all the glory to God, God this is all you, this is all you God.'

This religious faith is most clearly seen on two songs from the album, 'Blinded by Your Grace, Part 1' and 'Blinded by Your Grace, Part 2'.

Stormzy did not have an easy time growing up, and he witnessed and experienced drug dealing, gang violence and depression. When he sings the line, 'It's not about blood and it's not about birth', he seems to have come to a realisation that God loves him no matter who he is or what he has done.

Song Sheet

The religious theme found in this contemporary song is that God's grace, or loving forgiveness and help, can help to change a person or even save them.

THINK, PAIR, SHARE

Search online for one of the following contemporary songs.

See if you can find the lyrics online. In **pairs**, **think** about what religious themes you think are in the song.

- 'Pray' by Justin Bieber
- 'You've Got the Love' by Florence and the Machine

Share your thoughts with the class.

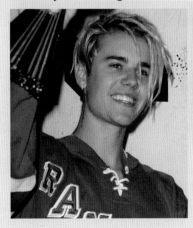

Father Ray Kelly

Father Ray Kelly is an Irish Catholic priest who became famous in 2014. A video of him singing Leonard Cohen's Song 'Hallelujah' while he was celebrating at a couple's wedding reception became a YouTube sensation. The clip has received over 61 million views. As a result, he released an album with Universal Music called *Where I Belong*.

In 2018 he auditioned for the show *Britain's Got Talent*, singing a song by REM called 'Everybody Hurts'. He said he was thinking of his younger sister, Regina, while he was singing. Regina had passed away from cancer at the age of 59. The priest said that the song had helped him to cope with his sister's death.

RESEARCH
Exploration

Search online to watch Fr Kelly singing 'Everybody Hurts' on *Britain's Got Talent*. Listen to the lyrics of the song. What could the words mean to someone who has a religious faith?

ACTIVITY
Reflection and Action

Think about a song that has special meaning for you. Does it remind you of a special place or person? What meaning do you get from the lyrics?

Write a piece about the song you have chosen and explain its importance to you.

Ed Sheeran

'Supermarket Flowers' is a song by English singer-songwriter Ed Sheeran. It featured on his third album, ÷ *divide*. He wrote the song about his grandmother, who passed away while he was making the album. He played the song at her funeral and it is written from the point of view of his own mother.

The lyrics of the song describe what happened and how his mother was feeling at the time. The family's sadness as they packed away memories of his grandmother's time in hospital is clear. He imagines that when God finally meets his grandmother in heaven, he'll say to her, 'Hallelujah, you're home.'

 RESEARCH   Exploration

Search online and listen to the song 'Supermarket Flowers'. Discuss what message it could have for someone who has a religious faith.

REFLECTIVE ACTIVITY

Think about your own attitude to how religious themes can be found in today's world in music and answer the following questions:

1 Why, do you think, is music a good way for people to express their religious faith?

2 Has music ever helped you to explain or understand your feelings about something?

3 Which of the songs mentioned in this chapter has the most meaning for you and why?

 PowerPoint summary

 Weblinks

CHAPTER 5
Religious Rituals

SOL: 3, 5, 8
LO: 1.6, 1.8

LEARNING OUTCOME

Examine and appreciate how people give expression to their religious belief in religious rituals, in formal places of worship and other sacred spaces.

KEY SKILLS YOU WILL USE IN THIS CHAPTER

- Working with others
- Communicating
- Being creative
- Managing information and thinking

WELLBEING INDICATORS IN THIS CHAPTER

LEARNING INTENTIONS

At the end of this chapter, I will

1 Understand what a sacred space is

2 Understand what going on a pilgrimage is like

3 Be able to describe what happens at Croagh Patrick in Co. Mayo

4 Be able to describe what a significant building is

5 Be able to describe the order of the Mass and how we participate in it

6 Be able to describe the Church of Ireland.

Associate:
Connect it with
something.

Sacred space:
Sacred means 'holy',
so this is a holy place
devoted to a religious
ceremony.

Do you have a
significant place you
like to go to?

Places often have a special meaning to us. This can be because we associate something nice with the place or because we have fond memories of being there once.

CLASS DISCUSSION Exploration

Think for a moment about a place that is special to you.
Why is this place special to you? What makes it like this?
Share your ideas with the class and discuss as a group.

Significant Places

Places can also become significant for religious reasons. They can be associated with an important person in a religion. The person may have been born there, lived there or visited the place during his or her lifetime. There may have been a vision or apparition that took place there. These places can become known as sacred spaces for religious followers.

The Western Wall, Jerusalem, Israel.

RELIGIOUS RITUALS 5

Pilgrimages help people to strengthen their relationship with God. This may have been damaged due to illness in the family, a disappointment or the loss of someone close to them.

Holy tree at the birthplace of Buddha in Nepal.

Pilgrimage

People learn a lot about themselves on a pilgrimage, as technology tends to be put away and people can be alone with their thoughts. They can fully relax and focus on the things that are important to them. Because of this it is easier to give special time to God as there are no distractions. If something is on their mind they can seek forgiveness or guidance. It also gives them the opportunity to thank God for something that they have received, which they may have prayed for.

People might also go on pilgrimage because they believe this is something that God wants them to do. All the major world religions have significant places that people from that faith journey to.

THINK, PAIR, SHARE

In **pairs**, **think** about other reasons why a person might go on a pilgrimage.
Share your thoughts with the class.

LITERACY LIBRARY

Devotion:
Loyalty to something or someone.

Ritual:
A religious or solemn ceremony that involves actions throughout.

Would you like to climb Croagh Patrick?

One example of such a place is Croagh Patrick in Co. Mayo. It is a place of pilgrimage for people in the Christian religion. People go to Croagh Patrick because they associate it with religion in a special way. They feel close to God when they have climbed to the top of the mountain.

Read the following passage on Croagh Patrick to learn more about it.

Croagh Patrick

Croagh Patrick is a mountain near the town of Westport in Co. Mayo. It is known by many people simply as 'The Reek' and has been a sacred site since ancient times. However, it was the patron saint of Ireland, St Patrick, who made it a place of significance for Catholics. Christian tradition says that Patrick went up this mountain and spent forty days praying, fasting and reflecting there.

Pilgrims now come from all over the world to pray in this sacred place, and the last Sunday in July is particularly special. It is known as Reek Sunday and each year at this time more than 25,000 pilgrims visit the mountain.

The first stop on the pilgrimage path is a statue of St Patrick. Many people stop and pray here, and it is special for those who cannot make the journey to the top of the mountain. The more able pilgrims continue up the mountain and many even make the trip barefoot as a sign of devotion. There are three pilgrimage stations on the way to the summit of Croagh Patrick. Each one has a sign with instructions for the proper prayers and rituals that pilgrims must make on the way.

CROAGH PATRICK

IRELAND'S HOLY MOUNTAIN

RELIGIOUS RITUALS

5

41

FIRST STATION

The first station is at the base of the mountain, where pilgrims walk around a mound of stones seven times, saying seven Our Fathers, seven Hail Marys and one Creed.

SECOND STATION

The second station takes place on the summit and has four different stages. The pilgrims first kneel and say seven Our Fathers, seven Hail Marys and one Creed. They then pray near the chapel where Mass is said every day for the pope's intentions. Next, they walk around the chapel fifteen times while saying fifteen Our Fathers and fifteen Hail Marys. Finally, they walk around the area known as Patrick's Bed seven times, again saying seven Our Fathers, seven Hail Marys and one Creed.

THIRD STATION

The third station takes place at Roilig Mhuire. Here the pilgrims walk seven times around each mound of stones, again repeating the sequence of seven Our Fathers, seven Hail Marys and one Creed. Finally, they walk around the whole enclosure of Roilig Mhuire praying.

WRITE THE ANSWERS Enquiry

1 Where is Croagh Patrick?

2 Why is it seen as a place of religious significance?

3 What is Reek Sunday?

4 Why is the statue of St Patrick so important to some people?

5 What happens at each of the stations?

View from the top of Croagh Patrick.

 Search online to find a virtual tour of Croagh Patrick.

Significant Buildings

Buildings can become places of significance too. All the major world religions have buildings that are important to them. Usually this is because these buildings are where followers gather together and worship their God.

Even though these buildings may be different in size or shape, they have certain common features or characteristics associated with their religion. Below is a table of the five major world religions and their place of worship.

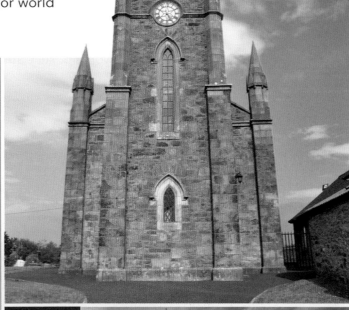

CHRISTIANITY Church

ISLAM Mosque

BUDDHISM Temple/Vihara

JUDAISM Synagogue

HINDUISM Temple/Mandir

GROUP ACTIVITY

Enquiry

In a group, find out more information on one of the above buildings of religious significance. Describe to the class why it is a building of religious significance and what happens there.

We will now look at a building of significance in the Catholic religion. This is a Catholic church in Abbeyleix, Co. Laois. People attend this church to go to Mass regularly and in so doing give expression to religious belief in religious rituals. The Church of the Most Holy Rosary was built in 1893. It can be found off the main street in the town of Abbeyleix.

A Catholic Church

This is a picture of the Church of the Most Holy Rosary Church in Abbeyleix. The cross on the top of the building identifies it as a Christian place of worship. All Catholic churches have a cross on the top of the spire.

1. THE ALTAR

2. THE AMBO

The altar is where the celebration of the Eucharist takes place. It is the main area of focus during the Mass.

The ambo, or lectern, is where the priest or Ministers of the Word read the readings and gospels.

3. THE PRESIDER'S CHAIR

The priest is called the presider because he is the one who leads the congregation.

The presider's chair is where he sits during the Mass.

4. THE TABERNACLE

The tabernacle is where the body of Christ is kept between Masses.

5. THE SANCTUARY LAMP

Churches usually have at least one lamp burning or lit constantly beside the tabernacle. It shows and honours the presence of Christ. It symbolises the light of Christ shining in our world. It is usually red.

6. STATUE OF OUR LADY

Statues are often found in different areas of the church and may be of Our Lady or different saints.

RELIGIOUS RITUALS

5

7. CANDLES

Candles are sometimes found in front of holy statues. People light them as a symbol of the prayers they say.

8. STATIONS OF THE CROSS

The Stations of the Cross consist of fourteen separate images found around the walls of the church. They depict scenes from the Crucifixion and the last important moments of Jesus's life.

9. STAINED-GLASS WINDOW

Stained-glass windows are colourful images that may show scenes from biblical passages.

10. CONFESSIONAL BOX

The confessional box is a place where people can receive the sacrament of reconciliation.

11. CRIB

At Christmas you will find a crib in the church. This is built to look like a barn or cave and depicts the story of Jesus's birth.

Sacredness

A place of worship such as the Church of the Most Holy Rosary in Abbeyleix, Co. Laois is very special to people of the Catholic faith. Going there helps them to feel close to God and to focus on their spiritual lives.

Christians believe that God is always very close by, always looking after them. People show great respect in these buildings of significance. They can be described as sacred or holy places.

Sacred spaces can also be found in other buildings besides official places of worship. Your school may have a sacred space such as a prayer room. You may be brought to this sacred space when your class organises a liturgy of some kind. This place is special as it allows you some time out to reflect and relax during your busy school day.

WRITE THE ANSWERS   Enquiry

1   The Church of the Most Holy Rosary was built in _____.

2   The _____ on the top of the building identifies it as a Christian place of worship.

3   The _____ is where the body of Christ is kept between Masses.

4   The Stations of the Cross consist of _____ separate images found around the walls of the church.

5   The confessional box is a place where people can receive the _____ of _____.

6   In small groups, choose a world religion. How would you create a sacred space for this religion? Describe this through a written or visual piece.

The Mass

At the Church of the Most Holy Rosary in Abbeyleix and other churches around the country, people gather together for Mass on Saturday evening or Sunday morning to pray. During Mass, Catholics take part in rituals when they gather together as a group to worship God.

A ritual is a religious ceremony involving a series of actions that are performed without any variation. These actions are symbolic and help people to express their beliefs, values and deepest concerns.

Religious rituals have a special meaning as they help people of faith become closer to God. They allow them to celebrate the presence of God in their lives. They are important because they allow people to gather together to experience something that has a special meaning.

When people want to talk to each other they can meet, but when they want to talk to God they do this by praying or taking part in a ritual. Rituals allow links to be made between the worshipper and God.

LITERACY LIBRARY

Eucharist:
The greatest act of worship for Catholics. The word 'Eucharist' means 'thanksgiving'.

Celebrating the Eucharist is the most important ritual for Catholics. At Mass people gather together in communal prayer and thanksgiving for the love that God shows to them. During the introduction to the Mass, the sign of the cross is made and the community asks for God's forgiveness through the penitential rite. They then listen to the word of God through scripture readings from the Old and New Testament.

The congregation kneels and stands together for the Liturgy of the Eucharist when they receive Christ's body and blood. Finally, they are dismissed into the wider community to love and serve God.

The Order of the Mass

Some of the responses people make to the priest have changed since 2011. Parishes around the country prepared for this for quite some time. It is important to note that the structure and order of the Mass have not changed.

There are four different parts to the Mass:

1 Introduction
2 Liturgy of the Word
3 Liturgy of the Eucharist
4 Conclusion.

Introduction

There are five parts to the Introduction of the Mass:

1 **Entrance procession and priest's greeting:** At this point people make the sign of the cross as a community of believers.
2 **Penitential rite:** The word 'penitence' means 'being sorry for sinning'. The congregation reflect on their wrongdoings and ask for God's forgiveness.
3 **Kyrie:** Together, the followers of Christ say 'Lord have mercy, Christ have mercy' after the priest.
4 **Gloria:** Through this prayer, Catholics praise God.
5 **Opening prayer:** The priest explains in the opening prayer what this Mass is about, for example graduation, class Mass or other kinds of special occasions.

Liturgy of the Word

1 The word of God is spoken from the Bible. The **first reading** is from the Old Testament, while the **second reading** is from the New Testament.
2 Between the two readings is the Responsorial Psalm. There are 150 to choose from in the Old Testament. Ministers of the Word read all these readings. (These are laypeople who volunteer to read in the church.)
3 After that, the **Gospel** is read. This can be taken from Matthew, Mark, Luke or John. The priest reads the Gospel.
4 The priest normally says a few words after the Gospel, when he comments on the readings. This is called the **homily**.
5 When the priest is finished, everyone stands for the **Creed**. The Creed explains what Catholics believe about the Church and God.
6 Members of the congregation read the **prayers of the faithful**. Here they pray for things like His Holiness the Pope, peace, their families and the community.

RELIGIOUS RITUALS

5

Consecrated:
Blessed or made holy.

Nourishment:
Something that feeds us, supports us and helps us to grow.

Liturgy of the Eucharist

1 Members of the congregation present the gifts of bread and wine at the altar. This is called the **offertory**.

2 The **Eucharistic** prayer follows. This is a prayer of praise and thanksgiving for Jesus Christ. The words of the Last Supper are spoken: 'This is my body … This is my blood … do this in memory of me.' Jesus is now present under the appearance of the bread and wine as believers pray.

3 The **Lord's Prayer** is spoken as the congregation stand together as a community of believers. 'Our Father who art in Heaven …'

4 The **sign of peace** is an important part of the ceremony, as it is an invitation to offer peace to other members of the congregation.

5 Believers receive the **body of Christ** from the priest or Minister of the Eucharist. Like food, the consecrated bread gives them nourishment and strength.

Catholics believe that Jesus is truly present at the Mass. Jesus is present when people read from scripture. During the Mass the bread and wine change into the body and blood of Christ. This is called **transubstantiation**.

Conclusion/End of the Mass

1 In his final blessing, the priest tells the people to 'go forth and spread the good news'.

2 The people leave with the knowledge that they are safe in the hands of God.

Participation

'To participate' means 'to take part in or take a role in something'. Catholics are encouraged to take an active part in the Mass. There are many ways people can participate or become involved in their local church. Laypeople can:

1   Become Ministers of the Word by saying the readings or prayers of the faithful at Mass. Most parishes have a rota system whereby people are encouraged to read every few weeks at Mass. A small course is run in the parishes that help to give people the confidence to read at Mass.

2   Become Ministers of the Eucharist by giving out the body of Christ at Communion time. Most parishes encourage people to take a course to become a Minister of the Eucharist. These minsters also visit people in their homes who are unable to receive Holy Communion at Mass.

3   Sing or play an instrument with the church choir. Most parishes have different types of choirs or folk groups that young and old can get involved in. When we sing, we pray twice.

4   Bring up the gifts at the offertory procession.

5   Get involved in decorating the church or helping to clean it.

Even if they don't have a particular job, people are still called through their baptism to take part in the ceremonies and rituals. They can do this by standing at certain times, joining in communal prayers such as the Our Father, kneeling at special times and even blessing themselves at the beginning and end of Mass. These are all ways of participating.

By fully participating in the Mass, Catholics come to understand more clearly the message of Christ. Therefore, they can go out into the world and spread the good news.

WRITE THE ANSWERS   Enquiry

1   Name the four parts of the Catholic Mass.

2   Describe each part in detail.

3   Do you think that any one part is more important than the others? Why?

4   Organise your own class Mass. Choose the readings, prayers, reflections and songs. Invite your local priest to say the Mass.

5   What does 'participation' mean?

 **GROUP ACTIVITY**   Reflection and Action

In small groups, and using a placemat, write down some ways a teenager can participate in his or her parish.

The Church of Ireland

The Church of Ireland is an important community of faith in Ireland. It is a Protestant church but has much in common with the Catholic Church. It is sometimes called the Anglican Church because it is part of an international group of Churches known as the Anglican community. However, it is important to note that the Church of Ireland is independent. Read the following interview with Reverend Chris Bennett to find out more.

REVEREND
CHRIS BENNETT

Q How long have you been a minister in the Church of Ireland?

A I have been a minister for 18 years.

Q What inspired you to take the step from layperson to minister?

A It was something I had wanted to do since I was about 15 or 16. A minister in my home church made a big difference in my life at that age, and I wanted to do the same for someone else some day!

Q What kind of work does your Church do at a local level?

A The Dock runs a pop-up café in the Titanic Quarter as a way of building community in a new part of Belfast. We run groups like book groups and knitting groups, which allow people to meet their neighbours. We're also open six days a week for people to call in, chill out and chat. We also have a Prayer Garden for people to take some time aside to think, pray or reflect. We run a weekly walk called the Dock Walk in which people discuss a Bible passage as we walk through the Titanic Quarter together.

Q What is the motivation for this work?

A I believe that the Church should be at the centre of building community and making a difference in this world. So I suppose you could say that the motivation is to make a difference in the Titanic Quarter and communicate the love of God through our actions.

Q What impact does this work have on other people and communities?

A Good question – you'd need to ask our customers! A lot of people in the Titanic Quarter wouldn't have anywhere to socialise and meet their neighbours if it wasn't for the Dock. A lot of students from the nearby college use the café as a 'home away from home', so it hopefully provides a sanctuary or safe place and a welcoming space for people in the middle of busy lives.

Q What is your own particular role within the Church?

A I'm the lead chaplain, so I co-ordinate a team of chaplains from different denominations as well as taking overall responsibility for running the café.

Q What kind of other roles do people take on in the Church community?

A We have a team of about 50 volunteers – about 25 of them are coffee shop volunteers (serving coffee and chatting to customers), some are on the management board and oversee the finances and technicalities. Some of them are on the Creative Team and fill the café with as much art and colour as possible, and some are chaplains who are happy to pray with people and discuss questions of faith.

Q What do you think are the challenges that face the Church of Ireland in today's world?

A I think the Church in general (and not just the Church of Ireland) now exists in a world where people are not only apathetic about Church and Christian belief – they are sometimes openly hostile. Church is seen as outdated, irrelevant and often corrupt or hypocritical. At the same time, people still have spiritual questions about life and death and the Churches need to find spaces and places where those questions can be asked and discussed. We also need to find ways to engage with our communities and make the world a better place – rather than hiding in 'holy bubbles'.

Leadership in the Church of Ireland/Anglican Church

Every community of faith is organised and run in a different way. The Church of Ireland has a very democratic style of leadership. It comes from the bottom up rather than the top down.

The joint leaders of the Church of Ireland are the Archbishop of Armagh and the Archbishop of Dublin. Their joint role is to be the official voice of the Church of Ireland and to lead their members by example. They consult with the other bishops and represent the Church on many international bodies. Reverend Dr Michael Jackson is the current Archbishop of Dublin. Bishop Richard Clarke is the current Archbishop of Armagh and Primate of All Ireland.

In September 2013, the Church of Ireland appointed **Rev. Pat Storey as its first female bishop**. Rev. Storey is the bishop of Meath and Kildare.

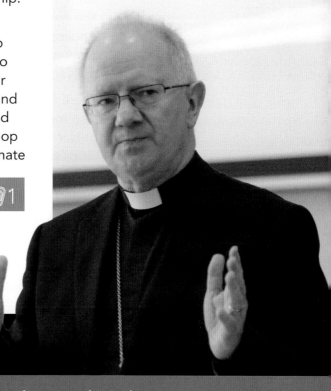

Archbishop Richard Clarke of Armagh, Primate of All Ireland.

LITERACY LIBRARY

Consult:
To discuss with and ask for advice from others.

Vestry:
A meeting attended by parishioners to discuss official Church business.

Synod:
A gathering of Church leaders to discuss the law of the Church.

Diocese:
An area of Churches led by a bishop.

Church of Ireland Leadership Structure

General Synod = House of Bishops and House of Representatives

↓

Diocesan Synod

↓

Select Vestry

↓

Annual General Vestry

1 Every lay member of a parish aged 18 years and over is allowed to attend and vote at the Annual General Vestry of the parish.

2 This General Vestry elects the Select Vestry (parish committees), which runs the parish.

3 Every third year, the General Vestry elects the parish's lay representatives to the Diocesan Synod.

4 Every third year, the Diocesan Synod elects the clergy and laity who will represent the diocese on the General Synod, the governing body.

5 This governing body consists of two houses, the House of Bishops and the House of Representatives, which is made up of clergy and laity.

Worship in the Anglican Church/Church of Ireland

Sunday service in the Anglican Church is led by the rector. He or she leads the prayers and bases the sermon around scripture readings. The congregation reflects on the readings and their main message. In the Anglican Church, everyone sings the hymns together and responds to the prayers. There is a Holy Communion service on the first and third Sundays of every month.

There are two main parts to the service. There are scripture readings, a sermon and prayers during the ministry of the word. Bread and wine are presented at the altar during the ministry of the sacrament. The words that Jesus spoke at the Last Supper are repeated. The congregation kneels before the altar and receives the bread first and then the wine from the chalice or cup.

WRITE THE ANSWER   Enquiry

Describe what happens at the Sunday service in the Anglican Church.

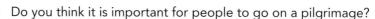

REFLECTIVE ACTIVITY

Think about your own attitude to religious rituals and answer the following questions:

1   What did you find interesting about this chapter?
2   Do you think it is important for people to go on a pilgrimage?
3   Do you think religious rituals are important for people?

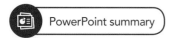
PowerPoint summary

Weblinks

St Patrick's Cathedral, Dublin

RELIGIOUS RITUALS

5

CHAPTER 6
Non-religious Rituals

SOL: 6, 8
LO: 1.7, 2.2, 2.10

 See also Chapter 9

LEARNING OUTCOME

Discuss how important non-religious rituals and celebrations are for people.

KEY SKILLS YOU WILL USE IN THIS CHAPTER

- Working with others
- Communicating
- Being literate
- Managing information and thinking

WELLBEING INDICATORS IN THIS CHAPTER

LEARNING INTENTIONS

At the end of this chapter, I will

1 Understand what a ritual is

2 Describe how using rituals can help people mark important events in life

3 Give an example of a non-religious ritual

4 Present the elements involved in a non-religious ritual.

LITERACY
LIBRARY

Acknowledge:
To recognise or accept.

Ceremony:
A formal marking of something,
usually performed in a group.

There are certain moments or events along the journey through life that are so important they must be marked or celebrated in some way. Whether they are moments of great joy or great sadness, they call on something inside us to take some time out from our busy lives and acknowledge their impact on us.

GROUP ACTIVITY   Reflection and Action

In small groups, discuss moments of joy or sadness in life that people mark or celebrate in some way in society today.
Share your thoughts with the rest of the class.

Rituals

For many years in Ireland, people turned to religion to help them show the importance of these moments in their lives. Rituals are a feature of all human societies.

A ritual is a sequence of activities that involves gestures, words and objects and it is performed in a certain place, in a particular way. Christian rituals, such as First Holy Communion and funeral Masses, have allowed people to take part in ceremonies at times when they needed to join with others to mark such occasions.

Many of these Christian rituals are still hugely important for believers today. Those who take part can find meaning in the rituals performed at such occasions.

Ritual ceremonies often have traditions associated with them that have been passed down from generation to generation.
This means that when people take part in these rituals, they know what to expect and can feel involved as they say the words or perform the actions.

Some rituals involve large numbers of people and this can give the event a communal feel. This sense of community at a ritual makes people feel united and stronger.

WRITE THE ANSWER   Enquiry

Think about a ritual you were involved in or witnessed.
Write about what happened at it and what part you or others played.

Why, do you think, are harvest times important to people?

Non-religious Rituals

Rituals don't have to be religious ceremonies or events. Rites of passage, dedication ceremonies, graduations and parades are all examples of rituals that don't have to be associated with religion.

Some rituals are seasonal, such as rituals relating to harvest times. Thanksgiving in the US is one example of a harvest festival. Another example is the harvest home festival, which is an English tradition. There is also a harvest festival every year in Waterford.

Whatever type of ritual it is, the reasons for it are the same: to gather with others and celebrate or mark an important moment in time.

In today's world, people of different religious beliefs and people of no religious beliefs live side by side. As a result, there is more of a need for non-religious rituals and celebrations to allow people of all faiths and none to mark important times in an inclusive way.

LITERACY LIBRARY

Rites of passage:
Any important act or event that marks the passage from one stage of life to another.

Dedication ceremony:
A ceremony that marks the official completion or opening of a public building or monument, for example.

Graduation:
A celebration held when someone completes a course of study in a college or school.

Inclusive:
Making sure everyone feels included.

LITERACY LIBRARY

Atheist:
A person who does not believe in a God.

Forgo:
To do without.

Chaos:
Something that is unpredictable and disorganised.

Fundamentally:
Necessarily or essentially.

Narrative:
A story or account of events.

Suzanne Moore is an English journalist who has written articles for the *Guardian* newspaper. She is an atheist, which means that she does not believe in God.

Suzanne Moore once wrote an article called 'Why non-believers need rituals too'. In it she spoke about wanting to create a ceremony after her child was born that would be meaningful to the people she invited who were from different faiths.

In the article she said, 'I love ritual, because it is through ritual that we remake and strengthen our social bonds.'

When it came to what she wanted for the ceremony, she said, 'I found myself turning to flowers, flames and incense. Is there anything more beautiful than the offerings made all over the world, of tiny flames and blossom on leaves floating on water?'

The writer went on to say, 'For me, not believing in God does not mean one has to forgo poetry, magic, the chaos of ritual, the re-making of shared bonds … It seems to be fundamentally human to seek narratives, find patterns and create rituals to include others in the meanings we make.'

Source: Suzanne Moore, The Guardian, *27 December 2013*

RESEARCH   Exploration

Find Suzanne Moore's article online. Read it and, in your own words, write down what you think she is trying to say.

6 NON-RELIGIOUS RITUALS

Search online for more information on this topic.

Anniversaries

Read the following story of how one family used a non-religious ritual to mark an important time in their lives.

Aidan's Day

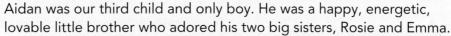

by Fiona

Aidan was our third child and only boy. He was a happy, energetic, lovable little brother who adored his two big sisters, Rosie and Emma. When he was six years old he learned to ride his bike without stabilizers and as a family we spent many happy weekends heading off on our bikes to explore the countryside around where we live.

Aidan loved sport. His favourite song was 'Ireland's Call', which he shouted out rather than sang at any football or rugby match we went to, even if it was two local teams playing in a friendly.

When Aidan was seven he began to complain of getting headaches. After many tests and hospital visits we were told the devastating news that Aidan had a very rare form of cancer. We were heartbroken. The illness progressed rapidly and our little boy passed away just six months later. The first few months after his death passed by in a blur of tears and sadness.

Coming up to the first anniversary of his death we decided as a family that we wanted to do something to mark the wonderful person that Aidan had been in his seven short years. Rosie and Emma came up with a lot of brilliant ideas.

Can you think of any other rituals the family could include in Aidan's Day?

We invited all our extended family and friends over to the house to help us remember Aidan and celebrate his life. Everyone brought their bikes and we headed off on a cycle together – all forty of us! – along one of Aidan's favourite routes.

When we came home we had a picnic in the back garden, eating all Aidan's favourite foods. People shared their memories of Aidan and we laughed together at some of the funny things we remembered him doing.

Just as the sun set in the evening, we each released a blue balloon into the sky and we all sang 'Ireland's Call' at the top of our voices.

Aidan has been gone for four years now and each year on his anniversary we carry out the same rituals with our family and friends. We call it Aidan's Day and while we will always miss him terribly, there's something very comforting and special about the way we remember Aidan every year.

WRITE THE ANSWER Enquiry

After reading Fiona's story, why, do you think, do the rituals they have created for Aidan's anniversary bring so much comfort to the family?

NON-RELIGIOUS RITUALS

6

Croke Park

Coveted:
Really wanted.

Spectators:
Viewers, people who
are watching.

Formality:
Something official
or fixed.

Are there any non-
religious rituals that take
place in your school, such
as assemblies or prize-
giving ceremonies? What
happens at them?

Rituals and Sport

For over one hundred years, on a Sunday in late August or early
September, sport-loving Irish people all over the world focus their
attention on Croke Park. It is one of the most exciting days in the GAA
calendar: the All-Ireland Senior Football Championship Final. Up for grabs
is the coveted Sam Maguire Cup.

Over the years, many rituals and traditions have built up around this
event. For many families it is an important date in their calendar and if
their home county is playing in the final it is almost like a national holiday.

On the day itself there are a number of rituals that are followed and are
well known to anyone who has attended the final or tuned in on their
television from home. It begins with the players from both teams running
out on the pitch to roars of support from the thousands of spectators.

The team photo is taken and then the teams line up for a very important
moment. The President of Ireland is introduced to each player and shakes
their hand. The teams then line up behind the Artane Boys' Band, who
lead them around the pitch.

Then the teams break apart and stand to attention while the national
anthem is played. Finally, they take up their match positions and the ball
is thrown in for play.

When the final whistle is blown, all GAA fans know what is coming next.
The President of the GAA makes a speech and presents the Sam Maguire
Cup to the captain of the winning team. Traditionally, when the captain
makes his speech, his opening lines are spoken in Irish. It is then the turn
of every player to hold up the cup to roars of applause from the crowd.

The traditions continue the next day with a homecoming celebration in
the winning county. In recent years, another tradition has become part of
the event: the players from the winning team bring the cup to Our Lady's
Children's Hospital in Dublin and visit some of the sick patients.

These non-religious rituals of the All-Ireland Football Championship are
very important for the people involved. It gives the event a sense of
formality and importance. People look forward to experiencing all the
different parts of the occasion and there is a great sense of unity and
celebration on the day.

RESEARCH Exploration

In small groups, choose one of the following types of non-religious rituals and research the different elements that may be involved.

1 A graduation ceremony

2 A harvest festival

3 A non-religious wedding ceremony

4 A dedication ceremony

5 A citizenship ceremony.

Present your findings to the class, making sure to address the following:

- Where it takes place
- When it happens
- What is being marked or celebrated
- What words or actions are involved
- Who participates and why.

Remember, there may be rituals that take place in other countries around the world.

LITERACY LIBRARY

Secular:
Non-religious.

The Sunday Assembly

In Edinburgh, Scotland, there is a group called the Sunday Assembly. In an interview with BBC News Scotland, the group's chairperson, Mark McKergow, describes it as 'a church with no religion'.
The movement began in London in 2013. The elements of worship and the community aspect of religion appealed to the founders, but they did not believe in God.

There are approximately forty-five Sunday Assembly groups around the world, found in eight different countries. They sing secular songs, listen to guest speakers and encourage each other to live better lives. It is a celebration of life.

One member said, 'It gives us a chance to come together as a family. My husband and I are both atheists, but we like coming together and hearing others' stories, listening to poems and reflections about life and singing with others.'

WRITE THE ANSWER Enquiry

Explain, in your own words, why you think belonging to a Sunday Assembly group might appeal to some people.

 PowerPoint summary

 Weblinks

 Do some research on the internet to find out more about the Sunday Assembly.

REFLECTIVE ACTIVITY

Think about your own attitude about the importance of non-religious rituals for people and answer the following questions:

1 How does ritual help people to mark important times in their lives?

2 What is the most meaningful ritual you have ever witnessed or participated in?

3 Which of the non-religious rituals that you have read about in this chapter appealed to you the most? Why?

CHAPTER 7
Prayer

SOL: 5
LO: 1.8, 2.8, 2.9

LEARNING OUTCOMES

Describe the role of prayer in the lives of people of faith.

KEY SKILLS YOU WILL USE IN THIS CHAPTER

- Working with others
- Communicating
- Being literate
- Managing information and thinking
- Being creative

WELLBEING INDICATORS IN THIS CHAPTER

LEARNING INTENTIONS

At the end of this chapter, I will

1. Understand why a person of religious faith uses prayer

2. Be able to explain what the following terms mean: 'personal prayer', 'communal prayer', 'formal prayer' and 'informal prayer'

3. Give an example of how prayer is important in the life of a person of faith

4. Present the meaning and role of two prayers associated with one of the major world religions

5. Explain what is involved in prayer in either the Jewish or Muslim faith.

In order to have a relationship with other people or groups, we must communicate. To communicate means to keep in touch with and to connect with someone else.

THINK, PAIR, SHARE

Imagine your best friend moved to a different country and you could not visit them.

Think of all the different ways you could communicate with them.

Work in **pairs**. **Share** your answers with the class.

What kinds of things are important for you to communicate with your friend about?

LITERACY LIBRARY

Communication:
Sharing information with other people.

Prayer

To have a religious faith means that a person has a relationship with their God.

Just like other relationships, the relationship with God needs communication. Without communication a relationship will suffer and possibly break down.

People of religious faith need a way to communicate with their God in order to keep the relationship alive. They do this by praying.

Praying is simply a conversation between a believer and their God. Some conversations are brief and to the point. Other conversations are deeper and more formal.

There are also conversations that are casual and informal. Just like there are different types of conversations, there are different types of prayers.

PRAYER 7

Communal and Personal Prayers

Formal prayers follow a set pattern of words and are known to most people in the community of faith. They are usually said when people gather together for worship. This is called communal prayer.

Communal prayer often happens in a place of worship, such as a temple, church or synagogue. An example of a communal prayer in Christianity is the Our Father. A formal prayer in Judaism is the Amidah (the Standing Prayer).

> Do you have a favourite prayer?

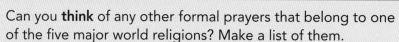

THINK, PAIR, SHARE

Can you **think** of any other formal prayers that belong to one of the five major world religions? Make a list of them.

Work in **pairs**. **Share** your ideas with your partner and see if they have named any formal prayers you have not heard before.

LITERACY LIBRARY

Synagogue:
A Jewish building used for worship.

Amidah:
A formal Jewish prayer, also called the Standing Prayer.

Informal:
Casual, unofficial.

The role of communal prayers for believers is for them to share their faith with others. Some religions believe that praying with others makes their prayers stronger. In the Christian Gospel it says, 'Where two or three are gathered in my name, there am I with them.'

Another type of prayer is informal prayer. These prayers are usually said when a person is on their own and they can be said anywhere. In informal prayer a person can use any words they wish and the prayer can be as long or short as they want.

The role of informal prayers for a believer is that they get to talk to their God in a more personal way. It is a private conversation between a person and their God.

Prayer in the Life of a Person of Faith

People of faith pray for many different reasons. Some pray because their religion tells them to pray at a certain time, in a certain way. In other words, it may be part of their religious beliefs.

> **RESEARCH** Exploration
>
> Split the class into five groups.
>
> Each group will take one of the five major world religions below and find an example of two prayers associated with the chosen religion.
>
> 1 Buddhism
> 2 Christianity
> 3 Hinduism
> 4 Islam
> 5 Judaism
>
> Explain what the prayer means, when it is used and why members of the religion say it.
>
> Report your findings on a poster or using PowerPoint.

> If you have a religious faith, do you pray at certain times of the day?

To find out what the role of prayer is in the life of a person of faith, read the following piece written by a member of the Christian religion, Mary, a working mother of two young boys who lives in the midlands.

Prayer was something I was taught from a young age by my parents. It was part of my everyday life. I wouldn't describe myself as an overly religious person, but I do have a strong faith. I see prayer as a way to simply chat to God.

When I wake every morning, my first stop is the bathroom. I find myself looking in the mirror and having my first conversation of the day. That conversation is with God. It starts by thanking God for everything I have: my husband, my children, my family and my home. I thank God for all the gifts of life and living for today.

In my prayers I ask God to be present with me and help me to live in the moment so that I can truly see all the beauty that surrounds me. I ask him to help me be present in every moment of my life, which can sometimes be difficult in the busy world we live in.

I believe that God is the creator of all things and he has created the world that I live in. It has good times and bad times and I can have moments when I feel alone. I ask God to help me through the difficult times and help me to learn from all situations so that I can live every day to the best of my ability.

> **WRITE THE ANSWERS** Enquiry
>
>
>
> 1 What does Mary think prayer is?
> 2 When does Mary pray?
> 3 Name three things Mary prays about.
> 4 Mary says that she has a strong faith. Explain why you agree or disagree with this statement after reading her piece.

PRAYER 7

Another person of faith for whom prayer was very important was a Catholic priest named St Maximilian Kolbe. Read his story and then answer the questions that follow.

St Maximilian Kolbe (1894–1941)

St Maximilian Kolbe was born Raymond Kolbe in Poland in 1894. In 1910, Maximilian joined the Franciscan Order. As a priest, he had a deep devotion to Mary and published a monthly magazine to tell others about the mother of Jesus.

In 1941, when the Nazis had control of Poland, Maximilian was arrested for hiding refugees, including Jews, and was sent to the concentration camp in Auschwitz. But Maximilian believed it was the will of God and his Blessed Mother that he should be there. He felt that there was nowhere else on earth that was in such need of spiritual strength and encouragement. He wanted to be there for the prisoners, day and night. While there, he gave away many of his own possessions and often gave his food to younger prisoners who he felt needed it more than him.

After a while prisoners began to come to him from all over the camp. He spoke words of love and prayed with those who were losing their faith. His message was that one must not give in to hatred, no matter how awful things are. One fellow priest who went to him to confess his sins came away saying he had met a living saint.

Maximilian was fifty-seven years old and was in poor health, yet he was forced to work every day. One morning one of the prisoners in his group escaped. As a punishment to the other people in the camp, the guards picked ten prisoners to be starved to death.

Then an extraordinary thing happened. Maximilian offered himself instead of one of the men who had a wife and family. He was sent to an underground cell with the other prisoners to wait to die. While there, he said prayers and sang hymns with the other prisoners to give them all support and strength, even though it angered the guards.

After days of being starved, Maximilian was the last prisoner alive. The Nazis killed him by injecting him with poison. Moments before his death, Maximilian could be heard praying.

Jesus once said, 'A man can have no greater love than to lay down his life for his friends.' Maximilian knew that his days on earth were at an end. He gave up his life as a sacrifice. It was an act of total goodness that shone through an act of evil.

Prayer played a huge role in Maximilian's life. He turned to prayer in times of need and he taught others how prayer could give them courage and strength.

WRITE THE ANSWERS Enquiry

1 What sort of life did Maximilian live in Auschwitz?

2 Describe the type of person he was.

3 Do you think he deserves the title of saint? Give reasons for your answer.

4 Describe how you think the prisoner felt when Maximilian took his place to die.

5 Explain what role prayer played in the life of Maximilian Kolbe.

Auschwitz concentration camp.

PRAYER 7

Cian Lynch

Cian Lynch is a hurling player with a strong faith. He plays at inter-county level with Limerick. He was on the team that beat Galway in 2018 and won Limerick's first All-Ireland in forty-five years. His strong faith comes from his Catholic family. Going to Mass and praying are a part of his everyday life. Cian has six siblings and his parents brought them to Mass every Sunday.

'If it was a feast day, we'd be in Mass to celebrate it or we might say a few prayers. But every Sunday I'd be down for Mass.'

Cian feels that going to Mass and praying gives structure to his life and keeps him grounded. He finds it especially helpful during the highs and lows of winning or losing matches.

If he can, Cian likes to go to Mass on the day of a game: 'Even if we we're meeting early, I'd go the night before. I'd be saying a few prayers at night anyway.'

Source: Adapted from an article by Marisa Kennedy for Pundit Arena.

WRITE THE ANSWER   Enquiry

In your own words, describe why and how prayer is important in the life of Cian Lynch.

📎1

RESEARCH   Enquiry

Break into small groups. Each group should pick one of the following people of faith and research the part prayer played in their life. Focus on why and how they used prayer.

1 Ignatius of Loyola
2 Muhammad
3 Siddharta Gautama
4 Pope Francis

RESEARCH   Reflection and Action

Look up information on the following sports stars who have a strong religious faith and see what difference it makes (or made) to them:

1 Stephen Curry, basketball player
2 Muhammad Ali, boxer
3 Venus and Serena Williams, tennis players
4 Katie Taylor, boxer

Jewish Prayer

The Jewish community in Ireland is a small but <u>vibrant</u> one. Read the following piece from the Office of the Chief Rabbi of Ireland about the role of prayer in the life of Jewish people of faith.

LITERACY LIBRARY

Vibrant:
Full of energy and life.

Prayer is a central and important feature of Jewish life, both in a communal setting and a private one. Every single day of the year begins and ends with prayer, shorter on weekdays and longer on the Sabbath and festivals. Once a year, on the Day of Atonement, prayer takes up most of the day.

Although God speaks all languages and accepts all prayers, Jews do have a fixed liturgy, printed in a **siddur** (prayer book for daily prayer) or a **machzor** (prayer book for festival prayers), which can be recited individually or with a group.

The prayers change depending on the time of day, the day of the week and even the number of people in attendance. In Orthodox tradition, many of the prayers can only be recited if at least ten adult males are present (a **minyan**), whereas non-Orthodox movements may allow fewer than ten or a mix of genders.

There are three daily services: **Shacharit** (the morning service), **Mincha** (the afternoon service) and **Arvit** or **Maariv** (the evening service). To make things easier, many synagogues will hold the evening service immediately after the afternoon one, so there are prayers once in the morning and only once in the evening.

A synagogue is not necessary for prayer, and many do choose to pray privately at home during the weekdays, although the Sabbath services are usually all held in the synagogue. Aside from the set liturgy, Jews are urged to pray whenever they want to communicate with God, without the need for a special building, text or time.

Because the prayers need to occur within a certain timeframe, Shacharit in the morning and Mincha in the afternoon, for example, you can often see groups of ten or more men joining for an impromptu prayer session in a football game, on an airplane or at a motorway rest-stop. However, even without the minimum number of ten, individuals will still stop to pray on their own.

Less traditional Jews may only pray on the Sabbath or on festivals, and similarly in non-Orthodox movements, but it is largely a personal decision. Orthodox places of prayer will also have separate seating for men and women, whereas other movements will have mixed seating.

Most of the prayers are said aloud, except for one prayer known as the **Amidah**, which is recited silently. On three days of the week – Monday, Thursday and the Sabbath – the prayer service also includes a public reading of the weekly portion from a Torah scroll.

Apart from the longer prayer services, the Jewish day is filled with shorter prayers, such as one said first thing in the morning to thank God for being alive; a prayer is said before and after eating or drinking to thank God for what He provides; and there is even a prayer said after using the bathroom to thank God that our bodies are healthy! A prayer a day (hopefully) keeps the doctor away ...

Prayer in the Life of a Muslim

The Islamic religion has very specific rules and guidelines when it comes to praying.

Prayer is one of the Five Pillars of Islam, which are five duties every Muslim must carry out. Prayer is a way of life for Muslims and not something separate from it.

Muslims see prayer as way for them to get closer to their God and to become better people. They must pray five times a day, which can involve much planning and preparation. The different parts involved in prayer form a ritual.

Wudu

Wudu is the washing that takes place before prayer. Muslims must make sure that the area where they perform their prayers is clean.

Wudu consists of removing the shoes, then washing the hands, mouth, nostrils, face, arms up to the elbows and feet up to the ankles. It also involves passing a wet hand over the head and wiping the inside and outside of the ears with a wet finger.

As prayer involves kneeling on the ground, Muslims pray on a prayer mat, which they can bring anywhere.

Facing the Kaaba in Mecca

Muslims must face in the direction of the Kaaba in Mecca in Saudi Arabia when they pray. Muslims in our part of the world must face southeast during prayer.

In the mosque there is a hollow in the wall called a mihrab. This is at a point nearest to Mecca and shows the believers which way to face.

If a Muslim is praying at home, their prayer mat may have a compass on it so they can work out the right direction to face.

LITERACY LIBRARY

Specific:
Definite or certain.

Mosque:
An Islamic building used for worship.

Mihrab:
A hollow in the wall of a mosque, facing Mecca.

Adhan

The Adhan is the call to prayer. When Muslims pray in the mosque or in a group, this call is given at the start of prayer time.

Ra'ka

Each Muslim must perform a set of movements in a particular order and say verses from the Qur'an to form a ra'ka, which is like a standard unit of prayer.

To begin the prayer, they raise their hands to their ears or shoulders. As the prayer continues, they bow, sit and kneel at certain stages and turn their head to the right and the left at the end.

Prayer Times

The five daily prayers take place at the following times:

Fajr   Dawn

Zuhr   Early afternoon, when the sun is about halfway before setting

Asr   Late afternoon before sunset

Magrib   Immediately after sunset

Isha   Evening time after darkness has set in

As you can see, the position of the sun plays a big part in prayer times. It is used to mark the beginning and end of prayer times. Because of this, the time for prayer will change slightly depending on the time of year. For example, in Ireland the sun rises earlier in the summer months, so Fajr will be at an earlier time in summer than in the winter.

WRITE THE ANSWERS   Enquiry

1 How many times a day should a Muslim pray?

2 What way do they face when they are praying?

3 Explain what wudu is.

4 How do Muslims perform a ra'ka?

5 Why do the prayer times change depending on the time of the year?

REFLECTIVE ACTIVITY

Think about your own attitude to the role of prayer in the lives of people of faith and answer the following questions:

1 Why, do you think, is prayer important for a person who has a religious faith?

2 How might not praying affect someone who has a religious faith?

3 Which person of faith did you most enjoy reading about in this chapter and why?

4 Has your view on prayer changed after reading this chapter?

 PowerPoint summary

 Weblinks

CHAPTER 8
Interfaith Dialogue

SOL: 6, 8
LO: 1.10

LEARNING OUTCOME

Discuss the importance of dialogue and interaction between major world religions and within major world religions in promoting peace and reconciliation in the world today.

KEY SKILLS YOU WILL USE IN THIS CHAPTER

- Being literate
- Being numerate
- Working with others
- Communicating
- Managing information and thinking
- Being creative
- Managing myself

WELLBEING INDICATORS IN THIS CHAPTER

LEARNING INTENTIONS

At the end of this chapter, I will

1 Be able to explain what reconciliation is

2 Be able to discuss how important reconciliation is to all major world religions

3 Be able to explain what interfaith dialogue is

4 Be able to explain how important interfaith dialogue is to Pope Francis

5 Know about the Centre for Interreligious Dialogue in Dublin City University.

LITERACY LIBRARY

Argument:
A discussion where people disagree with each other over something.

Reconciliation:
Actively embracing the person who has sinned against us and welcoming them back into our lives.

Think about your own world religion and what reconciliation message it is telling you.

Have you ever had an argument or a disagreement with your friend?

If so, how did that make you feel? How do you think he or she felt? How did you resolve the issue that caused the disagreement in the first place? How are things between you now? Have you moved on from the disagreement to live in harmony or peace with each other?

Talk to the person beside you about your thoughts on these questions.

These are important questions for us to ask ourselves. They are also important questions for members of religions today all over the world to ask of themselves and other world religions. Communication and discussion are important key elements between world religions.

Reconciliation and World Religions

Together let's look at how world religions get on with each other to promote peace and reconciliation. Many of us belong to one of the five major world religions: Christianity, Judaism, Islam, Buddhism or Hinduism.

Christianity, Judaism and Islam share several basic principles. Each of these religions:

	Believes in one God	Has a founder	Has a sacred text	Has a place of worship	Has important rules
Christianity	God	Jesus	Bible	Church	The Beatitudes
Judaism	Yahweh	Abraham/ Moses	Tenakh	Synagogue	Ten Commandments
Islam	Allah	Muhammad	Qur'an	Mosque	Five Pillars of Islam

WRITE THE ANSWERS   Enquiry

1. What world religion believes in Yahweh?
2. What world religion was founded by Jesus?
3. What sacred text do you associate with Islam?
4. In your copybook, fill in the blanks:
   (a) Christians worship in a _____.
   (b) Jewish people worship in a _____.
   (c) Muslims worship in a _____.
5. Find out more about the Ten Commandments and the Five Pillars of Islam. What relevance do they hold for us today?

LITERACY LIBRARY

Dialogue:
A conversation between two or more people.

Dialogue

When there are shared values, it makes it easier to sit with someone and have a conversation or discussion. The word dialogue means to talk to others and to listen to what they have to say in return.

Dialogue is an important part of helping individual people and groups to understand each other and grow. **Interfaith dialogue** is communication and understanding between people from different major world religions, not just between Catholics and Protestants (Christian Churches).

When people communicate with each other, they talk and they listen to each other. This is important because they are willing to hear what the other person is saying. They hear what is happening in the other person's life and are willing to learn from their experiences.

Ireland has changed greatly over the last number of decades and interfaith dialogue is even more important than ever. This is because we have lots of different people from different countries and religious faiths living side by side. When people travel from one country to another, they bring their religious beliefs with them. Today in Ireland there are people of many different faiths being educated together in schools.

WRITE THE ANSWERS   Enquiry

1   What does 'dialogue' mean?

2   Do you think dialogue is important? Why do you think this is?

3   Talk to someone in your family who is older than you (for example, a grandparent) and ask them how Ireland has changed over the last few decades.

Make notes of your conversation and report this to your class.

World Council of Churches

One example of world religions working together to promote peace and reconciliation in the world today amongst different faiths is the **World Council of Churches (WCC),** which was established over seventy years ago, in 1948.

Although some of its work involves ecumenism, in recent times it has become more involved in interfaith dialogue.

Ecumenism:
Attempts that Christians make to understand and respect each other and to grow together in a more unified way.

Pastoral support:
Spiritual guidance and help.

Reaffirm:
Explain again strongly.

In August 2018, the World Council of Churches visited Nicaragua during a political crisis. The visit there arose as a result of the World Council of Churches' Pilgrimage of Justice and Peace. The aim of the visit was to offer pastoral support to the churches in Nicaragua, where the people have suffered much pain and trauma, and to help find solutions to these issues.

A message issued by the members of the delegation reads, 'We have sought to support dialogue as a means to resolve differences and to reaffirm and strengthen calls for justice, peace and respect for diverse ways of thinking in contemporary societies'.

Peaceful protest against social security reforms in Nicaragua, 2018.

The World Council of Churches promotes contact between Christians and people of different faiths. It aims to build trust and to help people find solutions to common challenges through dialogue.

During the past few years, the WCC has organised several Hindu–Christian, Christian–Muslim, Buddhist–Christian and Jewish–Christian dialogues. As well as discussing religious topics, the participants also share ideas on issues of justice and peace.

Interfaith Youth Core

In July 2018, there was a gathering of young people in Chicago organised by the Interfaith Youth Core to improve relations among people of different faiths. 'Bringing students together who are Muslim, Hindu, Christian, pagan and many other world views, the conference will teach skills like how to have difficult conversations, how to work together despite fundamental differences and how to take action to create pluralistic communities.'

Muslims and Jews breaking the Ramadan fast together.

Interfaith Encounter Association

For over two decades the Interfaith Encounter Association has been dedicated to promoting peace in the Middle East through interfaith dialogue.

Interfaith dialogue is not about making all religions the same: it is about showing respect and celebrating the differences between religions.

Everyone needs to be involved in this process of working together. If religion has been part of the problem, it should also be part of the solution.

There are many groups involved in bringing peace about: religious groups, healthcare groups, women's groups and educators. These groups want people of all religions to come together and discuss things in a respectful way.

The Interfaith Encounter Association describes their vision as that 'of a society in which the otherness of "the other" is not only accepted, but truly understood and respected.' 'The other' means someone who is from a different culture than your own and who may have ideas that you don't agree with or find hard to understand.

WRITE THE ANSWERS   Enquiry

1   Give an example of world religions working together.

2   What does the word 'ecumenism' mean?

3   How does ecumenism differ to interfaith dialogue?

4   What, do you think, is meant by the following quote: 'Interfaith dialogue is not about making all religions the same: it is about showing respect and celebrating the differences between them'?

 Search online for more information about these topics.

Pope Francis I visits a synagogue in Rome.

Pope Francis and Interfaith Dialogue

Pope Francis has done a lot to promote interfaith dialogue. He believes collaboration is essential to building and forging relationships.

In Rome in August 2017, he spoke to rabbis from Israel, the United States and Europe. At this meeting he praised the fruitful dialogue between Catholic and Jewish communities. 'We have grown in mutual understanding and deepened our bonds of friendship,' he told those gathered.

Pope Francis has visited a synagogue in Rome and has walked through the concentration camp in Auschwitz. He has praised the Torah as 'a manifestation of God's love for man', encouraging further interfaith dialogue.

In July 2016, Pope Francis visited the Nazi death camps of Auschwitz-Birkenau, walking beneath the gates inscribed with the words *'Arbeit macht frei'* ('Work sets you free').

Here Pope Francis sat alone for several minutes of sombre contemplation and prayer. He wanted his visit to be in silence. He believed it was important to visit in this way as it would help him to pray in the silence of it all without the fanfare of crowds. His only public words for the visit were written in the guest book at Auschwitz: 'Lord have pity on your people. Lord forgive so much cruelty.'

LITERACY LIBRARY

Collaborate:
Work together.

Torah:
Means 'teaching or instruction'. It refers to the five books of Moses, also called the Pentateuch.

Pope Francis sits alone in prayer and contemplation during his visit to Auschwitz.

INTERFAITH DIALOGUE

8

During the visit he met some former prisoners of the camp who had risked their own lives to save Jews during the Nazi occupation of Poland. One example of someone he met was Valentina Nikodem (camp number 8737). She was born in 1922 in Lodz in Poland. In July 1942 she and her mother were taken to Auschwitz after her father killed members of the Gestapo (Hitler's secret police force). During their time there, her mother died at the camp.

Valentina, who was put to work in the camp packaging department, helped women who gave birth in the camp and became godmother to many of those children.

This visit of Pope Francis was significant in building relationships between Catholics and Jews. Reflecting on his visit a few hours later, he asked young people, 'Is it possible that man, created in God's image and likeness, is capable of doing these things?' Pope Francis sees the significance of world religions working together in harmony to make the world a better and safer place for everyone.

Pope Francis meets Auschwitz survivors during his visit in 2016.

WRITE THE ANSWERS — Enquiry

1 What has Pope Francis done to encourage interfaith dialogue?

2 What is the Torah and what did Pope Francis say about it?

3 Who did Pope Francis meet at Auschwitz?

4 Why was the pope's visit to Auschwitz significant?

RESEARCH — Enquiry

Research other former prisoners of the camp that Pope Francis met at Auschwitz that day in July 2016.
What is their story?
Share your information with the class.

ACTIVITY — Enquiry

1 As Pope Francis sat alone at Auschwitz, what, do you think, was going through his mind?

2 Research other ways that Pope Francis has participated in and encouraged interfaith dialogue in the Catholic Church.

 Do some research online to find out more about Auschwitz.

The Centre for Interreligious Dialogue

In Dublin City University, you will find the Centre for Interreligious Dialogue (CIRD). This is an academic centre committed to the study and practice of interreligious dialogue today. The centre seeks to support research, teaching and public engagement in the area of interreligious dialogue in Ireland and beyond, especially in relation to Islam, Judaism and Christianity and the religious–secular dialogue today.

The CIRD draws on the rich engagement of interfaith studies and research among academic staff in the school. It builds on existing public events, such as the 2013 Christian–Muslim Conference on 'A Common Word'.

In November 2018, some students travelled to the Jewish Progressive Synagogue. This was founded in 1946 by members of the Irish Jewish Community. While there these students were given a talk on Judaism by the community leader, Hilary Abrahamson. She spoke to the students about Jewish festivals and the lunar calendar. She also explained the interesting and tragic history of the Jewish people. After this, the students joined the large public community for a lecture sponsored by the Irish Council of Christians and Jews.

This was a true example of interfaith dialogue today.

The Inter Faith Centre at Dublin City University

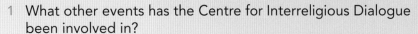

RESEARCH   Enquiry

In small groups, research the Centre for Interreligious Dialogue. Find our the following from the Dublin City University website:

1 What other events has the Centre for Interreligious Dialogue been involved in?

2 Who are the members of the team that work in the CIRD?

REFLECTIVE ACTIVITY

Think about your own attitude to interfaith dialogue and answer the following questions:

1 What part of this chapter did you find most interesting?

2 Do you think reconciliation is important?

3 Do you think interfaith dialogue is important between churches? Why/why not?

PowerPoint summary

Weblinks

INTERFAITH DIALOGUE 8

CHAPTER 9
Justice, Peace and Reconciliation

SOL: 6, 8
LO: 1.11

See also Chapter 8 and Chapter 27

LEARNING OUTCOME

Research a religious or non-religious organisation working at a national or international level to promote justice, peace and reconciliation and consider how their work is an expression of their founding vision.

KEY SKILLS YOU WILL USE IN THIS CHAPTER

- Being literate
- Being numerate
- Working with others
- Communicating

WELLBEING INDICATORS IN THIS CHAPTER

LEARNING INTENTIONS

At the end of this chapter, I will

1 Be able to recall what reconciliation is
2 Be able to show how Pope John Paul II demonstrated reconciliation in his life
3 Understand what the Sacrament of Reconciliation is.

Let's remind ourselves of what reconciliation is...

Reconciliation means to welcome someone who has sinned against us back into our lives. This can often be hard, as depending on what the person has done to us, we may or may not feel like welcoming them back.

THINK, PAIR, SHARE

Think of some examples where you might find it hard to welcome someone back into your life who has sinned against you.

In **pairs**, share your examples.

Share these examples with the class and discuss the reasons why it might be hard to reconcile with someone.

What do others think of your arguments for or against welcoming the person back into your life?

Forgiveness and Reconciliation

Jubilee:

An anniversary celebrating something special, held every 25 years.

For Christians, reconciliation is much more than the simple process of forgiving and forgetting. The fact that people don't hold grudges against other people does not mean that they are living up to the true Christian ideal of reconciliation.

Pope John Paul II was testament to this in both his words and actions. True reconciliation is achieved not simply by tolerating those who may have hurt us, but by actively embracing them in love and welcoming them back into our lives. Jesus calls on his followers not to judge others who have sinned when he said, 'Let he who is without sin cast the first stone.'

There are many examples from the Bible that show people that God is a forgiving God, so forgiveness of sin should be at the heart of all Christian beings. The greatest example of forgiveness is when Jesus was nailed to the cross on the hill of Calvary with criminals on either side. In St Luke's Gospel we are told that, nearing his death, Jesus called out to his Father: 'Father, forgive them; they do not know what they are doing.'

In the Jubilee Year in 2000, Pope John Paul II's mission for his followers was reconciliation. Not only had the pope preached on forgiveness and reconciliation, but he had shown it in his life too. Throughout his life, Pope John Paul II lived by the message of St Paul to the Corinthians (2 Corinthians 5:18): 'It is all God's work; he reconciled us to himself through Christ and he gave us the ministry of reconciliation.'

Canonise:

To declare someone a saint.

1

Pope John Paul II

Karol Wojtyla was born in Krakow, Poland, in 1920. As a young man, he did really well at sports and had a great love of the theatre. For some time, he even considered acting as a career. However, he was ordained a priest in 1946. By 1964 he was a cardinal.

In 1978, he was elected pope, taking the name John Paul II. Because he was so full of life and was so friendly, he started a new era in Catholic affairs. He was recognised as world leader of the Catholic Church. During his ministry he travelled widely, visiting Ireland in 1979. There, where he appealed to the men of violence to give up their arms and return to a time of peace.

Above all, Pope John Paul II wanted to be the people's pope. He always wanted to get close to the crowd. This almost cost him his life in May 1981. Leaning out of his vehicle in St Peter's Square, he was shot and seriously wounded by a Turkish man called Mehmet Ali Agca. Mehmet had committed a sin that he would have to be punished for. The pope spent a long time recovering from his injuries. Afterwards, he visited Mehmet in his prison cell, where he forgave and embraced him. He welcomed him back into the family of God, reminding the whole world that God has welcomed us back. Pope John Paul II was a man of integrity. His moral vision was based on the faith of Jesus Christ.

Despite poor health in later years, Pope John Paul II made many journeys around the world to spread the good news. Often the places he visited had political as well as religious problems, but he always felt the need to reach out to all. When he travelled to his native Poland to visit the graves of his parents and brother, huge crowds of people turned out to see the man they believed was a living saint.

Throughout his life he worked tirelessly to maintain the dignity of all humankind. In the Church's Jubilee Year of 2000, he encouraged everyone to embrace the ministry of reconciliation. Pope John Paul II died in 2005 and was canonised as a saint in 2013.

WRITE THE ANSWERS   Enquiry

1. Why is reconciliation much more than a simple process of forgiving and forgetting? Do you think that this is a difficult thing to do?

2. Give an example of forgiveness from the Bible.

3. Can you think of examples where you have been asked to reconcile with someone? Write about this experience.

4. In your opinion, did Pope John Paul II fulfil his dream of being 'the people's pope'?

5. When the pope visited Mehmet Ali Agca in prison, what might both men have said to each other?

6. In your opinion, have Catholics today embraced the message of reconciliation left by Pope John Paul II?

Restoration of Relationships

For full reconciliation to happen, there has to be an action. The relationship that has been broken needs to return to where it was before the offence took place. Reconciliation is the fixing of relationships. It welcomes the offender back into the life of the offended, just as God has welcomed his people back into his life.

The story of the Prodigal Son is testament to this. The father remained faithful to his son, even though the son had left and shown no respect for his father. On his return with nothing left, the Prodigal Son was welcomed with open arms and his father held a feast in his honour. God forgives all the wrong things people do and embraces them back into his family. He does not keep people at arm's length, but places them at the centre of the table with the Father, Son and Holy Spirit.

Offering reconciliation may be one of the most difficult things Christians are asked to do. They may be able to forgive, but can they forget? Can they move on to invite the person who has sinned against them back into their lives as if nothing has happened? Christians must remember the words of the Our Father: '… forgive us our trespasses as we forgive those who trespass against us.' They cannot expect forgiveness from God unless they too are willing to forgive those who have done them wrong.

'… forgive us our trespasses as we forgive those who trespass against us.'

JUSTICE, PEACE AND RECONCILIATION

9

Sacrament of Reconciliation

See also Chapter 24, pp.261–262

How to make a good confession today:

1 Find a church that you like to visit. Sometimes the priest will have a set time to hear confession at.

2 Say hello to the priest and make a sign of the cross.

3 Tell the priest what is on your mind and what you have done wrong. Trust God, as he is always there at difficult times in our lives.

The sacrament of reconciliation brings people closer to God.

4 Say 'I am sorry for the wrong things that I have done.'

5 Accept your penance for any wrongdoings and move on. Try hard not to repeat these behaviours again.

Healing of Relationships

Reconciliation is about bringing the Christian community closer together and closer to God. Reconciliation heals any hurt that people feel and, in doing so, makes it easier for people to love again without any barriers.

Choir performing at a remembrance day service in Glencree.

9 JUSTICE, PEACE AND RECONCILIATION

'If we wage peace with the intensity with which we waged war, there would be no wars.'

Glencree Centre for Peace and Reconciliation

The Glencree Centre is a group that has peace and justice as its main aims. Its motto is: 'If we wage peace with the intensity with which we waged war, there would be no wars.'

The Glencree Centre was founded in 1974 in response to the violent conflict in Irish society. People wanted to believe that there was a better way than violence, vandalism, intolerance and sectarianism. Concern for what was happening in Northern Ireland in the 1970s was not enough. Reconciliation was the key. Creating a peaceful society is of interest and value to us all. The Centre for Peace and Reconciliation welcomes all traditions in Ireland that have the same hopes of building peace. It is a non-governmental organisation (NGO). Its people see peace-building as a way to understand the nature and meaning of conflicts. It also gives people a chance to resolve differences without using violence.

The centre's programmes are based on the belief that new ways can be found to deal with diversity and conflict in a democratic society. In Glencree, the job of reconciling very old differences requires enormous effort and courage as well as time and patience.

Since it was set up, Glencree has been the scene of important events and projects. These have been in the fields of education, recreation, fundraising, work camps and hosting a flow of visitors. They not only help to build peace in Ireland, but also in other countries around the world. They have links with groups working for peace in places like Israel and Palestine. They have even travelled to places like Haiti to help teach people about ways to resolve conflict and bring about peace.

LITERACY LIBRARY

Intensity:
With a lot of energy and strength.

Resolve differences:
To end conflict, to come to agreement.

Diversity:
Of many different kinds.

WRITE THE ANSWERS   Enquiry

1 What do you think of the slogan 'If we wage peace with the intensity with which we waged war, there would be no wars'?

2 What, do you think, is responsible for the success of the Glencree Centre?

3 Do you think a place like Glencree is important in today's world? Why?

 Search online for the video of The Glencree Story, which illustrates the rich history and important work of the centre.

JUSTICE, PEACE AND RECONCILIATION

9

Read the following extract.

Enniskillen Bombing

On the first Sunday in November 1987 people gathered in Enniskillen, Northern Ireland, to remember those killed in past wars. As people gathered at the war memorial a bomb exploded, showering the area with debris. Gordon Wilson and his 20-year-old daughter Marie, a student nurse, were buried several feet under the rubble.

In the dark and chaos, father and daughter just managed to reach out and hold hands. Gordon asked his daughter, 'Are you all right, Marie?' Marie squeezed her father's hand, saying, 'Daddy, I love you very much.' These were her last words. The bomb killed eleven people, including Marie, who later died in hospital. Gordon Wilson, her heart-broken father, was injured in the explosion but amazed reporters who interviewed him that evening when he said, 'I bear no ill will ... I bear no grudge' towards the bombers, as it is 'not going to bring her back to life'. He said that because his daughter's last words were words of love, he would pray for the people responsible for the bombing and be thankful for the strength of God's never-ending love.

Throughout the rest of his life, Gordon Wilson was often called upon to speak about this experience. Through the meetings he attended, the interviews he gave and his writing, Gordon Wilson worked hard to bring about peace and overcome bitterness between people.

Source: Adapted extract from Revolutionary Christians who Live the Gospel *by Clare Richards*
© 2000 Kevin Mayhew Ltd.

The memorial to the war dead in Enniskillen was the site of the Remembrance Day bombing in 1987.

WRITE THE ANSWERS — Enquiry

1 Describe **one** way in which forgiveness can be seen in the above extract.

2 Explain how either integrity or religious faith can be seen in the above extract.

REFLECTIVE ACTIVITY

Think about your own attitude to justice, peace and reconciliation and answer the following questions:

1 What did you like learning about in this chapter?

2 Do you think it is important for people to reconcile with one another?

3 Do you think the Glencree Centre is an important part of Ireland's reconciliation story?

PowerPoint summary

Weblinks

9 | JUSTICE, PEACE AND RECONCILIATION

CHAPTER 10
Synthesis: Expressing Beliefs

SOL: 6, 8
LO: 1.12

LEARNING OUTCOME

Synthesise and consider the insights gained about how people express and live out their beliefs, religious or otherwise.

KEY SKILLS YOU WILL USE IN THIS CHAPTER

- Being literate
- Being numerate
- Working with others
- Communicating
- Managing information and thinking
- Staying well
- Managing myself

WELLBEING INDICATORS IN THIS CHAPTER

LEARNING INTENTIONS

At the end of this chapter, I will

1 Understand what insight means

2 Be able to tell the story of what happened to a football team in Northern Thailand in June 2018

3 Understand what veganism is.

Introduction

As we draw near the end of Strand 1, we should begin to reflect on what we have learned. This strand has taught us much about how we express our beliefs.

To have a belief means that we accept that something exists or that it is true. Our beliefs guide us on our journey through life. Everyone's beliefs are individual. It is important that we respect each other's beliefs, even if they are different to our own.

We can express our beliefs in many different ways, for example through prayer, music, our culture or our heritage. Our world religion teaches us the golden rule to love one another and that each of us should try to live this rule out as best we can. We understand the importance of all world religions working together to achieve this.

RESEARCH — Reflection and Action

In small groups, research the following:

1 Write five points from each chapter in Strand 1.
2 What is your favourite chapter so far? Why? Write a sentence on this.
3 Which is your least favourite chapter so far? Why did you choose this chapter?

Before we read a story together, think for a moment about the word 'insight'. What does it mean?

Insight

When you have insight, you have a feeling or a thought that helps you to know something important about a person or a thing. When you gain insight, you are using your intuition. This means you can understand something automatically without the need for conscious reasoning. It is important that we trust our intuition.

Think of a time when you had insight into something. Talk to the person beside you, then share the knowledge with the class.

LITERACY LIBRARY

Insight:
Ability to gain a deep understanding of someone or something.

Endurance:
Ability to endure something difficult without giving up.

Did you follow this story on the news at the time?

Read the following story about a football team in Thailand. Think about the insights they might have gained while they were trapped together in a cave for several weeks during the rainy season.

Human Endurance

Every day people around us make choices about what is best for them and others.

On 23 June 2018, a group of boys aged 11–16 and their coach entered a cave in Northern Thailand during heavy rains after football practice. All they brought with them were torches. They did not think they would need anything else, as they were planning to spend only about one hour in the cave. What happened over the next few weeks is a remarkable story of friendship, human endurance and the length that someone will go to to save the child of someone they don't even know.

When the boys did not return home that night, their parents became concerned and they reported the boys as missing. The following day, football boots, footprints and handprints were found near the cave. Rescuers entered the cave to see what they could find, but they were forced back by heavy floodwater. A vigil was kept at the entrance to the cave by the parents and relatives of the boys.

Swallowed up by an unforgiving mountain and surrounded by darkness, the boys and their coach lost all sense of time. Fear and terror must have been to the forefront of their minds, but they worked together to stay safe. Their football coach, Ake (who had once been a monk), taught the boys meditation techniques that helped them to stay calm. Strength was conserved by teaching the boys to lie still. They had each other and that was important for their survival.

Press conference in Thailand after the boys' ordeal.

The rescue effort.

Over the next few days, experts from around the world arrived to help with the search and rescue operation. A sense of community was felt. Everyone wanted to help. On the evening of 2 July, a miracle occurred as the twelve boys and their coach were found alive. Crowds cheered the good news, but attention soon turned to the difficult rescue effort ahead of them. Over the next week the boys were brought out in small groups in a carefully planned operation.

On 11 July, dressed in hospital gowns and wearing face masks, the boys sat up in their hospital beds and waved to the world. This is a story of ordinary people doing extraordinary things.

After the boys had been rescued, experts from around the world spoke about how the boys and their coach may be feeling in the months to come. Some believed the coach would go back to be a monk for a while, as Thais typically do this as a sign of penance.

Whatever happens, it is very important that each of them takes time out to reflect on their experiences, both individually and collectively.

LITERACY LIBRARY

Community:
Group of people working together to achieve something.

Penance:
Act of devotion that shows sorrow for a sin committed.

Ceremony in memory of former navy SEAL, Saman Kunan, who died trying to save the boys.

WRITE THE ANSWERS   Enquiry

1   When did the boys' parents become concerned?

2   How important, do you think, were the meditation techniques that their coach taught them while they were in the cave?

3   What thoughts do you think were going through their minds as they sat together in the cave?

4   What miracle occurred on 2 July?

5   How do you think the boys felt when they were rescued?

6   Did you know about this story before you read about it here? How would you have felt if it were you or a sibling in this situation?

7   What insights do you think the boys gained while they were in the cave and after their rescue?

LITERACY LIBRARY

Intuition:
Understand something automatically.

Epiphany:
A moment when something is revealed or shown.

Vegan:
A person who does not eat or use any animal products.

Mistreatment:
Treating someone or something badly.

Do you know anyone who is vegan?

Insight is important to us. When we gain insight, we are using our sixth sense or our intuition. Insight is often called an epiphany or a moment when we see things very clearly for ourselves. Insight can lead us to the solution to a problem we have been worrying about for some time. This can give us great comfort and relief.

Let's look at an example of this.

Veganism

Today in Ireland some people have chosen to become vegans. Veganism is a way of living that seeks to eliminate, as far as possible, all forms of mistreatment of, and cruelty to, animals used for food, clothing or any other purpose.

vegan

There are many ways to embrace vegan living today, but one thing all vegans have in common is a plant-based diet. They avoid all animal foods, such as meat, dairy and eggs, as well as products like leather.

Often people become vegans as they have this sixth sense about eating meat or wearing leather. They talk to people around them and find out more information on what they are feeling or thinking. They begin to see things clearly for themselves and find the solution.

Veganism is not just about a diet. There is much more to it.

Read the following piece about Sarah, who has been vegan for the last few years.

Ever since I was a little girl, I remember struggling with something that I felt just wasn't right, especially towards meat. In my family growing up there was meat everywhere: at dinner, breakfast and lunch. There were no vegetarians in my family. My family drank glasses of milk with their meal every evening as it was a great source of calcium and we needed to grow up to be big and strong.

I never knew the word 'vegan' until I was at college and heard about it at one of my lectures. The whole area fascinated me. I listened to the lecturer as he told his story, which sent shivers down my spine. Even thinking about them today does the same to me. I admired my lecturer's love and respect for animals, for his health, for nature around him and the planet we live on.

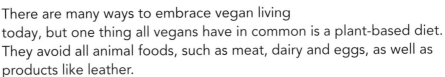

After I left college I followed vegans on Twitter and Instagram and decided to give it a go myself. I educated myself on what to eat that would give my body the calcium and other nutrients that it needed. Five years on I am still vegan. I live on a plant-based diet and I don't miss meat or anything associated with it.

I enjoy family occasions now as I am more relaxed and my family knows I won't join them in the glass of milk with dinner!

WRITE THE ANSWERS Enquiry

1   What did Sarah struggle with as a child?
2   What does 'veganism' mean?
3   Who influenced her in this area?
4   How did she feel about it to begin with?
5   Did she become a vegan straight away?

What kind of foods would you eat as a vegan? Copy the following KWL table into your copybook and fill it in.

K What I know	W What I want to find out	L What I have learned today

---

RESEARCH Enquiry; Exploration

Interview a vegan in your school or at home. Find out why they decided to become vegan. Report this information to your class or year group at assembly.

REFLECTIVE ACTIVITY

Think about your own attitude to how people live out their beliefs and answer the following questions:

1   What did you find most interesting about this chapter?
2   Do you think insight was an important thing for the boys in the cave to have?
3   According to *The Economist*, '2019 will be the year of the vegan.' Have you noticed an increase in people turning to plant-based diets?

PowerPoint summary

Weblinks

STRAND 2
EXPLORING QUESTIONS

One of the most important abilities we have as human beings is being able to ask questions. Asking questions allows us to learn more about ourselves, others and the world around us. The words 'how' and 'why' can lead us to finding answers and help us to understand more.

Throughout history people have asked questions about the meaning and purpose of life. Questions about why and how the earth was created or what our purpose is on earth have caused people to wonder for thousands of years. Some people have turned to religion in their quest to find answers to these questions, while others have searched using non-religious means.

In this strand you will explore some of the questions of meaning, purpose and relationships that people wonder about and you will discover how people with different religious and non-religious beliefs respond to these questions.

CHAPTER 11
The Search for Meaning

SOL: 6, 8
LO: 2.1

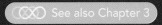 See also Chapter 3

LEARNING OUTCOME

Research artistic, architectural or archaeological evidence that shows ways in which people have searched for meaning and purpose in life.

KEY SKILLS YOU WILL USE IN THIS CHAPTER

- Staying well
- Managing myself
- Working with others
- Being creative
- Being literate

WELLBEING INDICATORS IN THIS CHAPTER

LEARNING INTENTIONS

At the end of this chapter, I will

1 Be able to explain what the Invictus Games are

2 Be able to tell the story of Captain Trevor Greene

3 Understand how important it is to question

4 Be able to understand how archaeological evidence shows us ways that people have searched for meaning and purpose in life.

Searching for Meaning

Every day people search for meaning in their lives. For some it can be a simple question they may ask of themselves. For others it can be because of something big that has happened to them in their life. This can cause them to make profound changes to how they do things.

One such example of this is the men and women that participate in the Invictus Games.

The Invictus Games

In Toronto on 23 September 2017, Prince Harry, the Duke of Sussex, said, 'I knew it was my responsibility to use the great platform that I have to help the world understand, and be inspired by, the spirit of those who wear the uniform.'

LITERACY LIBRARY

Resilience:
The ability to recover quickly.

Prince Harry meets with competitors during the Invictus Games in Toronto, Canada in 2017.

In 2008 Prince Harry had a life-changing experience. He flew a helicopter with three British soldiers on board who had been severely injured in the war in Afghanistan. In 2013 at the Warrior Games in the US, he saw first-hand how sport could help people physically, psychologically and socially. He said, 'The way I viewed service and sacrifice changed forever and the direction of my life changed with it.'

Today Prince Harry serves as the patron of the Invictus Games, which is a sporting event for wounded, injured and sick service men and women. In 2018 the games were held in Sydney, Australia, where Prince Harry and his wife Meghan, now the Duchess of Sussex, attended.

Invictus means 'unconquered' in Latin. The games represent the resilience of the human spirit. The Invictus Games were inspired by the poem 'Invictus' written by William Ernest Henley in 1875. Its final two lines read, 'I am the master of my fate: I am the captain of my soul.'

What emotions do you think Prince Harry was feeling on the helicopter in Afghanistan in 2008?

11 THE SEARCH FOR MEANING

Yellow and black are the two colours associated with the Invictus Games. Yellow is the brightest colour of the visible spectrum, so we associate it with positivity and optimism. Glowing through the darkness of black, yellow reflects the very essence of what these games are about.

There have been many stories told about the participants in these games. Let's look at one of these stories.

CAPTAIN **TREVOR GREENE**

Retired Captain Trevor Greene of the Canadian Armed Forces was attacked by a Taliban rebel in March 2006 in Afghanistan. Because of this he suffered an axe wound to his head. 'When I got home the docs took one look at me and said if I lived – which they doubted – I'd be a vegetable the rest of my life,' Captain Greene said at the emotional opening ceremony of the Invictus Games in Toronto in 2017.

'My armed brothers fought for me against all the odds. They believed in me in the fight and they still do. I had a choice: to accept the prognosis and give up, or to fight like a soldier. I chose to be the captain of my destiny, master of my fate.'

Captain Greene has spent many years recovering in hospital and rehab. This recovery and rehabilitation are the purpose of the Invictus Games and the Invictus Foundation.

Motivation is key. No one should be defined by their injuries: each person should be recognised for their achievements instead.

WRITE THE ANSWERS Enquiry

1. What life-changing moment did Prince Harry have?
2. What are the Invictus Games?
3. What inspired the Invictus Games?
4. What does 'I am the master of my fate: I am the captain of my soul' mean?
5. Do you believe you are the 'master of your fate' and 'the captain of your soul'? Why do you believe this?
6. What two colours are associated with the Invictus Games? Do you think they are worthy colours?
7. Who are the 'armed brothers' that Captain Greene mentioned in his speech at the Invictus Games?
8. How important, do you think, is motivation to someone who was injured in war?

GROUP ACTIVITY Enquiry and Exploration

Find out more information on the Invictus Games of 2018 (Sydney).

Share the information with your class group or in small groups in your class.

THINK, PAIR, SHARE

Think about what it must be like to have a disability. Would it change your life?

Pair with your neighbour or someone in the class.

Share your ideas with the class.

THE SEARCH FOR MEANING

11

The Questioner

'The important thing is not to stop questioning. Curiosity has its own reason for existing. One cannot help but be in awe when one contemplates the mysteries of eternity, of life, of the marvellous structure of reality. It is enough if one tries merely to comprehend a little of this mystery every day. Never lose a holy curiosity.'

Albert Einstein, physicist (1879–1955)

LITERACY LIBRARY

Curiosity:
A strong desire to learn or know something.

Awe:
A feeling of great respect and wonder at the greatness of something.

Contemplate:
To think deeply about something.

Eternity:
Endless time.

Merely:
Even, just, only.

Comprehend:
Understand.

One of the things that make human beings different from other animals is our ability to ask questions. As humans, we ask many questions each day. We learn a lot from the questions we ask. Some of our questions are more important than others. Some are more easily answered than others.

It can be frustrating or annoying if we cannot find answers to our questions in life, but that does not mean we should stop asking. It is by asking questions that we grow as people and learn new things about ourselves and others.

BIG QUESTIONS PEOPLE ASK

Is there a God?

What happens after we die?

What is life all about?

Why am I here?

Why do bad things happen to good people?

A Time to Reflect

Throughout history, people have always asked questions. During times like the Renaissance and the Reformation, people began to question many things.

The Renaissance took place during the fourteenth to the seventeenth centuries in Europe. It was a time of rebirth in art, architecture, sculpture and so on.

The Reformation began in the sixteenth century. The Reformation led to many changes in the Church. Many Christians started to think about what was happening in the Catholic Church.

Some of the greatest discoveries in the world have come about because people asked **why** or **how** and tried to find answers. Just think of all the experiments on display at the Young Scientist and Technology Exhibition. Many great things will be discovered because of students' questions.

The world would stay the same and be a very boring place if people stopped asking questions. Your day in school is all about finding out the answers to questions you and your teachers ask.

A copy of Italian Renaissance artist Michelangelo's *David* in Florence.

Caoilfhionn Ní Dheorain and Martha Nic Ionais from Coláiste Chillian, Clondalkin at the BT Young Scientist & Technology Exhibition.

THE SEARCH FOR MEANING

11

Finding Our Purpose in Life

By questioning what is happening around them, people are looking for meaning. Meaning refers to a sense of purpose. It helps people to make sense of the different situations they find themselves in. If people don't have a sense of purpose or a goal, life can seem meaningless for them.

People can find meaning in their lives through their connections with family, friends, music, architecture, art, religion and archaeology, among other things.

GROUP ACTIVITY   Reflection and Action

Divide the class into seven groups. Each group must select one topic from the following list:

- Family
- Money
- Architecture
- Religion
- Friends
- Music
- Art

Discuss the following using your group's placemat:

1. What words do you associate with your topic?
2. How important do you think your topic is as a source of meaning in your life?
3. Decide on the three most important or relevant points in your group.

RESEARCH: BRAINSTORM — Enquiry

1 From your study of history, can you remember what an
   archaeologist is?
2 What kind of items do archaeologists find in the ground?
If your class use 'show-me boards', you can use them for this activity.

Now let's look at archaeology and how evidence shows how people have searched for meaning and purpose in life. Imagine it is 4,500 years ago and you are living during a period in history called the Neolithic period or the New Stone Age.

What do you think life was like then?

THINK, PAIR, SHARE

Think about what life was like 4,500 years ago.
Pair with your neighbour.
Share your ideas with the class group.

Archaeological Evidence

Archaeologists believe that new settlers came to live in Ireland around 4000 BCE. They were farmers who probably came from Britain. They kept animals (cattle and sheep) inside the walls they built. They also grew crops such as wheat, oats and barley. Neolithic people left us no written records, so we get all our information about them from archaeological sources.

Copy the following KWL table into your copybook and fill it in.

K — What I **know** about archaeology and this period in history	W — What I **want** to find out about this period in history	L — What I would like to **learn** about this period in history

THE NEOLITHIC PEOPLE AND THEIR BURIAL TOMBS

Many ancient people did not see death as an end to life. They believed that the spirit left the body and moved on to live somewhere else. Neolithic farmers in Ireland believed in an afterlife.

We know this to be true because they built sophisticated tombs for their dead. These tombs are called megalithic tomb, as the stones that were used to build them were very big. We can learn a lot about Neolithic people and their beliefs from the tombs. The fact that they have survived all these years shows us how skilled the builders of this period were, even though their tools were made of stone.

There are three types of megalithic tomb: court cairn, dolmen and passage tomb. Passage tombs are the most impressive of the megalithic tombs, so we will focus only on this type.

Court cairn in Donegal.

PASSAGE TOMB

A passage tomb is very striking to the eye. It looks like a hill or a circular mound of earth. Inside there is a long passage that leads to the chamber, where archaeologists have found the remains of cremated human bodies. There are about 200 of this type of burial tomb in Ireland and they vary in size. The most famous is Newgrange in Co. Meath. Newgrange is about 8 kilometres west of Drogheda on the north side of the River Boyne. In 2018, another 5,500-year-old megalithic passage tomb was discovered in the Brú na Boinne heritage site in Co. Meath.

Some of the materials that were used to build Newgrange came from as far away as Co. Wicklow. It is older than either Stonehenge or the Egyptian pyramids.

Stonehenge in England.

Stonehenge is one of the most famous landmarks in the United Kingdom. It consists of a ring of standing stones, each 13 feet high and 7 feet wide. It was built in many stages. Human remains have been found here, which suggests it was used as a burial ground.

Search online for the following:
1 Stonehenge builders' village
2 Newgrange passage tomb.

NEWGRANGE

In the 1960s, archaeologists began to excavate at Newgrange. Why the Neolithic farmers built Newgrange is still a mystery to many, but it may have been built as a place of worship. As well as being a burial place, there were ritual gatherings here where ancestors were honoured. Newgrange is one of several passage tombs built on the River Boyne.

By using a technique called carbon dating to date objects found at Newgrange, it is believed that it was built between 2675 BCE (before Christ was born) and 2485 BCE. The tomb is very large, so archaeologists believe that it took over 400 men to build it over a period of sixteen years. During the excavation of Newgrange, some astonishing and wonderful discoveries were made.

Many of the stones at Newgrange are decorated with Megalithic art. No one can say for certain what the drawings represent, but it is clear that they were of spiritual significance to the people who created them. Historians believe that the builders noted the changing seasons in their artwork and that time and major solar events were very important.

Newgrange was probably built so that Neolithic farmers could use it as a calendar. They could tell when the shortest day of the year was. The stones along the passage and in the chamber are decorated with spiral, circle and diamond designs and shapes.

Newgrange is best known for the brightness of its passage and chamber when they are lit by the winter solstice sunrise. Above the entrance point to the passage, there is an opening called a roof box. This roof box was a great surprise to those who discovered it. Its purpose is to allow sunlight to enter the chamber on 21 December, the day of the winter solstice and also the shortest day of the year. Each dawn from 19 to 23 December, a narrow beam of light enters the roof box and reaches the floor of the chamber, slowly extending to the back of the chamber. As the sun rises higher, the beam widens within the chamber so that the entire room lights up. The event lasts just seventeen minutes, but its accuracy as a time-telling device is remarkable.

The Neolithic people who built this tomb understood the apparent movement of the sun and astronomy. They believed in an afterlife and had great respect for their dead.

LITERACY LIBRARY

Impressive:
Something or someone that is really great or awesome.

Excavate:
Dig.

Carbon dating:
Scientific method used to find the age of an object that was once alive. All living objects, for example plants, have carbon in them. When they die, the amount of carbon decreases.

WRITE THE ANSWERS   Enquiry

1 When was Newgrange excavated?

2 How many years did it take the farmers to build the tomb?

3 What designs are found on the stones?

4 What is a roof box?

5 What is the shortest day of the year?

Our Sense of Purpose

LITERACY LIBRARY

Remains:
What is left of a person when they have passed away.

By questioning what is happening around us, we are looking for meaning. Meaning refers to a sense of purpose. It helps us to make sense of the different situations we find ourselves in. If we don't have a sense of purpose or a goal, life can seem meaningless for us.

The idea of searching for meaning is important when we study Newgrange and ask ourselves why it was built. Why did these farmers choose this area of the Boyne Valley? The notion of passage is also important when we think about Newgrange. Passage symbolises a journey in time. The passage itself at Newgrange is over 19 metres long and the chamber is 6 metres in height. The passage from darkness to light was central to the people of the time.

Newgrange was a burial tomb, as human remains were discovered there. It is believed that only important people were buried there, as very few remains were found. In capturing the sun, the farmers protected the fertility of the land and the growth of the crops.

Newgrange was important for community gatherings. It is believed that the project of building Newgrange was handed down from one generation to the next, as people at that time died young. For the people of the time, Newgrange was a place to honour and value their ancestors who had gone before them.

Copy the 3-2-1 box below into your copybook and fill it in.

3-2-1		
3	2	1
things I have learned	things I found interesting	thing I want to learn more about

GROUP ACTIVITY   Enquiry

In small groups, research artistic or architectural evidence that shows ways in which people have searched for meaning and purpose in life.

Report the information you discover to the class group in a Powerpoint format.

REFLECTIVE ACTIVITY

Think about your own attitude to the search for meaning in life and answer the following questions:

1 What did you like learning about in this chapter?

2 If you met someone who was participating in the Invictus Games, what would you say to them?

3 Can you think of any other 'Big Questions' that you would like to ask? If so, what would they be?

PowerPoint summary

Weblinks

CHAPTER 12
Life's Big Questions

SOL: 5, 7, 11
LO: 2.2

 See also Chapter 10

LEARNING OUTCOME

Consider responses from one major world religion and from a non-religious worldview to some big questions about the meaning of life, such as:

- Why are we here?
- How should we live?
- What happens when we die?

KEY SKILLS YOU WILL USE IN THIS CHAPTER

- Staying well
- Managing myself
- Working with others
- Being creative
- Being literate
- Managing information and thinking

WELLBEING INDICATORS IN THIS CHAPTER

LEARNING INTENTIONS

At the end of this chapter, I will

1. Understand the importance of questioning and reflection
2. Be able to explain the following terms: theism, atheism, agnosticism, secularism, materialism and individualism
3. Understand Sister Stanislaus Kennedy's relationship with God and the meaning of life for her
4. Be able to explain what 'blasphemy' means.

Most people question things in life. Often this happens when something occurs in your life.

This could be because you know someone who was in a road traffic accident or you hear of someone who has been given devastating news about a serious illness.

These feelings are natural. It is important to question why these things happen and what you can do to support those involved. It is also important to understand that we don't always have the answers to the questions we ask.

THINK, PAIR, SHARE

Think for a moment – have you ever thought about why bad things happen to good people? Why natural disasters occur? Why a young mum dies of cancer? Why a young man is knocked down on his way home from work and dies on the operating table?

What answers do you have to some of the world's greatest questions?

Pair with your neighbour and share your opinions and ideas.

Share what you have discussed with the class.

Read the following report on the Indonesian earthquake that happened in September 2018.

On 28 September 2018, a 7.5 magnitude earthquake rocked the Indonesian island of Sulawesi, triggering a devastating tsunami. It is believed that 1,500 people were killed, with many more unaccounted for. Hundreds of people were said to be buried in mud that was slowly drying.

Diseases like typhoid and cholera were a concern. The earth's soil moved like it was water and swallowed everything that was in its path.

Entire families were reported missing, as houses were swept away following the tsunami. The waves of the tsunami were said to be six metres high. It is said that 70,000 people are now homeless. Aid agencies are doing all they can to help the people, but access to the small airport proved difficult.

The aftermath of the 2018 earthquake in Lombok Island, Indonesia.

RESEARCH
Exploration

Research why tsunamis happen.

1 Ask your Geography teacher to explain to your class how tsunamis occur.

2 Research the tsunami that occurred in Indonesia in December 2018.

3 Watch the film *The Impossible* about the tsunami in Thailand in 2004.

Collate all the information you gather and, with your teacher's permission, report this to your class on a poster.

WRITE THE ANSWERS   Enquiry

1 Where did the earthquake occur?
2 How many people had reportedly been killed?
3 What diseases were people worried about?
4 What hampered the aid effort?
5 How many people were said to be homeless?
6 Can you name another place where a tsunami occurred?
7 Research the diseases typhoid and cholera.

Share what you learn with the class.

Reading the above story would lead you to ask why bad things happen in this world. In this situation, what seemed like a normal day turned into anything but normal. Families were torn apart and they will find it hard to rebuild their lives again.

GROUP ACTIVITY   Enquiry

Research a natural disaster other than a tsunami and tell the class about it. Find out the following:

• What happened?
• When did it happen?
• Where did it happen?
• How are things today for the people of the region or city?

Reflection

Reflection means thinking deeply about something. Reflecting on an idea or topic helps us to develop our opinion on it. By reflecting, we can be comfortable with what we believe.

What we believe about God and religion is very important. It can shape our lives and help us to make decisions. Not everyone includes God and religion in their world view. Some people don't see God as having anything to do with the world, while others believe he is the reason we are here.

It is important to reflect on the existence of God. There are different responses to this question.

Experiencing God

When some people reflect on the world and their experiences in it, they may find that God plays a part in it. They may experience God in a very real way through moments in life such as birth and death. For these people, their world view is often based on what they believe about God.

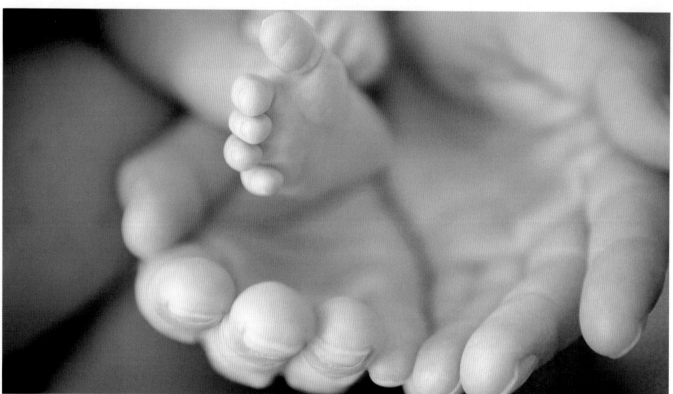

Theism

The word 'theism' means 'belief in God'. Christians and followers of other monotheistic faiths believe in one God – a God that created each and every one of us. They also believe he created the world for us. God is present as a guide and a friend leading us to the Promised Land.

Christians believe that God revealed himself through his son, Jesus Christ. The Jewish community believes that God revealed himself through the prophet Abraham and then Moses. Muslims believe that God revealed his message through the Angel Gabriel to the prophet Muhammad.

ATHEISM

Atheism

Atheists don't believe that any gods exist. Atheists believe that the world is natural, and that we are good and kind and loving or bad for natural reasons. Atheists believe that long ago, people made up stories about gods to explain things that they did not understand. It is okay to believe or not believe that gods exists.

- Some people are atheists because they have reflected on the issue and have made an informed or well-thought-out decision. For example, they might look at the world and conclude that there is not enough evidence to believe in any gods.
- Some people are atheists mainly because they live in a non-religious society, just like some people are religious mainly because they live in a religious society.
- Some people used to be religious, but they now think that religion is false or harmful and that people don't need it.

HOW ATHEISM COULD AFFECT A PERSON'S RELIGIOUS BELIEFS

A person's religious beliefs could be tested by atheism.

- An atheist might say that there is no proof that any gods exists. They might ask why an all-powerful god cannot give the same message to everyone. They might ask why a god would create such a huge universe just for people on one tiny planet.
- An atheist might say that if an all-good god did exist, then there would not be bad things in the world. But instead the world is a mix of good things and bad things, and good, loving people and bad, selfish people, some of them religious, some of them atheists.
- An atheist might say that faith is an unreliable way to find out what is true because it results in different people coming to different beliefs. An atheist might say that science is more reliable because it results in different people coming to the same beliefs.
- A reasonable religious person would consider all these arguments carefully and fairly, just as a reasonable atheist would consider religious arguments carefully and fairly.

A person's atheism or religious belief may be strong at certain times in their lives and weaker at other moments. Atheism may cause people to question their religion, and religion may cause people to question their atheism.

We must not be afraid to reflect on what we believe, as it can help us to come closer to understanding what is most likely to be true. While reflecting, we should be fair, just and kind to both atheists and religious people.

Agnosticism

Agnosticism is the belief that we cannot truly know for certain whether or not God exists. Agnostics argue that the human mind cannot know something that is so beyond its understanding. There is not enough evidence to prove it one way or the other. Therefore, we can only know what is happening in the present world and not in the afterlife.

As God cannot be seen, touched or heard directly, we cannot be certain he exists. Agnostics believe that we cannot prove God exists, but equally we cannot prove he does not exist. Agnostics recognise that there is a lot of doubt when it comes to religious beliefs, so they cannot say a definite yes, like theists, or a definite no, like atheists.

Agnosticism could challenge a person's religious beliefs in very similar ways to atheism.

Secularism

Secularism is a belief that public life should be carried out without reference to religion. A secularist is against the influence that religion has on our society. Some secularists don't want public figures to make reference to God. For example, during her first term as President of Ireland, Mary McAleese often used the words 'God willing' or 'with God's help' in her public statements or speeches. Before she was inaugurated for a second term, secularists asked her to stop making references to God in her public statements.

Does this mean that God does not have a place in modern Ireland? The President was simply using language that she had used throughout her life. She was not expressing a particular theological point of view or saying one belief was right over another. Some people say secularism is a move away from traditional religious values towards more modern ways. Others would argue that religion can have a place in the modern world and does not need to be separated from it.

The annual Secular Europe Campaign.

Conscience:

The voice in our head or a feeling we have helping us to understand what is right and wrong.

For a secularist, the most important thing is that religion does not have any influence on the laws of the country. Those ruling a country should not allow a particular religious way of thinking to influence the decisions they make. A secularist does not want any sign of religion in public places such as hospitals, airports, schools and workplaces. Secularists say that people should be free to practise any religion or no religion. It is all about equality.

For some time in Ireland, there have been calls to stop the Angelus bell being broadcast on RTÉ television and radio. Some people believe that the Angelus prayer has no place on the schedule of the state broadcaster. However, the Angelus is only a few minutes of quiet reflection. It gives an opportunity for people of all religions to take some time out and to think about what is happening around us. It could even be time out to think for an atheist!

Materialism

Materialism is the belief that only the things that we can see, smell and feel are real. As a result, materialists don't believe in God, as he is not made up of physical matter. Something is real only if it can be felt, touched, weighed or measured. None of these can be done to God. Materialists look to science for answers instead of religion. They don't believe in an afterlife or spiritual things.

Materialists explain everything that happens in the world in terms of the laws of nature and science. They see man as a material machine with no soul or spiritual side. Anything that is unthinkable to them cannot exist. Materialism is **not** the same as being materialistic, which is a love of possessions and money.

Individualism

Individualism values independence and self-reliance. Individualists believe that the interests of an individual or person are more important than those of the state or a social group. People should be free to express themselves as they want rather than doing what religion tells them they should.

Individualists believe that a person should not take into account what society thinks when making decisions. An individual's own view is what counts. They place great value on privacy and respect. Every individual should be given the freedom to follow their own interests and the state and Church should have very little say in their lives. They believe in following their own conscience rather than any rules when it comes to deciding between right and wrong.

WRITE THE ANSWERS

Enquiry

1 Do you think that it is important to reflect on the existence of God? Why/why not?

2 Explain the following terms in your own words: theism, atheism, agnosticism, secularism, individualism and materialism.

3 Do you think that these values bring people true happiness? Why/why not?

4 Do you think that the experience of God in one's life is more important than material goods? If so, state why.

5 Do you think that the everyday phrases regarding God spoken by President McAleese were unfair? Who do you think would be offended by them?

6 What does an individualist believe?

7 Fill in the blanks in the following sentences.

   (a) To believe in God is _____.

   (b) Monothesim is a belief in _____ God.

   (c) _____ deny the existence of God.

   (d) _____ is the belief that the human mind is not capable of knowing whether or not God exists.

   (e) _____ is the way we make our choices in life that excludes God.

   (f) A materialistic life is about _____.

01 Sr Stanislaus Kennedy (Sr Stan) Discusses the Meaning of Life

Sr Stanislaus Kennedy is a visionary and social innovator. She has been a member of the Congregation of Religious Sisters of Charity since 1958. Born Treasa Kennedy near Lispole on the Dingle Peninsula, she was one of five children. She grew up among fishermen and farmers in an Ireland that had high unemployment and emigration.

Her parents owned a small farm and it was here, amongst the animals and a strong Catholic community, that her sense of faith grew. She knew from an early age that she wanted to help people, especially the poor of society. The Congregation of Religious Sisters of Charity is committed to looking after the poor and the disadvantaged.

In 1985 she founded Focus Ireland, which at one time was the largest voluntary organisation in Ireland. In 2001 she also set up the Immigrant Council of Ireland as a response to the needs of new immigrants living in Ireland.

On interviewing Sr Stan about the meaning of life, this is what she had to say:

1 **What is the meaning of life for you?**
To carry on the work of God, who created the world out of love. Each of us are called to continue that work of creation, making the world a better place – we are all co-creators.

2 **How do Jesus and God make people better?**
Jesus came on earth to show us what God was like and to teach us how to live good lives. He showed us God as an all-loving father (mother) and he taught us to live a life of love and compassion as our father (mother) in heaven. If we listen and follow Jesus, we will lead good lives.

3 **What rules should people follow in Christianity?**
The rule of love: to love God above all things and love our neighbours as ourselves.

4 **Have you ever doubted your faith?**
Yes, I have, but I watched and listened to people with faith and they helped me.

5 **What happens when we die?**
I don't know, but I believe that we came from God's embrace and we will return to the same loving embrace of God.

6 **Define 'happiness'.**
Happiness comes from inside us, not outside us. We are happy when we accept and are grateful for who we are and what we have.

7 **What is right, what is wrong in today's world?**
What is right? Love, peace, hope and justice.
What is wrong? Hatred, anger, violence, injustice, inequality.

8 **Why do bad things happen to good people?**
Most bad things in the world are caused by people. For example, conflict, war, hunger, famine, poverty, inequality, etc. are caused by people. Some things, like sickness, loss and death, earthquakes and tsunamis, we cannot understand or explain.

9 **What do you think God is going to do in the future?**
I have no idea except God will always love us all unconditionally.

10 **What will you say to God when you finally meet him?**
Thank you for bringing me to this day and for your great love which sustained me in life.

11 **Is there life after death?**
Yes, I believe life is eternal, it goes on forever.

Sr Stan is a true example of a loving, caring and spiritual person who gives of herself to the poor and needy of society. Answer the following questions on the above text.

WRITE THE ANSWERS   Enquiry

1. Where and when was Sr Stan born?
2. What was Ireland like in the 1950s?
3. What religious order did she join?
4. Why did she choose this religious order over other ones?
5. How does she define 'happiness'?
6. How does she explain why bad things happen to good people?
7. What does she plan to say to God when she meets him?
8. What would you say to God when you meet him?

GROUP ACTIVITY: RESEARCH   Exploration

In groups find out more about the work of a charitable organisation in Ireland.

You can choose from the list below, or you may wish to choose a charitable organisation that is local to your area.

- Peter McVerry Trust
- Focus Ireland
- Capuchin Day Centre
- Simon Community
- Society of St Vincent de Paul
- Any local shelter for homeless people

Contact a representative from the organisation you have chosen to research and ask them to visit your class.

GROUP ACTIVITY: RESEARCH   Enquiry

In groups, research the work of the Immigrant Council of Ireland.

Report your findings to the class in PowerPoint, Prezi or poster format.

FOCUS
Ireland

Blasphemy

On 26 October 2018, there was a referendum in Ireland on whether or not to remove the offence of blasphemy from the Constitution.

Blasphemy can be defined as anything that is grossly abusive or insulting in relation to matters held sacred by any religion, thereby causing outrage among many followers of that religion. The Minister for Housing, Planning and Local Government, Eoghan Murphy, said, 'Whatever your views are on the proposals in the referendum, can I take this opportunity to encourage voters to go to their polling station during this 15-hour period on 26 October and have your say in the outcome of the referendum.'

Referendum:

A vote in which all people in a country or an area decide on an important question. They vote yes or no to the question asked.

The Defamation Act of 2009 made blasphemy a crime punishable by a €25.00 fine. In reality, no one had been prosecuted for blasphemy in Ireland since 1855.

Constitution:

These are the laws of the country written down in a book. In Ireland our Constitution is called **Bunreacht na hÉireann (Basic Law of Ireland).**

The turnout on the day was low (43.97%). Of the people who voted, 64.85% voted in favour of removing the offence of blasphemy from the Constitution, while 35.15% voted to keep it as part of the Constitution. These results show that Ireland is moving from being a deeply Catholic society to being a more secular one.

Secular society:

A society where the powers of Church and state are separate.

GROUP ACTIVITY   Enquiry

Find out what arguments were put forward on both sides.

What are your thoughts after hearing both sides of the argument?

Debate this topic with your classmates.

Having read about Sr Stanislaus and her faith and belief in God, it is now important to look at another person who has a non-religious worldview of the big questions in life.

Stephen Fry

Stephen Fry is an English comedian, actor, writer, presenter and activist. He was born in August 1957 in Hampstead, London. His mother was Jewish, but he was not brought up in a religious environment.

He has many times expressed his opposition to organised religion. He describes himself as an atheist and a humanist. In 2015 he was interviewed by Gay Byrne on the programme *The Meaning of Life*. In this series of programmes, Gay Byrne interviewed a prominent public figure about what they believe the meaning of life to be. Other guests who appeared on the programme were Gerry Adams, Ronan Keating, Tommy Tiernan and Martin Sheen.

During the programme Gay Byrne asked Stephen Fry what he would say to God when he walked up to the gates of heaven. Fry answered by saying that he would say to God, 'How dare he create a world that had children with bone cancer? What is the meaning of this, how can this be?' He continued to say that the misery in this world is not our fault. He believes the world we live in is full of injustice and pain.

RESEARCH

Research some other public figures that have been on *The Meaning of Life* with Gay Byrne on RTÉ.

What do they say about their understanding of the meaning of life?

Share their views with the class.

Gay Byrne joked with him and said, 'Do you think you will get in?' Fry answered that he did not want to. He said that he sees God as a maniac, totally selfish, monstrous and deserving of no respect. He believes when God is banished life becomes simpler, purer, cleaner and more worth living.

Within days of the programme airing, it was viewed five million times. Fry said that he did not refer to any specific religion and commented, 'I said quite a few things that were angry at this supposed God. I was merely saying things that Bertrand Russell and many finer heads than mine have said for many thousands of years, going all the way back to the Greeks.'

In May 2017 it was announced that Fry and RTÉ were under criminal investigation for blasphemy under the 2009 Defamation Act. The case was later dropped.

WRITE THE ANSWERS

Enquiry

1 Who is Stephen Fry?
2 What religion was his mother?
3 What did he say about God on the programme *The Meaning of Life*?
4 Do you agree with him when he says that God is selfish and deserves no respect? Why/why not?
5 Why were Stephen Fry and RTÉ investigated for blasphemy?

THINK, PAIR, SHARE

Read the following quotes on the meaning of life.

'Difficulties in your life don't come to destroy you, but to help you realise your hidden potential.'

Anonymous

Whatever we are, whatever we make of ourselves, is all we will ever have – and that, in its profound simplicity, is the meaning of life.'

Philip Appleman

'Without hard work, nothing grows but weeds.'

Gordan B. Hinckley

'If God brings you to it,
He will bring you through it.'

Anonymous

'Life is like riding a bicycle. To keep balance, you must keep moving.'

Albert Einstein

'The meaning of life differs from man to man, from day to day, from hour to hour. What matters, therefore, is not the meaning of life in general but rather the specific meaning of a person's life at a given moment.'

Victor E. Frankl

Which of the above quotes has meaning for you? Why?

Think about the above quotes. **Pair** with your neighbour and talk about the quotes and their meaning.

When you are ready, **share** your thoughts with the class.

REFLECTIVE ACTIVITY

Think about your own attitude to life's big questions and answer the following questions:

1   What did you like learning about in this chapter?

2   Do you think it is important for people to take some time out and reflect on what is happening around them? Why/why not?

 PowerPoint summary

 Weblinks

CHAPTER 13
Creation Stories

SOL: 6, 8, 19
LO: 2.3, 2.4

LEARNING OUTCOME

Explore how different stories, both religious and non-religious, express an understanding of how the world was created.

KEY SKILLS YOU WILL USE IN THIS CHAPTER

- Communicating
- Being creative
- Being literate
- Managing information and thinking
- Working with others

WELLBEING INDICATORS IN THIS CHAPTER

LEARNING INTENTIONS

At the end of this chapter, I will

1 Understand what 'narrative' means and why it is important to different cultures

2 Describe the Jewish and Christian creation narratives

3 Explain a scientific view of creation

4 Explore the relationship between religion and science and what they say about creation

5 Present a non-religious creation narrative.

The word 'narrative' basically means story. Narrative is found in all societies. We see it wherever humans are creative: music, film, radio, literature, video games.

When a sequence of events is presented to us in a creative way, this is called a narrative.

The Importance of Narrative

Many cultures use storytelling as a way to keep a record of their histories and values. These stories carry the shared experience and history of the culture within them.

People from some cultures, such as indigenous Americans, use storytelling to teach children the values and lessons of life. While storytelling provides entertainment, in this instance its main purpose is to educate.

CLASS DISCUSSION   Reflection and Action

Can you think of any stories you were told as a child that included a lesson about life?

LITERACY LIBRARY

Indigenous:
The first people in a particular place.

Pondered:
To think or wonder about something carefully.

Origins:
The beginnings of something, where something came from.

Oral tradition:
Passed on by word of mouth.

Myths:
Popular beliefs or traditional stories concerning the early history of a people or the world.

Profound:
Having a deep meaning, something very important.

Literal:
Following the strict meaning of the word, actual or factual.

Creation Narratives

Since the early days of civilisation, humanity has pondered the origins of the universe. All human societies tell stories of how the world began. Through oral tradition and writing, we can learn about these creation myths.

Creating a narrative around an event can often help humans to understand it better, especially when it is something as huge and mysterious as how the world began. A creation myth is usually regarded by those who believe in it as containing profound truths. This means it may not be factually true in a historical or literal sense, but rather that it can teach us important things about who we are and how we got here.

Monotheistic:
Belief in only one God.

To explore this further, we will look at four different creation narratives. Some are based in religion, while others are not.

Religious Creation Narratives

The three monotheistic major world religions – Judaism, Christianity and Islam – all share the view that God created the universe and everything in it. The Jewish and Christian religions both take their creation narratives from the Book of Genesis.

DAY ONE:
God divided light from darkness and so made day and night.

DAY THREE:
God made earth and sea. He commands the earth to produce grass, plants and trees.

DAY FIVE:
God created birds and sea creatures.

DAY SEVEN:
God rested and made this day holy.

DAY TWO:
God made the sky.

DAY FOUR:
God made the stars in order to create days, seasons and years.

DAY SIX:
God created animals, man and woman and commanded them to be fruitful and multiply.

ACTIVITY
Exploration

Draw your own picture or chart of this story of creation into your copybook to help you remember what happened on each of the seven days.

For hundreds of years, many people accepted the religious creation narrative as literally true. Religion seemed to provide all the answers to the questions people had about the world.

However, as time passed some people began to realise that the creation story was written to help people understand **why** the world was created, not **how**. The religious creation narrative was trying to show God as a powerful, loving creator.

Remember also that they were writing at a very different time, when people and the world were not as advanced as they are today.

Many people who have a religious faith may not take this creation narrative literally, but they do believe there is value in the Genesis account of creation. This is because, for them, it teaches important truths about God and why the world was created. They believe the religious narrative of creation was concerned with **why** the world was created, not how. They often turn to science for the answers to the **how** questions.

Search online to find a video of the Genesis story of creation.

Scientific Creation Narratives

LITERACY
LIBRARY

Species:

A sort or type, a class of plants or animals who share the same characteristics.

Evolved:

Developed over time.

Cosmic:

To do with the universe and what happens in it.

Expansion:

The action of becoming larger.

THEORY OF EVOLUTION

Charles Darwin was a British scientist. He became famous for his theory of evolution in 1859. It explained how different species came into being.

According to Darwin, all plant, animal and human life evolved through a process called natural selection. This means that in order to survive, plants and animals changed or adapted to suit their environment. They had all originally come from one living organism and had developed over millions of years.

THE BIG BANG THEORY

Most scientists believe that the universe was created between ten and twenty billion years ago from a cosmic explosion in outer space. This explosion hurled matter in all directions. This started the formation of atoms, which eventually led to the formation of stars and galaxies.

This theory, which came about in the 1920s, became known as the Big Bang theory. Experts believe that rather than an explosion, there was an expansion. The universe continues to expand today.

It could be said that time had no meaning before the Big Bang. If the Big Bang was the beginning of time, then there was no universe before it, since there could not be any 'before' if there was no time.

Other ideas state that the Big Bang was not the beginning of time. Instead, some believe that there was a completely different universe before the Big Bang and it may have been very different from the one we know today.

CREATION STORIES

13

Search online for a more detailed explanation of the theory of evolution.

Religion and/or Science?

In the past there has been a division between the religious view of creation and the scientific view of creation. However, as time passed people began to see that there was no need to choose between the two. Both contain great lessons.

The difference is that they are teaching two different things. Science is concerned with **how** the world came about, whereas religion is concerned with **why**. Science gives us explanations, while religion gives us meanings.

What they do have in common is that both are seeking truth. Both are trying to help us understand ourselves and our lives better. In fact, many believe that the only way to get a full and true meaning of the world is to accept what both have to say.

The scientist Albert Einstein once said, 'Science without religion is lame; religion without science is blind.'

> Do you think the world would be a better place if people looked to both science and religion for answers?

WRITE THE ANSWERS   Enquiry

1   Who became famous for the theory of evolution?

2   Explain what the theory of evolution means.

3   Explain in your own words what is meant by the Big Bang theory.

4   What is the difference between religion and science when it comes to creation narratives?

GROUP ACTIVITY   Exploration

In groups, design a quiz with questions about the religious and scientific views of creation. Test each other's knowledge on the topic by asking another group your questions.

CREATION STORIES

13

Creation Narratives from around the World

Creation myths often share a number of features. They are often considered to be sacred accounts. All are stories with a plot and characters who are either gods or human-like figures or animals who often speak and transform easily.

Creation myths develop in oral traditions and so often have multiple versions. Myths attempt to explain the unknown and sometimes teach lessons. Creation narratives give the people in a culture a worldview that guides how they should relate to the natural world and to each other. They often contain symbols.

We will now look at two creation narratives from around the world.

PAN GU AND THE CHINESE CREATION NARRATIVE

Pan Gu is an important figure in Chinese creation mythology. The myth tells of how in the beginning the universe was nothing but chaos and the heavens and earth were all mixed up. It is described as a big black egg.

Pan Gu was born inside this egg and slept for 18,000 years. When he woke he cracked the egg and pushed it apart. The upper half of the egg became the sky above him and the lower half became the earth. The longer he held the egg apart, the bigger they grew.

After another 18,000 years, Pan Gu died and his body formed the various parts of the earth:

- His breath became the wind, mist and clouds.
- His voice became thunder.
- His left eye became the sun; his right eye, the moon.
- His head became the mountains.
- His blood became the rivers.
- His muscles became fertile lands.

- His facial hair became the stars and the Milky Way.
- His fur became bushes and forests.
- His bones became valuable minerals.
- His sweat became rain.
- The fleas on his fur carried by the winds became animals and humans.

According to this myth, Pan Gu was the first supreme being and the originator of the heavens and earth. Pan Gu is worshipped at a number of shrines in China. Some Chinese people believe that Pan Gu sacrificed his life to create the world and his body to enrich it and beautify it.

AUSTRALIAN ABORIGINE CREATION NARRATIVE

The Aborigines of Australia are considered to be one of the oldest surviving cultures in the world. Many different creation stories exist among the different Aboriginal groups. According to the Aboriginals there was a time called the Dreaming Era, which was when spirit beings formed creation. One of the stories goes like this:

There was a time when everything was still. Almost all the spirits of the earth were asleep. The Father of All Spirits gently woke the Sun Mother. He told her he had work for her to do. She was to go down to earth and wake the sleeping spirits and give them forms.

The Sun Mother glided down to earth, which was bare, and began to walk in all directions. Everywhere she walked, plants grew. She rested when she saw what her work had been done, but the Father of All Spirits told her to go into the caves and wake the spirits. So she ventured into the dark caves on the mountainsides. The bright light coming from her woke the spirits and insects of all kinds flew out.

She thought her work was finished, but again the Father of All Spirits urged her on to do more.

She went into a very deep cave, spreading her light around her. Her heat melted the ice and rivers and streams were created. Then she created fish and snakes. Next she woke the spirits of the birds and animals. The Father of All Spirits was pleased with the Sun Mother's work.

She called all the creatures to her and told them to enjoy the wealth of the earth and live peacefully together. Then she rose into the sky and became the sun.

At first the creatures lived together peacefully, but after a time they began to argue. The Sun Mother had to come down from her home in the sky. She gave each creature the power to change their form to whatever they chose.

She was not happy with the forms some of them took. The Sun Mother decided she must create new creatures. She gave birth to two children. The god was the morning star and the goddess was the moon. Two children were born to them and she sent them to earth. They became our ancestors.

GROUP ACTIVITY   Enquiry

In groups, choose either of the creation myths in this chapter.

Illustrate it using words and images.

You can present your work on a poster or in a PowerPoint presentation.

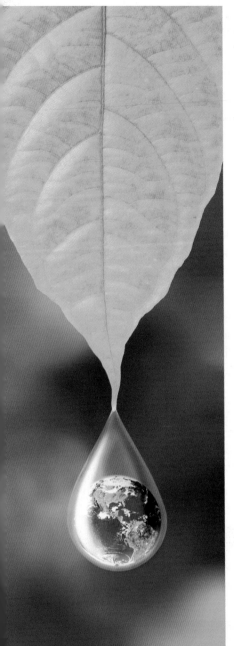

Meaning and Relevance of Creation Narratives Today

As you can see, most of the creation narratives from both religious and non-religious viewpoints started hundreds of years ago. Some of the scientific ones were discovered in more recent times.

However, just because something comes from the past does not mean it does not have value. Creation narratives can teach us about who we are and help us to think about how we got here and why. For example, one lesson we can learn from creation narratives is how important it is for all creatures to live together in a caring way. This is especially true in today's world: we can see the effects of global warming when people don't care for the earth.

None of the creation narratives can be proven to be completely true or completely false. Even the Big Bang Theory has a certain amount of faith involved in it. What came before the Big Bang? There is no way for scientists to know since there is no remaining evidence. Scientists have only been able to go back in time so far.

Many people who have a religious faith believe in the scientific element of the Big Bang theory, but they also believe that there is a God who made it happen. For these people, science answers the **how** questions and religion answers the **why** questions. There are some people who believe the religious creation narratives literally. These people come from fundamental religions where believers take the teachings of the religion to be true, word for word.

As science develops even more in years to come, we may be provided with new theories about creation. It is up to us as individuals to decide what to embrace as the truth. Creation narratives can help us give meaning to things we don't fully understand.

WRITE THE ANSWERS   Enquiry

1. Write a piece about which creation narrative appeals to you the most.

2. Explain what the narrative teaches people about creation and why you like this particular narrative.

REFLECTIVE ACTIVITY

Think about your own attitude to religious and non-religious stories about creation and answer the following questions:

1. Why, do you think, is it important for people in today's world to think about how the world was created?

2. How do you think the world was created?

3. Do you think people in the future will have different creation narratives? Why do you think this?

4. What was the most interesting thing you learned about creation narratives from reading this chapter?

 PowerPoint summary

 Weblinks

CHAPTER 14
Understandings of God

SOL: 6
LO: 1.1, 1.9, 2.4

LEARNING OUTCOME

Research and present understandings of God from the viewpoint of two major world religions.

KEY SKILLS YOU WILL USE IN THIS CHAPTER

- Being literate
- Managing information and thinking
- Working with others
- Being creative

WELLBEING INDICATORS IN THIS CHAPTER

LEARNING INTENTIONS

At the end of this chapter, I will

1 Understand what the Bible teaches Christians about their God

2 Understand what the Qu'ran teaches Muslims about their God

3 Research one of the other three major world religion's understanding of God.

14

At the heart of any religion is what the people believe to be true about their God or gods.

Some religions believe in a transcendent power rather than a God. Their beliefs about God will often influence how people worship. These beliefs may affect how they live their lives and the choices they make.

We are going to look at two major world religions and find out what their understanding of God is. In order to do this, we will research what their sacred text says about their God.

Monotheistic Religions

Three of the five major world religions are what are called monotheistic faiths. This means that they believe in only one God. Judaism, Christianity and Islam all worship the same God. They all believe that this God revealed himself to a man called Abraham.

God is known by many different names: Dios in Spanish, Gott in German, YHWH in Hebrew and Allah in Arabic. The three monotheistic religions share many of the same beliefs about God. They may express their beliefs differently, but at the centre of these faiths is one true, loving God.

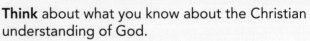

THINK, PAIR, SHARE

Think about what you know about the Christian understanding of God.

In **pairs**, write down what you know.

Share your ideas with the rest of the class.

LITERACY LIBRARY

Transcendent: Otherworldly, beyond human understanding.

Where did your knowledge of the Christian understanding of God come from?

RESEARCH   Enquiry

Look up the word for God in as many different languages as you can. Can you find any similarities between the words? What are they?

Christian Understanding of God

Where might you see a copy of the Bible?

The sacred text or holy book of any religion is where you will find its most important beliefs. For Christians, this is the Bible. The Bible was written thousands of years ago. It is not just one book, but is made up of over sixty books. These books contain poems, letters and stories all related in some way to God.

The Christian Bible is split into two main parts: the Old Testament and the New Testament. The Old Testament is an account of the time before Jesus Christ and the New Testament continues the story of the religion from the time of Jesus. Christians believe that God is a spiritual being who cannot be seen or touched, but his work can be seen in the wonders of the universe.

See also Chapter 15, pp.144–149

UNDERSTANDINGS OF GOD

14

What Does the Bible Say about the Christian God?

1 ONE GOD

The Bible tells its followers that there is only one God. This important teaching about God can be found in the Old Testament in a book called Exodus. The teaching comes from a list called the Ten Commandments.

The Ten Commandments are a set of rules God gave to the people of Israel through a leader named Moses. They were written on stone tablets and are still important today for the Jewish and Christian religions, as followers of these religions believe the Commandments came directly from their God. The First Commandment states,

'I am the Lord your God, you shalt not have any strange Gods before me.'

This Commandment means that Christians should not worship false gods and must not believe in any more than one God. Christians are reminded of the importance of this Commandment in the Book of Luke, Chapter 4: 'It is written, "The Lord thy God shalt thou worship, and him only shalt thou serve." '

2 GOD THE CREATOR

Christians believe that God is the creator of the universe and everything in it. This belief can be found in the very first book of the Bible, the Book of Genesis. Genesis 1:1 says, 'In the beginning, God created the heavens and the earth.' This means that before this time, nothing existed. The Christian understanding is that God designed all things. This belief is mentioned again in a later book called Isaiah, which says, 'Do you not know? Have you not heard? The Lord is the everlasting God, the Creator of the ends of the earth.' Throughout the Bible there are more than sixty-two verses about God being the creator.

WRITE THE ANSWERS Enquiry

1 Name three monotheistic faiths.

2 What is the sacred text of Christianity called?

3 What does the first of the Ten Commandments tell people?

4 What do Christians mean when they say God is a creator?

3 ALL-POWERFUL, ALL-KNOWING AND EVERLASTING GOD

Christians believe that God has three important characteristics: that he is all-powerful, all-knowing and everlasting. To say that God is all-powerful means that he has the ability and power to do anything. In other words, his power is unlimited.

In the Bible, Psalm 147:5 says, 'Great is our Lord and mighty in power; his understanding has no limit.' This quote also tells believers that their God is all-knowing. His intelligence and wisdom are above human capabilities. This is why people of faith cannot fully explain their God.

Isaiah 55:8–9 says, ' "For my thoughts are not your thoughts, neither are your ways my ways," declares the Lord. "As the heavens are higher than the earth, so are my ways higher than your ways and my thoughts than your thoughts." '

Christians also believe that God is eternal. He has always been and forever will be. Psalm 90 says, 'Lord, you have been our dwelling place in all generations. Before the mountains were brought forth, Or ever You had formed the earth and the world, Even from everlasting to everlasting, You are God.'

LITERACY LIBRARY

Capability:
The ability to do something.

Unconditional:
Complete and not limited in any way.

4 A LOVING GOD

One of Jesus's apostles, John, said, 'God is love.' This means that God's most important concern is the wellbeing of others. Christians believe it was because of this love that God sent his son Jesus to earth.

Christians see God's love as being different from human love, as it is unconditional. It is not based on feelings or emotions. God does not love people because they are lovable or because they make him feel good. He loves people because he **is** love.

LITERACY LIBRARY

Divine:
Heavenly or godlike.

The Bible clearly speaks of God the son, God the Father and God the Holy Spirit. Yet there is only one God. How can this be?

If we were to imagine it in terms of maths, it would not be $1 + 1 + 1 = 3$. It would be $1 \times 1 \times 1 = 1$. In the book of Genesis, God says, 'Let **us** make man in **our** image … male and female **He** created them.' There is a mixture of singular and plural nouns here. The word 'trinity' comes from two words: 'tri', meaning 'three', and 'unity', meaning 'as one'.

The understanding of God as Trinity is also explored in a prayer in the Christian religion called the **Nicene Creed**. This is a statement of religious beliefs.

THE NICENE CREED

We believe in one God, the Father, the Almighty, maker of all that is, seen and unseen.

We believe in one Lord, Jesus Christ, the only Son of God.

We believe in the Holy Spirit, the Lord, the giver of life.

EXPLANATION

This describes God as Creator. It gives us an image of God as Father.

Christians believe Jesus is both human and divine. This is how God experienced what it was like to be human.

The Holy Spirit is the power of God that people experience in their lives.

Matthew's Gospel, 28:19 says, 'Jesus commands his disciples to baptise in the name of the Father, the Son and the Holy Spirit.' It is a mystery how God can be all three things at once, but it is one of the most important things Christians believe about their God.

GROUP ACTIVITY Enquiry

Find the following Bible references:

Old Testament	New Testament
Psalm 136:26	Romans 11:33
Isaiah 46:9–10	Hebrews 13:8
Nehemiah 9:6	

Say whether the above Bible references shows God as:

1 One God   3 All-knowing   5 Love

2 God the creator   4 Eternal

RESEARCH Exploration

Find 1 Corinthians 13:4 in the Bible. (**Hint: It is in the New Testament!**)

In a PowerPoint presentation using images or photos, explain what this passage says about love.

You might like to do this in groups.

Islamic Understanding of God

Christianity and Islam have a lot in common when it comes to their understanding of God, who Muslims call Allah. The sacred text that Muslims refer to for information is the Qur'an. Muslims believe the Qur'an is the direct word of Allah and that it was revealed to Muhammad by the Angel Gabriel.

The Qur'an contains all Muslims' beliefs and moral codes. It cannot be changed and has been kept in its original form.

The Qur'an was originally written in Arabic and Muslims use it in their worship. It is made up of 114 chapters, or **surahs**.

What Does the Qur'an Say about Allah?

1 ONE GOD

The belief in one God is the most important aspect of a Muslim's religious faith. The Qur'an says, 'Say, He is God the One, God the eternal. He begot no one nor was he begotten. No one is comparable to him' (112: 1-4). This is a clear statement by God describing himself to humanity.

To say that anything is as great as God or deserves worship like him is one of the greatest sins of Islam. The Islamic creed, the **Shahadah**, states, 'There is only one God worthy of worship and Muhammad is his messenger.' Some Muslims say this creed first thing in the morning and last thing at night because the belief is so important to them.

WRITE THE ANSWERS Enquiry

1 What is the name of the sacred text of Islam?
2 What language was this text written in?
3 How many chapters are in it?
4 Where did the words in the sacred text come from?
5 What does the Islamic creed state?

2 MERCIFUL AND COMPASSIONATE

Each chapter of the Qur'an, except for one, begins with, 'In the name of God, the merciful, the compassionate.' The prophet Muhammad once said, 'God is more loving and kind than a mother to her dear child.'

Muslims believe that Allah is a forgiving and loving God. They think anything is possible through Allah as long as they ask for his help and forgiveness. In order to gain Allah's mercy, the Qur'an tells Muslims that they must 'Obey Allah and the Messenger that you may obtain mercy' (3:132).

3 CREATOR

'All praise is due to Allah, Creator of the heavens and the earth' (35:1). Muslims believe that Allah created the heavens and the earth in six days.

As well as giving Allah the name of creator, the Qur'an also refers to him as 'Inventor', 'Fashioner' and 'Originator'. All these words highlight the fact that Muslims see everything that Allah created as a blessing, including the creation of humans.

LITERACY LIBRARY

Attribute:
A quality or trait something has.

Idolatry:
Worshipping something as if it was a god.

Islamic calligraphy with the name of Allah.

4 NINETY-NINE NAMES BUT NO IMAGES

In the Qur'an Allah is given ninety-nine different names. These names are believed to be attributes of Allah. Some of them include The Light, The First, The Wise, The Majestic, The Great and The King. While Muslims use names such as these to describe Allah, they have no visual representations of him.

Chapter 42:11 of the Qur'an says, 'Allah is the originator of the heavens and the earth … there is nothing like a likeness of Him.' This is taken by Muslims to mean that Allah cannot be captured in an image by human hand, such is his beauty and grandeur. To attempt such a thing is seen as an insult to Allah. This idea comes from the Muslim belief that images can give rise to idolatry.

5 MASTER OF THE DAY OF JUDGEMENT

According to Islam all humans who have lived on earth must answer for their beliefs and actions on the Day of Judgement. Allah alone is the one who will judge them. Chapter 99:7–8 of the Qur'an says, 'Then shall anyone who has done an atom's weight of gold, see it! And anyone who has done an atom's weight of evil, shall see it.'

Muslims believe that they will be rewarded for doing good by going to heaven and be punished for doing bad by being sent to hell, unless God forgives them.

Islam teaches that this life is simply a test to determine our place in the eternal life after death.

THINK, PAIR, SHARE

Think about what you know about Islam or Christianity.
Working in **pairs**, one of you will take the role of interviewer, asking the questions. The other partner will be the interviewee, the person answering the questions.

Choose either Islam or Christianity as the subject of the interview.

Design a set of questions and answers that could be used in an interview about a religion's understanding of God.

Share the interview by acting it out in class when you are ready.

GROUP ACTIVITY: RESEARCH   Exploration

In groups research what the either the Jewish, Buddhist or Hindu understanding of God/gods is.

Present your findings to the rest of the class.

REFLECTIVE ACTIVITY

Think about your own attitude to the understanding of God found in Christianity and Islam and answer
the following questions:

1   Do you think Christianity and Islam have a lot in common about their understanding of God? Explain your answer.

2   Is there any other understanding of God that you have, which you think is important, that is not mentioned in this chapter?

3   Was there any understanding of God that you learned about in this chapter that you did not know about before?

 PowerPoint summary

 Weblinks

CHAPTER 15

The Life of Jesus Christ and the Development of the Bible

SOL: 3, 5, 6
LO: 1.9, 2.5

LEARNING OUTCOMES

Create a biography of a founder or early followers of a major world religion, using religious and historical sources of information, and explain what was involved in the development of the Bible.

KEY SKILLS YOU WILL USE IN THIS CHAPTER

- Communicating
- Being creative
- Being literate
- Managing information and thinking
- Working with others
- Being numerate
- Managing myself

WELLBEING INDICATORS IN THIS CHAPTER

LEARNING INTENTIONS

At the end of this chapter, I will

1 Know the difference between a biography and an autobiography

2 Have learned about the Roman Empire

3 Understand who Moses was

4 Know the difference between the Old Testament and the New Testament

5 Have learned about the four Gospel writers

6 Understand what a parable is and be able to give examples of parables.

7 Appreciate the importance of the Bible today.

What Is a Biography?

A **biography** is a detailed description of a person's life that has been written by someone else. It covers more than simply details of their childhood, their education, their work and their relationships. A biography describes a person's experience of these life events.

Sometimes the subject (the person the biography is about) might help the writer, but that is not always the case. In fact, some biographies may be about people who died a long time ago. A biography is non-fiction, which means it is based on facts rather than imagination.

An **autobiography** is an account of a person's life that is written by the subject of the book themselves.

GROUP ACTIVITY — Reflection and Action

Imagine you have been asked by someone to help them write a biography of your life.

- What would you say?
- What important fact would you like to include?
- Who would you ask to help you put it together?

Here is how best to proceed:

1. Introduce yourself. Who are you? What is important to you? Always write this in the third person

2. What stage are you at in your education? Have you completed eight years at primary school? What exam are you preparing for now? When will you sit this exam?

3. What have you achieved to date? Do you play sport? Have you won anything? Do you play an instrument; if so, what grade are you at? Do you participate in your local community; if so, what do you do?

4. Give a closing statement about yourself. Mention what you think is important for people to know about you. What is unique to you that makes you different to someone else?

RESEARCH — Exploration

In groups, think about someone that you would like to find out more about: for example, a sports player, musician or fashion designer.

Together, research this person and make a summary, PowerPoint presentation or a video clip of why you chose that person and include some interesting facts about them.

Here are some recent biographies and autobiographies to help you start.

Draw the table below into your copybook and fill it in to keep a note of your progress.

What I already **know** about the person	What I **want** to find out	What I have learned upon completion of my task

Let's look at a biography of a founder of a major world religion using religious and historical sources of information. We need to go back over 2,000 years to learn about the life of Jesus Christ, the founder of Christianity.

Galilee, Samaria and Judea: The three provinces or areas under a certain rule of Palestine.

Bethlehem: The birthplace of Jesus.

Nazareth: The town where Jesus grew up.

River Jordan: The river where Jesus was baptised.

Sea of Galilee: The place where Jesus met his first disciples.

Jerusalem: The town where Jesus was arrested and put to death and where his resurrection took place.

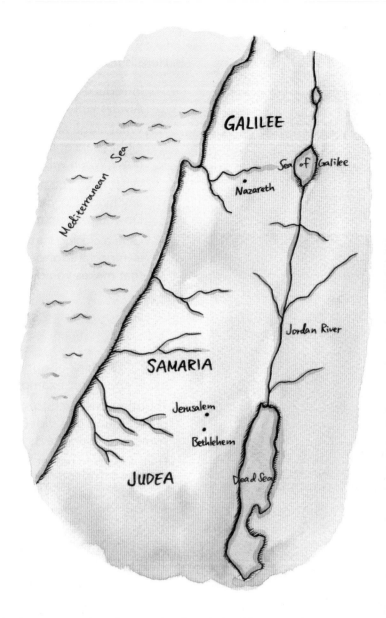

LITERACY LIBRARY

Founder:
A person who starts or sets up something from the very beginning.

The region or land where Jesus lived, preached and died became known as the **Holy Land**.

The Holy Land is where Jesus was born. Another name for the Holy Land is Palestine. The Holy Land is about one-quarter the size of Ireland. It is beside the Mediterranean Sea. Three continents surround it: Europe, Africa and Asia.

Today this country is called Israel. This map shows some of the most important places associated with the life of Jesus.

ACTIVITY Enquiry

Imagine being in the Holy Land/Israel today. What do you think it looks like? Why don't you look it up online?

Draw or trace this map into your copybook to help you remember it.

The Roman Empire

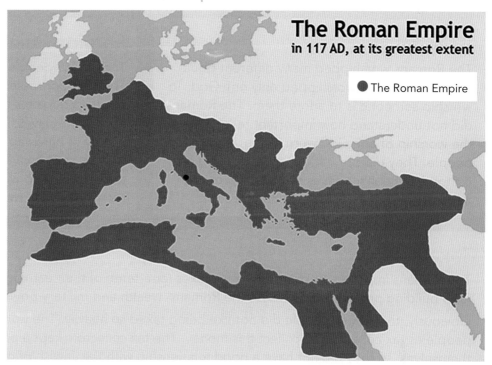

The Roman Empire
in 117 AD, at its greatest extent

● The Roman Empire

LITERACY LIBRARY

Dynasty:
A line of rulers all from the same family.

Palestine was under the control of the **Roman Empire** at the time of Jesus. With Rome as its centre, the Roman Empire stretched to Spain and France in the west, the Alps in the north, Greece, Turkey and the Holy Land in the east, and across North Africa and the Mediterranean Sea in the south.

Even though it was small, Palestine was an important area. It was split into three different provinces: Galilee in the north, Samaria in the middle and Judea in the south. To rule their lands effectively or properly, the Romans appointed, or picked, a governor, or procurator, in each province. The governor was the person who ruled a certain area.

At the time of Jesus, Pontius Pilate ruled over Judea and Samaria. Galilee, seen by Rome as the least important area, was governed by Herod Antipas. The Herod family was a ruling dynasty, or government, in Palestine at the time of Jesus.

FILL IN THE BLANKS   Enquiry

In your copybook, fill in the blanks in the sentences below:

1 The land where Jesus lived, preached and died became known as the
   _____ _____.

2 Another name for the _____ _____ is _____.

3 Palestine was under the control of the _____ _____ at the time of Jesus.

4 Palestine was split into _____ different provinces: _____,
   _____ and _____.

5 At the time of Jesus, _____ _____ ruled over _____
   and _____.

6 The _____ family was a ruling dynasty, or government, in Palestine at the time of Jesus.

The Jews and Romans did not get along for the following reasons.

Religion

The Romans worshipped many different gods, whereas the Jews worshipped only one God. To worship someone is to adore them. The Romans did not understand how important religion and the worship of one God were to the Jewish people. They did not understand their religious customs or habits, such as not working on the Sabbath, and this caused tension and stress.

Foreign Rule

The Jewish people wanted to rule themselves. They felt oppressed by Roman rule. To be oppressed means to feel helpless and almost like slaves. They had suffered a long history of hardship under foreign rulers. They wanted their own independent land, ruled by themselves, and were waiting for God to send them a Messiah to lead them to freedom.

Taxation

The Romans imposed, or charged, heavy taxes (one-tenth of their earnings) on the Jewish people to fund building projects and increase the Romans' wealth and military power.

Obviously, the Jewish people did not like being taxed so heavily. The Romans employed local people as tax collectors to collect this money. The tax collectors kept a portion of the taxes for themselves, so they did not have a good relationship with the Jewish people.

However, as a compromise, the Jewish people were allowed to follow their own customs and practise their own religion. When a compromise is made, an agreement is reached. The Romans were mainly interested in the Palestinian land because whoever controlled the roads in and out of these areas gained power and wealth.

LITERACY LIBRARY

Military power:
A country's military power is their armies, soldiers and weapons.

Copy the 3-2-1 box below into your copybook and fill it in.

3-2-1		
3	**2**	**1**
things I have learned	things I found interesting	thing I want to learn more about

Sculpture of ancient Roman gods.

WRITE THE ANSWERS Enquiry

1 Why did the Romans not understand the Jewish religion?

2 Why did the Jews not like being ruled by the Romans?

3 Explain how taxation worked at the time of Jesus.

Messianic Expectation

The Jewish people believed strongly that they had a special relationship with God and were his chosen people. They awaited the coming of the Messiah, a great leader who would restore their freedom. They believed God spoke to them through the prophets. Prophets (for example, Jeremiah) were holy men and women who carried messages from God. They told of God's promise to send a great, powerful leader who would guide and rule the Jewish people.

The Jews had experienced a troubled past. Their land had been invaded many times and their cities had been destroyed. For many years they longed for a united, prosperous and successful kingdom like the one they had when King David ruled them (from 1010 BCE to 970 BCE). He was Israel's greatest king and a faithful follower of God.

Ever hopeful, the Jews waited for the Messiah, or a leader, sent by God who would save them. They saw the Messiah as a great military leader, a king-like figure, strong and powerful. The Messiah would be the anointed one who would lead them to freedom. In the meantime, they prepared themselves for his coming by following the laws set down for them by the prophet Moses.

The ruins of a synagogue in Israel in which Jesus preached.

THE LIFE OF JESUS CHRIST AND THE DEVELOPMENT OF THE BIBLE

15

01 Who Was Moses?

Moses was a Jew who earned a living as shepherd. One day he saw a bush that appeared to be on fire. As he got closer he realised that even though the bush was on fire, it was not actually burning. Suddenly, he heard God's voice speaking to him. God told him he was to help the Jewish people. At first, he was frightened and was unsure that he could carry out what God had asked of him. However, he was a man of great faith, so he set off to see the pharaoh.

He asked the pharaoh to let the Jewish people go so that they could return to the Promised Land given to them by God. The Pharaoh refused. Wanting to show that Moses was chosen by him to help them, God sent ten plagues on Egypt. A plague is a terrible event and these plagues included swarms of locusts and hailstorms that ruined all crops. Still the pharaoh refused to free the Jews.

Finally, God sent the last and the most terrible plague. An Angel of Death passed over each house in Egypt killing the firstborn son. The Jews were told to sacrifice a lamb and smear the blood on their doors so that the angel would know they were Jews and pass over their houses.

After this plague, the pharaoh agreed to let the Jews go. They set off, led by Moses, but were soon chased by the Egyptian army because the pharaoh had changed his mind. When they got to the Red Sea, God parted the waters, allowing them to pass through. This event became known as the Exodus and is one of the most important moments in the history of the Jewish religion.

After that Moses travelled with the Jews to Mount Sinai, where he received the Torah. This gave details about how God wanted his people to live. The well-known Ten Commandments are part of the Torah.

This was the second covenant that God had made with his chosen people, the Jews. In the first covenant God promised to make Abraham the Father of a great people. He said that Abraham and his followers must obey God. In return for this, God would guide and protect them and give them the land of Israel.

The second covenant reinforced the first covenant that God had given to Abraham. God promised to stay with the Jews and never abandon them.

For the next forty years the Jewish people struggled to keep their covenant with God. At times they doubted him, but he was always present in their hour of need. In this way they learned to trust him and realised the importance of keeping their promises to him.

Their leader, Moses, died before they reached the Promised Land. He is still a role model today for Jewish people.

THINK, PAIR, SHARE

Think about the above text.

In **pairs**, write three pieces of information.

Share the three pieces of information with your classmates.

WRITE THE ANSWERS   Enquiry

1   What does 'Messianic expectation' mean?

2   What did the Jewish people long for?

3   The Jewish people prepared themselves for the coming of the Messiah. If you were a Jewish person at the time, how would you prepare for this coming?

4   What did Moses see while minding his sheep?

5   What did Moses ask the pharaoh to do?

6   What was the most terrible plague that God sent to Egypt?

7   What happened at the Red Sea?

8   What is the Torah?

Mount Sinai, Egypt.

THE LIFE OF JESUS CHRIST AND THE DEVELOPMENT OF THE BIBLE

15

01 ## Sources of Evidence about Jesus Christ

Evidence about Jesus comes from oral and written traditions. These sources include the Bible, historical documents and the four Gospel writers. Let's look at each of these to find out more about Jesus Christ.

LITERACY LIBRARY

Evidence:
Proof or information that shows something is real.

The Bible

We are used to thinking that the Bible is a single book, but as soon as we open it, it becomes clear that it is in fact a collection of books: seventy-two in total. Some of its stories are quite short, while others are long. Some of its books were written at the time of the Roman Empire, while others were written centuries earlier.

The material in the stories varies too. Some parts consist of historical material, while other parts contain wise sayings (the Psalms) and personal letters.

The Bible itself is divided into two parts: the Old Testament and the New Testament. The Old Testament is everything that happened before Jesus was born. The New Testament is the story of Jesus and his ministry on earth.

Each book in the Bible has a name and is organised into chapters and verses. Big numbers on the page are the **chapters** and the small numbers are the **verses**. For example, the Gospel of St John (name), 19 (chapter):15 (verse): 'But they shouted, "Away with him, away with him, crucify him." Pilate said, "Shall I crucify your king?" The chief priests answered, "We have no king except Caesar."' The book names can be shortened, for example Mark (MK) and Luke (LK).

In small groups around your table, find out what each of the following references say: John 18:10, Luke 24:8, Mark 3:6, Matthew 28:7.

THE LIFE OF JESUS CHRIST AND THE DEVELOPMENT OF THE BIBLE

15

THE OLD TESTAMENT (HEBREW SCRIPTURES)

The Old Testament tells the story of the coming of the Messiah. It consists of many books, from the story of Genesis, when we were created in the image of God, to the story of the **prophets**, who spoke on behalf of God. The most famous prophets are Jeremiah, Isaiah and Ezekiel.

The prophets reminded the Jewish people about the law of God and warned them against disobeying it. They were told that if they obeyed it, God would look after them. Because they had suffered for many years, the Jewish people wanted to live in peace and harmony. The Old Testament traces the history of the Jewish people.

WRITE THE ANSWERS	Enquiry

1. How would you describe the Bible?
2. How many books are in the Bible?
3. What sort of material is found in the Bible? Give examples.
4. What is the Old Testament (Hebrew Scriptures)?
5. Draw the books of the Old Testament, labelling them clearly.

Reading the torah using a *yad* (a hand pointer to help the reader follow the text).

LITERACY LIBRARY

Evangelist:
Means 'person of faith' and those who believe that Jesus is God.

THE NEW TESTAMENT

The Evangelists, namely Matthew, Mark, Luke and John, are the four Gospel writers. The Evangelists wanted to tell everyone the Good News. In time, the Good News came to be known as the **Gospel**. The four Gospels are mainly about the last three years of Jesus's life. They focus on the teachings of Jesus, his death and resurrection.

The Gospels came together in three separate stages:

1 The actual events that took place during Jesus's lifetime.
2 The disciples preaching about Jesus (oral tradition).
3 The writing down of the Gospels (written tradition).

WRITE THE ANSWERS
Enquiry

1 Name the four Gospel writers.
2 What did the Good News come to be known as?
3 What does the word 'evangelist' mean?
4 What are the main events of Jesus's life?
5 What are the three stages of the Gospels?

1. Actual Events in the Life of Jesus

Jesus the teacher travelled with the **disciples** all over Palestine (the Holy Land). The word 'disciple' means the 'chosen one'. Much of Jesus's teaching was based on what God had already told us in the books of the Old Testament.

In Matthew's Gospel we are told that Jesus himself said, 'Do not think that I have come to do away with the Law of Moses and the teachings of the prophets. I have not come to do away with them, but to make their teachings come true.'

Jesus took the teaching of the Old Testament and brought it to completion or made it perfect.
The Old Testament encouraged or asked us to love our neighbours as ourselves and Jesus also encouraged us to do this. He lived out this message of love in his life.

Everywhere he went, Jesus taught with authority. This means Jesus knew exactly what he wanted to talk about and explained it very clearly to those who listened. When he spoke to people, it was as if he knew them inside out.

In fact, Jesus made a big impression on everyone he met. Those who hated him recognised a power within him to make strong speeches and work miracles.

It was Jesus who was the crucified one, who died on the cross and rose from the dead three days later. After the resurrection, he appeared many times to the disciples.

2. Disciples Preaching about Jesus (Oral Tradition)

Today Jesus makes a huge difference to people's lives because he is living among them. After he rose from the dead and sent the Holy Spirit to the **Apostles**, they realised how powerful and good he was. They realised that Jesus was God made man, the Son of God.

The Apostles travelled all over Palestine, telling everyone the good news of the resurrection. When told, many people believed and became Christians. The story of the resurrection was told and retold for many centuries. It was passed from one person to the next by word of mouth. This is called **the oral tradition**, like the stories told by *seanchaí* in Ireland years ago.

When Christians hear the story of the resurrection, they are reminded that Jesus died on the cross so that they could be saved. God's love for them is so great that he gave his only son for them. Because Jesus is both God and man, his resurrection gives people the strength to one day rise from the dead by the power of God.

Many extracts in the Bible illustrate this oral tradition, such as 1 Thessalonians 2:13–16. In this story we see how the Apostles proclaimed the word of God to the people they spoke to. We see how the message of Christ continued through the Apostles when Christ died.

WRITE THE ANSWERS Enquiry

1 How has Jesus made a huge difference to people's lives?

2 What is meant by 'the oral tradition'?

3 How important was this phase, in your opinion?

4 Read the passage 1 Thessalonians 2:13–16 and explain its main message.

THE LIFE OF JESUS CHRIST AND THE DEVELOPMENT OF THE BIBLE

15

3. Writing Down the Gospels (Written Tradition)

LITERACY LIBRARY

Witness:
Someone who was present at the time and saw the event.

Chronological order:
Presented in the order in which something happened.

As news of the resurrection spread, it was impossible for the disciples to preach in all the areas where there was a demand for them. The Apostles were also getting quite old and some of them had died. It therefore became very important to start writing things down before it became too late.

The written Gospel would help future generations to get to know Jesus, the Messiah and the Chosen One. The details of some events, such as when Jesus healed the sick, were taken from witnesses.

Others who witnessed the miracles performed or the resurrection told their stories and they were written down first-hand. When the evidence was given, it was written down and then sorted and examined by the Evangelists. The Evangelists picked out what they thought would be important to future generations. As we have already mentioned, the four Gospel writers are Matthew, Mark, Luke and John. Their Gospels are in fact **documents of faith**.

Some people make the mistake of comparing the Gospels to a history book. If you think about the history book you study for your Junior Cycle, it is full of dates and times and everything is in chronological order: early Christian Ireland, the Middle Ages, the Renaissance, etc.

In the Gospels there are no dates and the events of Jesus's life are in no particular order. For this reason, Christians often refer to the Gospels as a story of faith instead of a precise history with exact dates. Often information is grouped together because a particular theme or topic is being addressed. For example, in St Luke's Gospel he devotes some time to parables.

The Gospel stories are mainly about the last three years of Jesus's life. In fact, little time is spent writing about his childhood. Just like his father, Jesus worked as a carpenter, yet we are told nothing of this in the Gospels. The Gospels are really documents that provide us with important written information. They provide us with information telling us that Jesus is God.

The Gospels are documents of faith to help future generations understand and believe in God. They are called documents of faith because the Evangelists believed that Jesus was the Messiah, the Chosen One, and they provided evidence to support what they wrote. They invited everyone to support this belief.

In the Gospels, names of people and places are often left out and no dates are given. Jesus's life is not written down exactly the way it was lived. The Evangelists believed that Jesus had risen from the dead and was living among them.

Many things were gathered that help us to learn more about Jesus through his teachings in the parables and the many miracles he performed.

The Evangelists – Matthew, Mark, Luke and John – studied everything that was brought to them. They were men of deep faith. They chose to include what they felt was important for Christian communities: Jesus's teaching, his miracles, his death and his resurrection. In doing this, they showed how Jesus's words and actions revealed that he truly is the Son of God.

WRITE THE ANSWERS
Enquiry

1 How important was the writing of the Gospels?

2 In your opinion, was it necessary to write them down? Why?

3 How important do you think evidence is to the writing of the Gospels?

4 What important news do the Gospels give us?

5 Explain, giving two reasons, why the Gospels are described as documents of faith.

6 Name the three stages in the development of the Gospels. What was involved in these three different stages?

GROUP ACTIVITY
Enquiry

Work in groups of three or four. What are the similarities and the differences between the oral tradition and the written tradition?

Historical Documents

Most of what we know about Jesus comes from our reading of the New Testament in the Bible. We also get information about Jesus from historical documents written at the end of the first century and the beginning of the second century. Two such examples are written by Josephus and Tacitus.

The historian Josephus.

The Historian Josephus (written approximately 93 CE)

There were many documents written at this time, but an important one was written by a man called Josephus around 60 years after the death of Jesus. He was a Jewish scholar and wrote a book about the history of the Jews. In this he described Jesus as a wise man and teacher. Also, he wrote about the crucifixion of Jesus by Pontius Pilate and his resurrection from the dead three days later.

The Historian Tacitus (written approximately 120 CE)

Like Josephus, Tacitus was also a historian. However, he was a Roman and was suspicious, or wary, of Christianity. In his case, he set down his beliefs about 80 years after the death of Jesus. Among the things he wrote about were the death of Jesus, how he was sentenced by Pontius Pilate and how Christians got their name from Jesus Christ.

Both these men were historians and were concerned with facts and details. They wrote many facts about events that happened and people who were present. Because they were not Christians, they had no personal interest in Jesus, the man or his message.

Both documents show that Jesus was a real person who did exist and lived among ordinary people in Palestine. The people who followed him were known as Christians. He was sentenced to death by the governor of Palestine, Pontius Pilate.

There are two sources of information that help us to learn about Jesus: Christian and non-Christian. The Christian sources of information are found in the Gospels of the New Testament. The non-Christian sources are found in the historical documents written for the Romans in the second century CE.

The Christian sources set out that Jesus is the Son of God. The historical documents from non-Christian sources confirm that Jesus did exist and that he was a historical person. Jesus founded a new religion.

The historian Tacitus.

WRITE THE ANSWERS　　　　　Enquiry

1 Who were Josephus and Tacitus?

2 How important are their writings?

3 From their writings, are you convinced that Jesus did exist?

The Four Gospel Writers

Gospel writer	Which group did he write for?		His symbol
Matthew	Jewish Christians		The angel
Mark	Christians living in Rome		The lion
Luke	Gentiles (non-Jewish); Christians		The ox
John	Christians throughout the Mediterranean world		The eagle

LITERACY LIBRARY

Precisely:
Carefully or exactly.

The Gospel of St Matthew

This Gospel was once believed to be the first Gospel written. However, research has shown that it was written after Mark's Gospel, in Antioch, where there was a large community of Jewish Christians. It is now believed that this Gospel was written around 85–90 CE. Matthew had a wide knowledge of the Jewish religion and the Old Testament. He saw Jesus as the new Moses, the **'one promised by God'**, the **Messiah** and the **'Son of David'**. Matthew taught his followers a new way of living.

The Gospel of St Mark

It is believed that Mark's Gospel was written for Christians around 65–70 CE. At that time Mark was well known to Peter, who was Jesus's closest disciple, so he could listen carefully to what Peter told him and record the information precisely. In this Gospel, Jesus is seen as a miracle worker and a teacher. Much of it is devoted to the miracles performed by Jesus.

Mark tells us that Jesus is indeed the promised Messiah who suffered at the hands of the authorities in Jerusalem. He also informs us that Jesus had feelings like everyone else.

The Gospel of St Luke

It is believed that Luke's Gospel was written around the same time as Matthew's one. Luke wrote his Gospel for Gentile Christians. He himself was a Gentile and wanted to spread the Good News about Jesus. Throughout this Gospel, Luke's caring side is clear. He had great sympathy for the oppressed and poor people of society.

Luke's Gospel helps us to see that Jesus is the saviour who brings God's love to all people. He also showed Jesus as someone who brings love and forgiveness to all.

His Gospel has a special place for Mary as the mother of Jesus. Another important aspect of this Gospel is prayer. Luke describes Jesus as a man of prayer.

The Gospel of St John

It is thought that John wrote his Gospel around 95 CE. However, this Gospel writer used different sources to describe the story of Jesus. He may have been a follower of one of Jesus's youngest disciples, who was also called John. We do know that Jesus had a special place for this disciple John, because when he was dying on the cross he asked him to take special care of his mother, Mary.

By all accounts John wrote this Gospel for Christians living throughout the Mediterranean world, namely in Turkey, Greece and Italy.

His Gospel helps us to see Jesus as a real human being, as he shares our pain and burdens, and is also there in good times to share our joys. He is the real Son of God. Much of this Gospel is spent telling stories that are not found in the other three Gospels.

WRITE THE ANSWERS Enquiry

1 Which Gospel writer wrote his Gospel first?

2 Write a summary about each Gospel.

3 Why, do you think, did these four men write Gospel stories?

4 How, do you think, did these Gospels make a difference to the lives of the people for whom they were written?

St John the Evangelist

THE SYNOPTIC GOSPELS

The Gospels of Matthew, Mark and Luke are all quite similar and therefore they are known as **Synoptic Gospels**. The word 'synoptic' means 'describing events from a similar point of view'. Sometimes these three Gospels are so similar that one might think they were copied from each other. Both Matthew and Luke use Mark's Gospel as the basis of their own work.

The Gospels of Matthew and Luke are longer than Mark's Gospel. This causes us to ask where all the extra information came from for them to write their Gospels.

Many Bible experts believe that this information came from a document called **the 'Q' or Quelle document** (*Quelle* means 'source' in German). This is a collection of Jesus's sayings from a much earlier date. Although many experts believe that 'Q' is a real document, none has ever been found.

The Beatitudes can be found in Matthew's and Luke's Gospels. These help us know how to behave the right way towards God and other people. They are not found in Mark's Gospel.

The Gospel of St John

The Gospel of John is different from the other three Gospels, as it uses other sources to tell the story of Jesus. There are **no parables** found in John's Gospel and **the Kingdom of God is only mentioned once**, whereas it has great importance in the other three Gospels.

This Gospel focuses more on **who Jesus is rather than what he says and does**. The opening lines of John's Gospel are from a poem: '…born not from human stock or human desire or human will but from God himself'. This shows God's power towards his people. Jesus revealed God to us in a way that an ordinary person could understand.

There are many 'I am' statements to be found in this Gospel, where Jesus makes the following statements about himself: 'I am the bread of life' (6:35), 'I am the vine' (15:1) and 'I am the light of the world'. In this way, John identifies Jesus with the God who appeared to Moses in the burning bush. When Moses asked God his name, God answered, 'I am who I am'.

In John's Gospel the themes of love and life are also evident. These are gifts given to us by God and ones that we receive willingly. To love God is to love one another. Jesus brings this gift to those who have faith in him.

WRITE THE ANSWERS   Enquiry

1   What does the word 'synoptic' mean?

2   Why are the three Gospels – Matthew, Mark and Luke – known as Synoptic Gospels?

3   How are Matthew's Gospel and Luke's Gospels similar?

4   What is the Quelle document?

5   What is so different about John's Gospel from the other Gospels?

THE LIFE OF JESUS CHRIST AND THE DEVELOPMENT OF THE BIBLE

15

Parables

A parable is a simple story with a moral or spiritual meaning. Jesus used parables, as he felt they helped people to understand his message more clearly.

Parables are easy to understand and easy to remember. This was the way people learned in biblical times, through story. Jesus was using a way of learning that the people already knew in order to teach them this new and difficult concept of the Kingdom of God.

Parables at times prompt us to **stop** and **think** about how we live our lives. Every parable that Jesus told highlights something different about the Kingdom of God. Jesus told parables using examples from the daily lives of his followers, for example the farmers and fishermen.

Reading one parable is not enough to understand what the kingdom is like, however. This is because the Kingdom of God is such a great way of life that no one story does it the justice it deserves.

In general, parables are used to teach us a lesson about life. Jesus used parables for different reasons:

1. To command attention from the disciples

2. To challenge their growth in faith

3. To use stories to explain difficult concepts or ideas so that they could understand, for example, stories about fishermen and tax collectors.

The parables made the disciples and others question their everyday lives and ask themselves if they were living a life that was worthy of the Kingdom of God.

THINK, PAIR, SHARE

If Jesus were to tell parables today, what examples from our daily lives could he use for his listeners?

- **Think** about this.
- **Pair** with your neighbour.
- **Share** your ideas with the class.

Let's look at some parables. The first one can be found on the next page.

Read the full story on the next page

1 The Good Samaritan (Luke 10:25–37)
This parable shows how important it is to **love** your neighbour in the Kingdom of God. Anyone can be a member of this kingdom.

2 The Parable of Talents (Matthew 25:14–30)
Jesus told this parable to encourage us to use the talents that we have been given.

3 The Mustard Seed (Mark 4:30–32)
This parable shows that God's love for us is a gift that is planted in our hearts, where it **grows** and matures. From small and insignificant beginnings, God can bring about wonderful conclusions.

4 The Prodigal Son (Luke 15:11–32)
This parable shows the unconditional love a parent has for their child. No matter what the child does, there is always a place for them to come home to, just like in the Kingdom of God.

Read the full story on p.234

THE LIFE OF JESUS CHRIST AND THE DEVELOPMENT OF THE BIBLE

15

Jesus told this parable about a kind-hearted man who helped a stranger at the side of the road.

THE GOOD SAMARITAN: LUKE 10:25–37

There was once a man who was going down from Jerusalem to Jericho when robbers attacked him. They stripped him and beat him up, leaving him half dead. It so happened that a priest was going down that road; but when he saw the man, he walked on by, on the other side of the road. A Levite also came along the same road, went over and looked at the man, and then walked on by, on the other side.

However, a Samaritan who was travelling that way came upon the man, and when he saw him, his heart was filled with pity. He went over to him, poured oil and wine on his wounds and bandaged them. Then he put the man on his own beast and took him to an inn, where he took care of him.

The next day he took out two silver coins and gave them to the innkeeper. 'Take care of him,' he told the innkeeper, 'and when I come back this way, I will pay you whatever else you spend on him.'

And Jesus concluded, 'In your opinion, which one of these three acted like a neighbour towards the man attacked by robbers?' The teacher of the law answered, 'The one who was kind to him.' Jesus replied, 'You go then, and do the same.'

The Samaritans were people that came from the province of Samaria. Although they were Jewish, they were looked down on by other Jews. Their customs and religious practices were different to other Jews. As a result, they were treated as outsiders by many. In Jesus's time they mixed freely with non-Jews (Gentiles).

In this parable it is the Samaritan who helps the man at the side of the road, while some religious people just pass him by. Being a good neighbour and friend has nothing to do with the colour of your skin, the clothes you wear or your religion.

Throughout his life, Jesus taught that people should love their neighbour as they love themselves. The Kingdom of God is a place of truth, justice, peace and love. It is the goodness in each person. The parable of the Good Samaritan shows us that it is often the most unlikely person who will come to our aid at the end of the day.

LITERACY LIBRARY

Levite:
A Jewish temple official.

GROUP ACTIVITY   Exploration

1 Brainstorm with your group about the main parts of the story of the Good Samaritan. Write these on your part of the placemat.
- Discuss these with the group.
- Decide with the group on what the three most important or relevant points are to the story.

2 Divide the class into four groups. As a group, select a parable from page 155 to read.
- Create a short role-play to illustrate the parable to the rest of the class. You should allow 10–15 minutes to prepare.
- Present your role-play to the class.
- Write the main points of the parables that the other groups have presented.

3 Find the other three parables in the Bible.

The Sacred Text or the Bible Today: Its Continued Significance in the Lives of Believers

The Bible continues to be significant for people today. It was written for people and not for a particular time in history. The Bible was written for the human heart to ponder over and seek comfort from its many stories.

The Bible demonstrates to us all that we are imperfect, as even David, who defeated Goliath with a rock, made mistakes in his life all the time. The Bible uses people's flaws or mistakes to display God's redemptive power at work in them. Matthew 26:31–75 tells the story of how Peter

denied Jesus three times and yet Jesus forgave him. Peter could be any one of us. We have all stumbled and fallen at times in our lives and we have been picked up to continue on the path of life.

The Bible helps Christians to find the answer to the problems we are facing in life, whether it is fear, worry, finance or something else.

Often people sit in silence and read the Bible stories. This gives them comfort at a time in their life that is difficult due to illness, bereavement, worry over exams or other difficult challenges.

RESEARCH   Reflection and Action

Reflect on the following passages:

- I Timothy 14:12
- Galatians 6:9
- Romans 15:13
- Philippians 4:6–7

1 Do these passages bring you comfort, peace or contentment?
2 What do you think each passage is saying?

REFLECTIVE ACTIVITY

Think about your own attitude to Jesus Christ and the Bible and answer the following questions:

1 What did you like learning about in this chapter?
2 If Jesus were alive today, what would you like to say to him?
3 Choose one thing from a sacred text that you would like to tell your class about.

 PowerPoint summary

 Weblinks

THE LIFE OF JESUS CHRIST AND THE DEVELOPMENT OF THE BIBLE

15

CHAPTER 16
Hinduism and Its History

SOL: 3, 6, 8
LO: 2:6

LEARNING OUTCOME

Construct a timeline of one major world religion, making reference to key people, times of expansion and times of challenge.

KEY SKILLS YOU WILL USE IN THIS CHAPTER

- Working with others
- Managing information and thinking
- Communicating
- Being creative
- Being literate

WELLBEING INDICATORS IN THIS CHAPTER

LEARNING INTENTIONS

At the end of this chapter, I will

1 Understand where Hinduism began
2 Be able to give examples of Hindu gods
3 Be able to tell the story of Mahatma Gandhi
4 Understand the caste system today.

Look at the timeline below. As you can see, many significant events have taken place over the last 4,000 years.

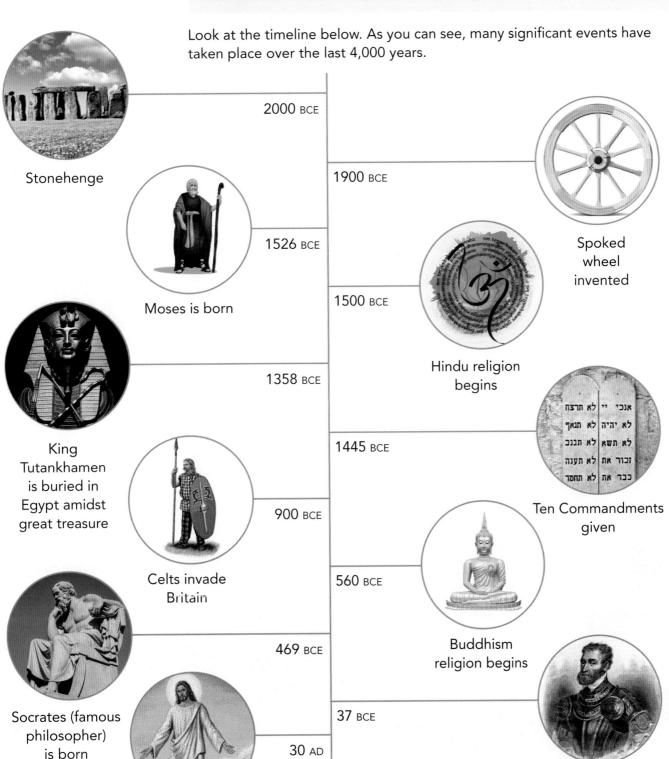

Stonehenge

2000 BCE

1900 BCE

Spoked wheel invented

1526 BCE

Moses is born

1500 BCE

Hindu religion begins

King Tutankhamen is buried in Egypt amidst great treasure

1358 BCE

1445 BCE

Ten Commandments given

Celts invade Britain

900 BCE

560 BCE

Buddhism religion begins

Socrates (famous philosopher) is born

469 BCE

37 BCE

30 AD

Life of Jesus Christ

Romans make Herod the Great King of Judea

16

The Cultural Context: Where It All Began

Hinduism is one of the world's oldest religions. It started 4,000 years ago in the Indus Valley in India. The name *Hindu* comes from the River Indus.

Archaeologists have found clay statues of gods and goddesses similar to those that are now worshipped by Hindu people all over the world.

There are over 900 million followers of the Hindu religion today. Hinduism is the main religion in India, Nepal and Bali.

> What do you think India looked like in those times?

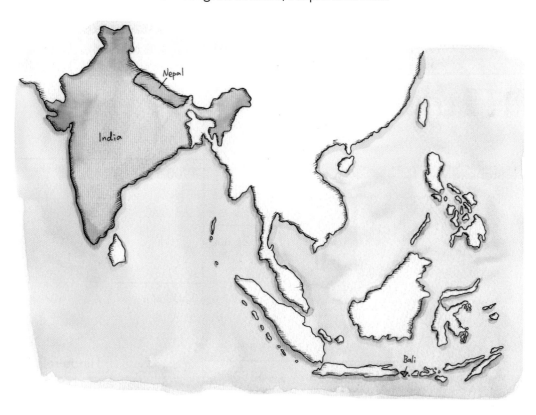

Founders and Beliefs

Unlike the other world religions, Hinduism has no single founder. It emerged from the rishis (sages of insight), holy men and saints, around 2000 BCE. This makes it quite unique. It is also one of the oldest surviving religions.

LITERACY LIBRARY

Rishi:
A Hindu wise person or saint.

Sage:
A wise person.

The Hindu religion stresses a way of living rather than a way of thought. The creed of a religion sums up what the followers of that religion believe. What is important to Hindus is their belief in a supreme soul or spirit that has no shape or form. This is called Brahman. Everything in the universe flows from this, so all life is part of Brahman.

There are many Hindu gods and goddesses, so this religion is an example of polytheism, which is a belief in many gods. The gods and goddesses represent the different parts of Brahman's power and character. Hindus are free to worship whatever Hindu god they like.

There are three important Hindu gods:

Brahma

This is the god who created the world. This god is identified with four faces and four arms. The faces symbolise the four Vedas, which are the writings of Hinduism. The Brahma's four arms face in different directions, showing that he is everywhere. In his hands, he holds:

- A water jar, as water is essential to life and life came from the ocean
- Beads that show time cycles
- A book that shows his intellect or knowledge.

His beard represents wisdom and the eternal process of creation.

Vishnu

This is the god who protects people from all evil and wrongdoing. He is known as an avatar. He has taken both animal and human forms. It is believed that he has visited the world nine times so far. On the tenth – and final – visit, the world will come to an end.

Shiva

This is the god who destroys and then rebuilds. Shiva has three eyes (the third eye is on Shiva's forehead), symbolising the moon, sun and fire. The universe goes through a process of birth, growth, destruction and rebirth. Shiva destroys the universe for it to be reborn.

LITERACY LIBRARY

Avatar:
The human form of a Hindu god.

Rebirth:
In the Hindu faith, this is also known as reincarnation.

See also pp.10–11, Chapter 1

What do you think this phrase means: 'a way of living rather than a way of thought'?

HINDUISM AND ITS HISTORY

16

Statue of Lord Vishnu.

When they pray to a particular god, most Hindus have a statue or a picture beside them. This helps them to focus. They believe that they must always do what is right and correct for themselves – this is called dharma. Hindus do what is right according to their social status or the stage they are at in life. Every form of life and every group of people has its own dharma. This is the law of its being. Dharma, or virtue, is following the truth of things. Adharma, or vice, is opposition to it. Duty is central to dharma. Doing one's duty is very important.

There are no set rules for being a Hindu, but most Hindus share the same beliefs. They believe that when you die, your soul is reborn in another body as an animal or a person. This cycle of birth and rebirth is called samsara. While Christians believe that you only live on earth once, Hindus believe that you are reborn over and over until you become perfect. Because of this belief, when you do good, good will come your way, and if you do bad, bad will follow you. This is called karma. Today, people often describe karma as 'what goes around comes around'.

WRITE THE ANSWERS   Enquiry

1 What is the main emphasis of the Hindu religion? Explain it in your own words.

2 Do you think that this is a good philosophy to have? Why/why not?

3 What does 'polytheism' mean?

4 Explain the word 'Brahman'.

5 What are the three important Hindu gods? Find out the names of other Hindu gods and goddesses.

6 Explain the following:
   (a) Dharma   (b) Samsara   (c) Karma.

Shore Temple in Tamil Nadu, India is also a UNESCO world heritage site.

LITERACY LIBRARY

Epic:
A long poem, usually about a hero.

Copy the 3-2-1 box below into your copybook and fill it in.

3-2-1		
3	**2**	**1**
things I have learned	things I found interesting	thing I want to learn more about

Sources of Evidence

Hindus have many holy books rather than one sacred text. Their scriptures were passed on by word of mouth (oral tradition) for many years before they were written down. The Hindu scriptures are written in Sanskrit. This is the language of ancient India, but it is no longer spoken.

The oldest Hindu sacred texts are from the four collections of prayers, hymns and magic spells called the Vedas. They were put together about 3,000 years ago and teach and guide Hindus on how they should live their lives. The four Vedas are:

- Rig-Veda
- Sam-Veda
- Yajur-Veda
- Atharva-Veda.

The Upanishads are another important Sanskrit text. They are teachings presented in the form of stories, poems and parables told by teachers to their students.

The two greatest stories / poems are the **Mahabharata** and the **Ramayana**. They are both epics that teach the importance of honesty, loyalty and courage. The Mahabharata tells the story of a war between two royal families and the ups and downs of their everyday lives. The Ramayana was written around the second century BCE. It tells the story of how the god Rama rescued his wife Sita from an evil demon king called Ravana. It teaches Hindus about love, courage and friendship.

Meditation is one way that Hindus pray. Designs or patterns like the yantra also help people to concentrate when meditating.

WRITE THE ANSWERS   Enquiry

1 How is prayer different in the Hindu faith from other world religions?

2 Compare the way Hindus pray to the act of prayer in another world religion.

A Disciple of the Faith: Mahatma Gandhi (1869–1948)

LITERACY LIBRARY

Renunciation:
Giving up or sacrificing.

Inherent:
Existing as a part of something, which it cannot be separated from.

Mahatma Gandhi was born Mohandas Karamchand Gandhi on the northwest coast of India on 2 October 1869. His mother was a very religious Hindu who regularly prayed to the gods and fasted. His father took care of a part of India for the British, who governed the country at the time. During Gandhi's youth, he regularly ate meat and stole from family members to buy tobacco. This changed when his father died.

At the age of 14, Gandhi was married to a girl called Kasturbai, who was 13. They stayed together until her death in 1944. After they were married, Gandhi wanted to go to London to study law. Once in London, he began to read sacred Hindu writings. The Bhagavad-Gita, an important Hindu text, had a strong impact on him. He cut down on his daily expenses, walked everywhere and ate less. In 1891, Gandhi returned to India as a qualified barrister.

There were too many barristers in India at the time, so he went to work for an Indian law firm in South Africa.

Mahatma Gandhi

In South Africa, Gandhi saw first hand the life of Indians living there. The turning point in his life came when he refused to give up his seat on a train to a white person, even though he had a ticket. He was beaten by the driver and thrown off the train. He spent that night sitting on the cold railway platform.

Gandhi was arrested many times in South Africa. From then on, Gandhi worked to defend the dignity of Indians.

What message do you think Mahatma Gandhi would have for the world today?

'Truth, purity, self-control, firmness, fearlessness, humility, unity, peace and renunciation – these are the inherent qualities of a civil resister.' Gandhi

Indians living in South Africa had to get their fingerprints taken and carry a permit at all times. Any Indian who broke this rule was fined, jailed or forced to leave the country. Gandhi encouraged them to stand up against this treatment. He developed a method of direct social action called satyagraha. This was based on the principles of courage, truth and non-violence. Gandhi always believed that how people behave is more important than what they achieve.

In 1915, Gandhi returned to India. Using the same idea of satyagraha, he led the campaign for India's independence from Great Britain. He was arrested in India many times. He believed it was honourable to go to prison for a just cause. Many times, Gandhi used fasting to convince other people of the need to be non-violent.

Finally, in 1947, India won independence from Britain. Gandhi had always hoped that India would be united and that Hindus and Muslims would live together in peace. However, there were many deep-rooted divisions between the two groups. The British responded to this by dividing ancient India into two independent countries: India, with a Hindu majority, and Pakistan, with a Muslim majority. Gandhi rejected this, as he believed both could live together in peace.

Above all, he believed the division of India was a tragedy. Religious riots soon broke out between the two groups. Gandhi once again began a fast to convince people to stop the fighting. After five days, the riots stopped and Gandhi began to eat again.

Some Hindus were not happy that Gandhi wanted peace with Muslims. At the beginning of 1948, Gandhi was walking to his evening prayer meeting. A young Hindu named Nathuram Godse approached him, pretending to seek Gandhi's blessing. He took a gun from his pocket and shot Gandhi three times. The 'Father of a Nation' died saying the word 'Rama', the name of a Hindu god. When he died that night, a light went out in the lives of the Indian people.

Mourners gathering around Gandhi's funeral pyre in 1948.

WRITE THE ANSWERS Enquiry

1 What does the quote at the end of page 164 say about Gandhi?
2 How significant was the turning point in Gandhi's life?
3 What does 'satyagraha' mean? Would this work in today's world?
4 Why, do you think, did Gandhi see the division of India as a tragedy?
5 Do you think that Gandhi died too early? Why/why not?
6 Find out about other people who follow or followed the Hindu beliefs of non-violence, truth, courage and so on.

GROUP ACTIVITY Exploration and Action

In groups, research one of the Hindu people in the images below.
Write down your key findings on the following and report this to the class:

- Place of birth
- Family background
- Career path
- Life beliefs and lessons learned
- Their life today.

1 Julia Roberts

2 George Harrison

3 Russell Brand

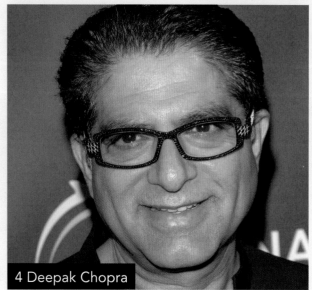
4 Deepak Chopra

16 HINDUISM AND ITS HISTORY

166

LITERACY LIBRARY

Ethnic origin:
Where the characteristics of a group come from.

Times of Expansion

During the twentieth century, many Indian Hindus moved to other countries. The biggest Hindu communities in Ireland are in the cities of Dublin, Cork, Galway and Limerick.

The main Hindu community in Ireland is of Indian ethnic origin. Other members of the community are from Nepal, the Philippines and other Asian countries. There are ethnic Irish Hindu followers too. The number of Hindus in Ireland is growing.

The number of Hindus in Ireland rose from 6,082 in 2006 to 14,332 in 2018, an increase of 135.6 per cent.

Hinduism can be compared to many faiths, including Christianity. All religions share the belief that we must regard other faiths with respect and treat all people equally.

- In the Hindu faith, we are told that we must not do anything to others that, if done to ourselves, could cause us pain.
- In the Buddhist faith, we are told to act towards others exactly as we would act towards ourselves.
- In the Christian faith, we are encouraged to treat others as we would like to be treated ourselves.
- In the Islamic faith, we are told that none of us truly believes until we wish for others what we wish for ourselves.
- In the Jewish faith, we are told that we must not do to others what is harmful to us.

The above statements can have an effect on our behaviour towards members of all world religions today. Actions that are carried out by any person can have good and bad consequences (karma).

FILL IN THE BLANKS   Enquiry

1   The biggest Hindu communities in Ireland are in the cities of _____, _____, _____ and _____.

2   Hinduism can be compared to many faiths, including _____.

3   In the Hindu faith we are told _____
    _____
    _____.

4   Actions that are carried out by any person can have good and bad consequences. This is called _____.

HINDUISM AND ITS HISTORY

16

Challenges Facing the Hindu Religion

The Social Hierarchy in India

Indian Hindus are born into a caste system, which divides people into different social classes. This is a very old system that dates back 1,500 years. It is based on the belief that people are born to have different roles in life. As such, people are not all equal. People have to marry within their caste.

- The Brahmins belong to the highest caste. They are the priests and scholars.
- The Kshatriyas are the soldiers and warriors.
- The Vaisyas are the merchants and the professionals, such as doctors and lawyers.
- The Sudras are the lowest caste. They are the servants and labourers.
- The Harijans are outside the caste system. They are known as the Untouchables. They are widely discriminated against.

The Caste System Today

The caste system is still in operation in India today, but it is much less strict. Much work has been done to improve the position of the Untouchables.

LITERACY LIBRARY

Merchant:
A person who buys and sells goods.

ACTIVITY   Exploration

Search online for the following video: Alex Drake 'The Caste System and Ancient Indian Society'.

After watching the video, brainstorm the following in small groups:

1   What are the main points made in this video?

2   What did you learn from this video?

WRITE THE ANSWERS   Enquiry

Read back over the text on the caste system and answer the following questions:

1   What is the caste system?

2   'People have to marry within their caste.' Do you think this is fair? Why/why not?

3   Research online to find out more about the Harijans and the work being done to help them today.

ACTIVITY   Reflection and Action

As you can see from reading this chapter, the Hindu religion is a fascinating one, dating back 4,000 years. Can you imagine living 4,000 years ago? Think about how different the world was then from how it is today.

Now think about living around the time of Mahatma Gandhi. Imagine sitting on the train that he was thrown off of.

1   Do you think you might have said something to him about this?

2   Would you say something to the driver of the train who beat him when he refused to give his seat to a white person?

REFLECTIVE ACTIVITY

Think about your own attitude to the history of Hinduism and answer the following questions:

1   What did you enjoy learning about in this chapter?

2   What, do you think, is meant when it is said that on the night Gandhi died, a light went out in the lives of the Indian people?

3   What are your thoughts on the caste system?

 PowerPoint summary

Weblinks

CHAPTER 17

How Christianity Addresses the Issue of Poverty

SOL: 6
LO: 1.1, 1.11, 2.7, 3.7

LEARNING OUTCOME

Explore how the religious teaching of Christianity addresses the issue of poverty.

KEY SKILLS YOU WILL USE IN THIS CHAPTER

- Staying well
- Managing myself
- Working with others
- Being creative
- Being literate
- Managing information and thinking
- Communicating

WELLBEING INDICATORS IN THIS CHAPTER

LEARNING INTENTIONS

At the end of this chapter, I will

1 Have explained what 'poverty' means

2 Understand what the Bible says about poverty

3 Have explored ways in which people can respond to poverty

4 Understand why Christians should respond to poverty

5 Be able to explain why Trócaire was set up and what work it does

6 Present a project on a Christian organisation that helps those in poverty.

What Is Poverty?

The world we live in today is fast-moving, technological and much more advanced than it was fifty years ago. Advances in medicine and communications have improved life for a lot of people around the world.

However, our world still has many issues and areas of concern that need to be addressed. One of these areas is poverty. Poverty is a condition where people's basic needs for food, clothing and shelter are not being met.

Concern:

A matter of importance or one that causes worry.

Address:

To focus on an issue or problem.

Condition:

A factor that affects the way people live.

Basic:

Something that is necessary, that a person must have.

GROUP ACTIVITY   Enquiry

Divide the class into groups of four. Using a placemat, write down your answers to the following questions:

1 What kind of poverty, do you think, is most common in Ireland today? Think about lack of food, clothes, shelter, education and medical needs.

2 Which members of society are most likely to be affected by poverty?

3 What people or groups could help to address this poverty?

4 What has caused this kind of poverty?

Discuss your answers and try to reach an agreement as a group. Use a ranking ladder to show what you think the most important points are.

Poverty has been a problem in our world for a long time. It is not something that only happened in recent times. All the major world religions try to help improve the lives of people who are affected by poverty. The reason they do this can be found in their religious teachings.

We are going to explore what the Christian religion has to say about this issue of concern for the world today.

HOW CHRISTIANITY ADDRESSES THE ISSUE OF POVERTY

17

Old Testament Teaching

The Old Testament, the first part of the Bible, was written over 3,000 years ago. The Old Testament clearly teaches that God has a special love and regard for the poor. In the Book of Deuteronomy 15:11, he told those who had more to share with the poor, 'There will always be poor people in the land. Therefore I command you to be open handed towards your brothers and towards the poor and needy in your land.' This shows that God wants his people to look after the poor and do what they can to help them.

In another book of the Old Testament, Leviticus, God goes on to tell his followers, 'When you reap the harvest of your land, you shall not wholly reap the corners of your field, nor shall you gather the gleanings of your harvest. And you shall not glean your vineyard, nor shall you gather every grape of your vineyard; you shall leave them for the poor and the stranger: I am the Lord your God.' (Lev 19:9–10)

God's people were called the Israelites. Many of the wealthy Israelites made their money by farming wheat or growing grapes in a vineyard. In this Bible passage God was telling these farmers that when they harvested their fields, they should leave some of their crops behind so that the poor and needy could come pick up what was left. God was trying to teach his people to only take what they needed for themselves and to avoid being greedy. He wanted the farmers to have a generous heart and to let the poor help themselves.

Further on in the Old Testament, the prophets wrote about the issue of poverty too. Prophets were people who were chosen by God to give a message to his people. Prophets such as Jeremiah and Isaiah called on the rulers and the people to see that justice was done and that those in need were helped.

Why, do you think, is it important for religions to speak about issues like poverty?

 GROUP ACTIVITY Exploration

In small groups, rewrite either Deut 15:11 or Lev 19:9–10 in your own words.

Write them on a poster and draw images to help explain them.
Display your posters in the classroom.

New Testament Teaching

The New Testament, the second half of the Bible, is about Jesus Christ and his life on earth. Jesus himself was a poor man who spent his ministry helping the poor. He was born in a cold and rough stable as there were no rooms free to give shelter to his parents, Mary and Joseph. Jesus always made a special effort to reach out to the poor and make them feel like they were equal.

At that time a lot of people believed that being wealthy meant that you had been blessed by God. A man who was rich was seen as being chosen by God and close to him. A poor man was seen as being under a curse from God.

People were shocked when Jesus told them through his teaching that this was not the truth. He asked the people to look at their values and how they were living their lives. He urged them to change their ways.

How do you think rich people in today's world view those who are poor?

One of his most famous lessons is **the Sermon on the Mount**, where he taught the people **the Beatitudes**. The Beatitudes described good ways of behaving towards God and other people.

His central message from the Beatitudes is simple: people should love God and their neighbour as they love themselves. In the Beatitudes he said, 'Blessed are you who are poor, for yours is the Kingdom of Heaven' (Luke 6:20–21). This meant that the poor would have a special place in God's kingdom.

17

Another great figure in the New Testament, St John, said, 'If anyone has the world's goods and sees his brother in need, yet closes his heart against him, how does God's love abide in him? Little children, let us not love in word or speech, but in deed and truth' (1 John 3:17–18). St John was saying here that we cannot simply talk about love, we must show it in our actions. One such action is to give the poor what they need.

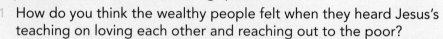

THINK, PAIR, SHARE

In **pairs**, **think** about the following questions:

1 How do you think the wealthy people felt when they heard Jesus's teaching on loving each other and reaching out to the poor?

2 How do you think the poor people felt when they heard this message?

Share your answers with the rest of the class.

How Can We Help?

When people see poverty around them they can often feel anger and frustration. They think it is unfair that some have so much while others have so little. Most people feel the need to reach out and help those in need.

There are many ways people can help those who are experiencing poverty. One obvious way to help the poor is by giving them the things they need. Many people do this by giving donations of food, clothes or money.

Another way is to volunteer your time to an organisation that helps the poor. Raising awareness of the issue of poverty is how other people choose to respond. You can do this by participating in events or asking those in power, such as government leaders, to change things for the better.

LITERACY LIBRARY

Illustrate:

Use a picture or image to help explain something.

Steward:

Caretaker.

Found:

Set up or start something.

Dignity:

Honour and respect.

THINK, PAIR, SHARE

Think about ways of helping those living in poverty.

In **pairs**, discuss ways that you or members of your family have helped those experiencing poverty.

Has your school ever been involved in events that have helped the poor in any way?

Share your answers with the rest of the class.

CLASS ACTIVITY   Reflection and Action

Design a large poster or collage illustrating the things people in your class have done to help those in poverty.

The Christian Response to Poverty

If a person is a follower of Christianity, then it is part of their religious beliefs to help those in need. God calls on his people to be stewards of the earth. This means that they must look after each other and share their money, time and skills as well as care for the environment we live in. Being wealthy is not wrong or a sin, but not using wealth wisely is seen as going against Christian beliefs and values.

John Wesley was an English man who lived in the 1700s. He founded a branch of the Christian church called the Methodist church. On the issue of responding to poverty he said, 'We should earn as much as we can, save as much as we can and give as much as we can.'

Even those Christians who don't have much themselves are encouraged to look around and see if they can help those who are worse off than themselves.

For Christians, responding to poverty is not just about giving material things to others: it is also about showing tenderness and compassion to those suffering from poverty. Christians should try to make the poor in society feel included and worthwhile. They must recognise the dignity of their fellow humans.

Singer/songwriter Glen Hansard leads the annual Christmas Eve busking session in Dublin city in aid of the Dublin Simon Community, December 2017.

HOW CHRISTIANITY ADDRESSES THE ISSUE OF POVERTY

17

Trócaire

One clear Christian response to the issue of poverty was the establishment of Trócaire in 1973.

In the 1960s the leader of the Catholic Church was Pope Paul VI (6th). He called on people to take notice and respond to the injustices that were occurring all around the world. In 1973 the country of Bangladesh in South Asia was destroyed by floods. An Irish priest, Cardinal William Conway, saw the need for a church agency that could organise charity donations from Ireland as so many people wanted to help.

The bishops in Ireland wrote a pastoral letter to their people about what Trócaire was and why it had been set up.

Marie Louise Umuhire (right), Trócaire Resource Rights Project Officer, talks to a water field officer.

EXTRACT FROM THE PASTORAL LETTER

The nations of the world can be divided into two classes: first, the developed nations, second, the developing nations.

Every year the gap between the two grows deeper and wider. The developing countries are the poor ones; the rich grow richer by leaps and bounds while the poor lag further and further behind.

Officially and in reality, Ireland is a developed country. It is true that there are inequalities within our society and we must never forget that some of our people are living in poverty. But our problems are small indeed when we compare them with the problems of the developing countries...

There are many countries ... today where the majority of the people go to bed hungry every night, where the majority have never learned to read or write, where a baby born today can expect to die twenty years earlier than an Irish baby.

We are a rich nation to some extent because others are poor. Part of our prosperity is due to the fact that people in the developing countries are not getting a fair deal. We may not like to acknowledge that our actions may have such adverse consequences for other people but as Christians we must face up to these facts.

We in Ireland who are followers of Jesus Christ must continually try to shape our lives by his teachings. He taught us to love one another, to feed the hungry, to clothe the naked, to care for the sick. He said: 'As you did it to one of the least of my brethren, you did it to me' (Matt 25:40).

It is our Christian duty as individuals to share our wealth and to help our needy brothers. It is equally our Christian duty to demand that the political authorities representing us act always with justice and responsibility towards less fortunate countries.

For this reason, the Bishops of Ireland have set up a fund which is called Trócaire, the Irish word for 'mercy'. The aim of Trócaire will be two-fold. Abroad it will give whatever help lies within its resources to the areas of greatest need among the developing countries. At home it will try to make us all more aware of the needs of those countries and of our duties towards them. These duties are no longer a matter of charity but of simple justice.

We pray to all merciful God to grant us all a share in his mercy. We pray to him to keep our hearts always open to those in hunger and need.

On behalf of the Hierarchy of Ireland,

Feast of the Presentation of the Lord,

2 February 1973.

Source: by kind permission of Trócaire

Milka Irungu, emergency programme coordinator for Trócaire, in Somalia.

LITERACY LIBRARY

Lag:
To fall behind, not able to keep up.

Prosperity:
Wealth, comfort, security.

Acknowledge:
To admit or be aware of.

Adverse:
Harmful or negative.

Brethren:
Fellow people, brothers and sisters.

Resources:
Stocks or supplies.

Grant:
Give or allow.

WRITE THE ANSWERS   Enquiry

1   What does it mean to say we are 'stewards of the earth'?

2   When was Trócaire founded and who set it up?

3   What does the term 'developing countries' mean?

4   Explain what duties Christians have to those in need according to Trócaire.

5   What was the aim of Trócaire when it was set up?

GROUP ACTIVITY   Enquiry

Split the class into four groups. Each group will produce a presentation on one of the following Christian organisations that works with those who experience poverty:

1   St Vincent de Paul   3   Global Missions
2   Christian Aid   4   Gorta – Self Help Africa

Your presentation should address the following areas:

- The history of the organisation
- The aims of the organisation
- How the organisation helps people who experience poverty.

REFLECTIVE ACTIVITY

Think about your own attitude to the teaching of Christianity on the issue of poverty and answer the following questions:

1   Do you think the reasons why Trócaire was set up still exist in the world today? Explain your answer.

2   Even if people cannot stop poverty from happening in our world, why, do you think, is it important that people don't give up on working to help those in poverty?

3   If you could set up your own charity to help those experiencing poverty, what would you call it and why?

 PowerPoint summary

 Weblinks

17

177

CHAPTER 18
The Positive Impact of Religious People

SOL: 6, 8
LO: 1.11, 1.12, 2.8, 3.7

 1

LEARNING OUTCOME

Present stories of people in the history of Christianity and Judaism who have had a positive impact on the lives of others because of their commitment to living out their beliefs.

KEY SKILLS YOU WILL USE IN THIS CHAPTER

- Communicating
- Working with others
- Being literate
- Managing information and thinking

WELLBEING INDICATOR IN THIS CHAPTER

LEARNING INTENTIONS

At the end of this chapter, I will

1 Understand what makes someone an inspiring person

2 Have explored the life of Martin Luther King Jr and be able to explain how he had a positive impact on others because of his commitment to his beliefs

3 Have explored the life of Moses and be able to explain how he had a positive impact on others because of his commitment to his beliefs.

The Western Wall, Jerusalem.

Inspiring People

@1

In the history of our world there have been many people who have made a positive impact on others because of the way these people have chosen to live their lives.

When someone has strong beliefs and they live their life by these beliefs, it can influence and have an effect on others. We can feel inspired by these individuals and their legacy can live on for hundreds or even thousands of years. Their actions have even changed the course of history in some cases.

THINK, PAIR, SHARE

Can you **think** of anyone who has changed people's lives for the better because of the way they lived their life?

In **pairs**, discuss your thoughts.

Share your answers with the rest of the class and record the most popular names on the board.

Some of the photographs below might inspire you.

All the major world religions have had rich and interesting histories. Their beliefs have shaped cultures and have been the cause of many major world events. Within the stories of these religions, certain individuals have stood out.

They have lived their lives by their religious beliefs, even if that meant facing danger and ridicule. By doing this they have had a positive impact on the people around them. They are seen as legends and their stories continue to impress people today.

We will look at two such individuals whose lives have been important in the Christian and Jewish religions: Martin Luther King Jr and Moses. They both showed huge commitment to living out their beliefs.

Nelson Mandela

Irena Sendler helped rescue 2,500 Jewish children during World War II.

Malala Yousafzai. You can read more about Malala on pages 219–220.

The Dalai Lama. You can read more about the Dalai Lama on page 287.

THE POSITIVE IMPACT OF RELIGIOUS PEOPLE

18

Baptist:
A branch of Christianity that believes in being baptised after you make a promise to follow the Christian religion.

Activist:
Someone who fights for their political or religious values.

Racism:
Hating someone from a different race, believing they are inferior.

Segregate:
Separate different races, keeping minorities apart from the majority.

Pastor:
A minister or priest in charge of a church.

Do you think racism is still a problem in today's world?

CHRISTIANITY
Martin Luther King Jr

EARLY LIFE

Martin Luther King Jr was an American Baptist minister and activist who was born in Atlanta, Georgia in 1929. His father was a minister in the church and his parents were both African-American.

At that time in America racism was very common. In many states black people were treated as second-class citizens and were segregated from white people. King experienced this segregation from an early age, as he had to attend a school for African-Americans while white children had their own schools.

He witnessed his parents being treated as second-class citizens and saw his father stand up to this treatment on several occasions. Growing up, he was full of anger at the way he saw his people being treated.

CALLING TO SERVE

At the age of eighteen, King decided to follow in his father's footsteps and become a minister. He said he had an 'inner urge to serve humanity'.

He went to college and earned a degree in theology. At the age of twenty-five he became the pastor of a church in Montgomery, Alabama.

Martin Luther King Jr went on to live his life in a way that inspired millions of people. He believed in the Gospel values of justice and equality. He saw Christianity as a way of life. He once said, 'We must keep God in the forefront. Let us be Christian in all our actions.'

Boycott:
To refuse to use
something or buy
something.

CHALLENGE

In 1955 King faced a huge challenge. He had to decide whether or not to be committed to living out his beliefs, even if that meant putting himself in danger. That year, a woman named Rosa Parks was sitting in the 'black' section of the bus. The bus became crowded and the bus driver demanded that Ms Parks and several other African-Americans give up their seats to let the white people sit down. She refused, was arrested and fined.

Martin Luther King Jr met with other local civil rights leaders and together they planned a citywide bus boycott. King began to give speeches as the leader of the group organising the boycott. He had a special way with words and believed that peaceful protest was the way to change things for the better. He often referred to the person of Jesus Christ when he spoke and it was clear that he was committed to living out his Christian beliefs.

So in 1955 the African-American population of Montgomery refused to take the bus. Many walked to work, and the few with cars offered lifts to others. The boycott continued for 381 days and it ended up costing the city a lot of money.

The Supreme Court ruled that the segregation laws on the buses were illegal. The non-violent, well-organised protest had worked. But it had not been easy. During the protest King's house had had a bomb thrown at it while his wife and daughter were home. King's response to this was, 'We must learn to meet hate with love.'

Rosa Parks seated towards the front of the bus, Montgomery, Alabama, USA, 1956.

THE POSITIVE IMPACT OF RELIGIOUS PEOPLE

18

LITERACY LIBRARY

Rally:
A large gathering of people for a common cause.

Acknowledged:
Showed thanks or appreciation for.

Assassinated:
Executed or murdered for political or religious reasons.

Convict:
A person guilty of a crime.

COMMITMENT

In 1957 King and other civil rights activists founded the Southern Christian Leadership Conference (SCLC). Their aim was to achieve full equality for African-Americans through non-violent protest. King travelled around the US, and indeed the world, giving lectures as well as meeting with religious and political leaders.

In 1963 King helped organise the March on Washington for jobs and freedom, a peaceful political rally. Over a quarter of a million people attended and it became one of the most important moments of the American Civil Rights movement. It was also the occasion of one of the most famous speeches in history: Martin Luther King Jr's 'I have a Dream' speech. In it he said, 'Now is the time to make justice a reality for all of God's children.'

King fought peacefully all his life for the Christian values he believed in: equality and justice for all. He showed people that they must stand up for what they believed in so that positive change would come about. He changed the lives of millions of African-American people. The positive impact he had on the lives of others was acknowledged when in 1964 he became the youngest person ever awarded the Nobel Peace Prize.

On 4 April 1968, Martin Luther King Jr was assassinated in Memphis by an escaped convict and racist, James Earl Ray. The third Monday of January is known as Martin Luther King Day in the US.

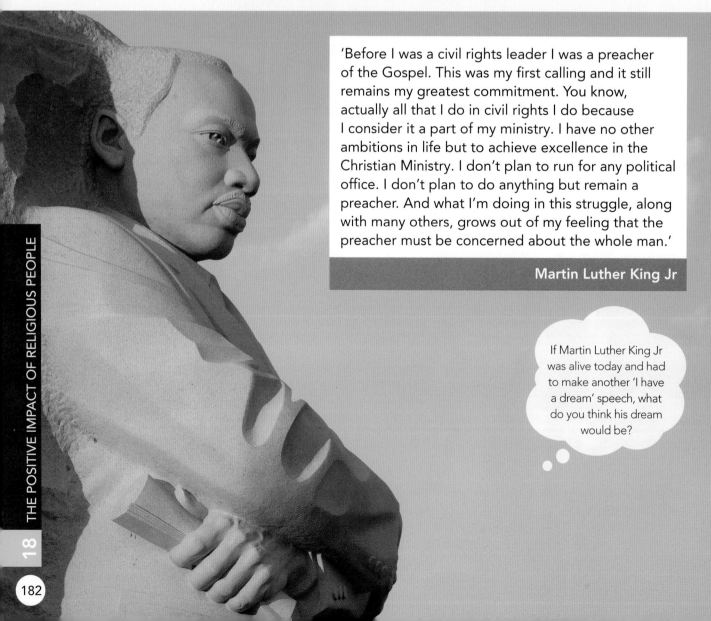

'Before I was a civil rights leader I was a preacher of the Gospel. This was my first calling and it still remains my greatest commitment. You know, actually all that I do in civil rights I do because I consider it a part of my ministry. I have no other ambitions in life but to achieve excellence in the Christian Ministry. I don't plan to run for any political office. I don't plan to do anything but remain a preacher. And what I'm doing in this struggle, along with many others, grows out of my feeling that the preacher must be concerned about the whole man.'

Martin Luther King Jr

If Martin Luther King Jr was alive today and had to make another 'I have a dream' speech, what do you think his dream would be?

WRITE THE ANSWERS　　　　　　　　　　Enquiry

1　Explain what 'segregation' means.

2　Give one example of how Martin Luther King Jr experienced segregation in his life.

3　Describe what happened to Rosa Parks.

4　What was the Montgomery bus strike?

5　In your own words, describe how Martin Luther King Jr had a positive impact on the lives of other people.

6　What, do you think, inspired Martin Luther King Jr to do the work he did?

THINK, PAIR, SHARE

In **pairs**, imagine you could interview Martin Luther King Jr about himself and his work.

Think of three questions you would like to ask him. Discuss your ideas with your partner.

Share your work with the rest of the class and write the ten most interesting questions on the board.

Black Lives Matter rally in July 2016 in New York.

Search online for Martin Luther King Jr's 'I have a Dream' speech.

THE POSITIVE IMPACT OF RELIGIOUS PEOPLE

18

JUDAISM
Moses

BCE:

Before the Common or Christian Era.

Famine:

Extreme hunger and starvation in a region.

Revolt:

To protest and rebel against something.

Intervened:

Tried to settle a disagreement.

Moses is a very important figure in the history of three of the major world religions: Judaism, Christianity and Islam.

However, Moses is most closely associated with the Jewish religion. The interesting story of his life can be found in the Torah. The Torah consists of the first five books of the Jewish Bible.

Moses had a positive impact on the lives of thousands when he lived in Egypt in the thirteenth century BCE. His people were called the Hebrews, and later the Israelites, and because of Moses and his commitment to living out his beliefs, they found freedom and a stronger faith in God.

EARLY LIFE

At the time Moses was born, his people, the Hebrews, had suffered through many years of hardship. Famine and fighting had forced them to flee their homeland and they had settled in Egypt. Their time there was one of slavery to the Egyptian rulers, who were called Pharaohs. They had no rights and were forced to work under terrible conditions. The Hebrews were growing in numbers and the Pharaoh was afraid they would join together and revolt. So he ordered all newborn Hebrew boys to be killed.

In order to save Moses, his mother put him in a basket, which she placed in the waters of the River Nile, hoping that someone kind would find him and give him a better life. That person turned out to be the daughter of the Pharaoh. She brought him home and Moses was raised as one of the Egyptian royal family, even though he was a Hebrew.

As he grew up, Moses witnessed how cruelly the Hebrew people were treated and he knew deep down that it was not right. One day he saw one of the Egyptian slave masters beating a Hebrew slave so badly that he intervened to help the slave. In the fight the slave master was killed and Moses fled to a place called Midian. He settled there and got married, leaving his royal life behind him.

CALLING TO SERVE

In Midian, Moses earned a living as a shepherd. One day, he saw a bush that appeared to be on fire. As he got closer, Moses realised that although the bush was on fire it was not actually burning. Suddenly he heard God's voice speaking to him. God told Moses that he was to help the Jewish people.

At first Moses was frightened and unsure if he could carry out what God had asked. However, he was a man of great faith, so he set off to see the pharaoh.

When he met the pharaoh, Moses asked him to let the Jewish people go, so that they could return to the Promised Land given to them by God. Without even thinking about it, the pharaoh said no.

God wanted to show the people that Moses was chosen by him to help them. So he set ten plagues on Egypt. These plagues included swarms of locusts and hailstones that ruined all the crops. Still the pharaoh refused to free the Jews.

Finally, God sent the last and most terrible plague. An Angel of Death passed over each house in Egypt, killing the firstborn son. The Jews were told to sacrifice a lamb and to rub the blood on their doors. The Angel would know they were Jews and pass over their houses.

See also Chapter 15, pp.142–143.

CHALLENGES

After this plague, the pharaoh agreed to let the Jews go. Led by Moses, they set off, but were soon chased by the Egyptian army. The pharaoh had changed his mind. When the Jews reached the Red Sea, God gave Moses the power to part the waters, allowing them to pass through safely. This event became known as the Exodus. It is one of the most important moments in the history of the Jewish religion.

After that Moses travelled on with the Jews to Mount Sinai. There, Moses received the Torah. This gave details about how God wanted his people to live. The well-known Ten Commandments were part of the Torah. This was the second covenant that God had made with his chosen people, the Jews.

For the next forty years, the Jewish people worked hard to keep their covenant with God. At times, they doubted him, but he was always present in their hour of need. In this way they learned to trust him and realised the importance of keeping their promises to him.

Their great leader Moses died before they reached the Promised Land. He is still a great role model for Jewish people. Throughout his life he showed commitment to living out his beliefs when called by God to lead his people. Even though he was afraid, he never gave up and always remembered his promise to God.

GROUP ACTIVITY   Reflection and Action

Divide the class into groups of four.

Together work on creating an oral presentation you will deliver telling the story of how Moses had a positive impact on other people because of his commitment to his beliefs.

You may use PowerPoint during your presentation.

REFLECTIVE ACTIVITY

Think about your own attitude to how Martin Luther King Jr and Moses had a positive impact on the lives of others because of their commitment to living out their beliefs and answer the following questions:

1   What lessons can we learn today from Martin Luther King Jr?

2   Do you think there are any similarities between the stories of Martin Luther King Jr and Moses?

PowerPoint summary

Weblinks

You might like to watch the story of Moses which is told in the film, *The Prince of Egypt*.

THE POSITIVE IMPACT OF RELIGIOUS PEOPLE

18

CHAPTER 19
The Stages of Faith

SOL: 5
LO: 1.8, 2.9

LEARNING OUTCOME

Describe how the faith of a believer can change at different stages in life.

KEY SKILLS YOU WILL USE IN THIS CHAPTER

- Communicating
- Managing myself
- Managing information and thinking
- Working with others

WELLBEING INDICATORS IN THIS CHAPTER

LEARNING INTENTIONS

At the end of this chapter, I will

1 Have explored what is important to people at different stages of their lives

2 Understand Fowler's stages of faith development

3 Be able to identify what stage of the faith development journey a believer is at.

What Is Important?

Do you think males and females think differently about what is important to them?

Stop for a minute and think about the things in life that are important to you now. They are probably different to the things that were important to you when you started primary school at the age of five.

Imagine what things might be important to you when you are thirty years old. Again, they probably will not be the same things that are important to you now.

GROUP ACTIVITY Reflection and Action

Copy the table below into your copybook. Take a few minutes to fill in the boxes about what things you think are important to people at different stages in their lives.

Put a tick in the box you think applies to how a person feels about each of the topics at the age given.

Afterwards discuss your answers as a class.

	Education	Health	Friends	Family	Hobbies/Pastimes	God/Religion	Politics in Ireland	World Events
Age 0–5								
Very important								
Slightly important								
Not important								
Age 6–12								
Very important								
Slightly important								
Not important								

	Education	Health	Friends	Family	Hobbies/ Pastimes	God/ Religion	Politics in Ireland	World Events
Age 13–18								
Very important								
Slightly important								
Not important								
Age 19–28								
Very important								
Slightly important								
Not important								
Age 29–39								
Very important								
Slightly important								
Not important								
Age 40+								
Very important								
Slightly important								
Not important								

Faith of a Believer

To have faith means to trust or have confidence in a set of religious beliefs. When you have faith you don't need proof that your God exists. It can obviously be difficult at times for a believer to have faith in something they cannot see or touch.

As we go through life our beliefs about things change. Just as our opinions and attitudes don't remain the same for our whole lives, a person's faith moves through different stages. It does not remain static. Life is a journey and a person's religious beliefs can go through ups and downs during this journey.

At certain times in life a person's beliefs may be very important to them, while at other times their beliefs may be weak or not important to them at all.

Stages of Faith Development

James W. Fowler was an American theologian and a minister in the United Methodist Church. He is best known for a book he wrote called *Stages of Faith* in 1981. In it, he developed a theory of the different stages of a person's faith as they go through their life. Fowler did a huge amount of research for his book, interviewing people of all different ages and all different religious backgrounds. He has won several awards for his work. His theory has six main stages, as outlined on the following pages.

> **Note** The names of each stage of Fowler's theory can be difficult to understand and remember. Don't worry, you can simply refer to them as Stage 1, 2, 3 and so on.

LITERACY LIBRARY

Static:
Does not change.

Theologian:
A person who studies religious faith and practice.

Theory:
An explanation of how something works.

Research:
Investigating and studying a topic to find out more about it.

LITERACY LIBRARY

Complex:
Difficult to understand.

Logical:
Reasoned and well thought out.

Literally:
To take something to be true, word for word.

Abstract:
A thought or an idea that does not actually exist.

Disillusioned: (p.192)
Disappointed that something is not quite what you had thought it was.

STAGE 1: INTUITIVE – PROJECTIVE FAITH (IPF)

This first stage generally applies to pre-school aged children. At this stage children don't see the world from anyone else's point of view. They are the centre of their world. They cannot understand complex ideas or logical arguments. They get their impressions of faith and God from their care-givers, who are usually their parents. They may have become involved with the rituals of their religious community, such as saying a prayer or attending a religious service, but they don't think about why they are doing it or what it means. They learn from those around them.

STAGE 2: MYTHIC – LITERAL FAITH (MLF)

This stage usually occurs between the ages of six to twelve. At this age children's source of religious authority starts to expand past parents to others in their community, such as teachers and friends.

Their faith becomes the stories told and the rituals practised. They take what they are told about religion and faith to be literally true. Later in this stage children may begin to understand that others might have different beliefs to them.

STAGE 3: SYNTHETIC – CONVENTIONAL FAITH (SCF)

This stage usually starts at around age thirteen until a person is eighteen years old. However, some people stay at this stage for their entire life. People are able to think in a more abstract way now rather than literally. They can find meaning in symbols, stories and rituals that they could not before. They also become aware of what others think about them and their faith.

People can begin to look outside of the family for guidance on religious issues and begin to look to friends more. However, their faith is usually still linked to that of their family.

THE STAGES OF FAITH

19

STAGE 4: INDIVIDUATIVE – REFLECTIVE FAITH (IRF)

This can be a difficult stage. It often begins in young adulthood. People begin to critically examine their beliefs and can become disillusioned with what they believed before. This can be the stage where people choose to leave their religious community if they cannot find answers to the questions they have.

However, they may become more mature through their questioning and become more confident in their own beliefs.

STAGE 5: CONJUNCTIVE FAITH (CF)

People don't usually get to this stage until their early thirties. Some answers have been found and the person is comfortable knowing that all the answers might not be easy to find.

People understand that they are not alone on their faith journey and see the importance of their religious community. They are also more open to other people's ideas and opinions on faith and don't feel threatened by them. They understand that life is a mystery.

STAGE 6: UNIVERSALISING FAITH (UF)

Only a small number of people ever reach this stage. They can become important religious teachers and can relate to anyone at any stage and from any faith. They put their faith into action and work to see justice done in the world. They are not afraid to stand up for what they believe in.

Mahatma Gandhi with his two granddaughters in New Delhi.

Mother Teresa of Calcutta.

THE STAGES OF FAITH

19

LITERACY
LIBRARY

Conference:
A formal meeting of people
with shared interests.

Read the following pieces by a selection of individuals on different stages of their faith journey. In your copybook, write down what stage of Fowler's faith development theory you think they are at.

1 Things have been so busy in work lately, but I'm glad I took the time to go to the concert in the church last night. It was lovely to see everyone from the parish there and the music helped to remind me that Christmas is about more than just shopping!

I've been praying a lot lately for my friend Clare, who is sick. I know God is with her giving her strength and that God will be with us all no matter what happens.

It is hard to understand why Clare is going through such a hard time, but maybe it is all part of God's plan.

Stage of faith development: _____

2 My mammy took me to the big building with the cross on top yesterday. I don't know who lives there but it is very quiet and you get to light candles, which I like doing. Mammy knelt down, so I did too.

Stage of faith development: _____

3 I have to get the train to Dublin tomorrow morning, so I'll be up early. There is a conference taking place for people from all different religious faiths to try to come up with ideas on how we can help with the terrible homeless situation at the moment.

I've been asked to speak on behalf of the Islamic church because of the work I've been involved in with my local community of Muslims.

Stage of faith development: _____

4 I've decided I'm not going to church with my family this Sunday. I just don't see the point when I don't think my prayers are being answered. I'm just not sure what I believe about God anymore.

Stage of faith development: _____

THE STAGES OF FAITH

19

193

5   When I went home from school today I told my little brother all about the story of Adam and Eve in the Garden of Eden that my teacher told me. He did not really understand how the snake could talk, but obviously back in those days animals were able to speak. I'm going to eat an apple every day so I will get more knowledge.

Stage of faith development: _____

6   I know that as a Muslim I'm supposed to pray five times a day and I do understand why it is important. But some of my non-Muslim friends don't understand and keep asking me questions about it. I don't feel comfortable talking about it with them, so I just change the subject when they ask.

Stage of faith development: _____

If you could rename each stage of Fowler's theory to explain it more clearly, what would you call each one?

You may have noticed in the information on Fowler's faith development theory that the word 'usually' or 'generally' appears a lot. This is because there are no hard and fast rules about when a person may enter the next stage of the journey.

Some people move through the stages very quickly, while others stay in the same stage for a long time or even forever. Every person is unique and therefore their faith development is unique too.

At difficult times in life some people turn to their faith for comfort and support, while other people going through a hard time may turn away from their faith. The important thing is to respect that everyone is on their own faith journey.

If you have a faith, what stage of the faith journey do you think you are at?

REFLECTIVE ACTIVITY

Think about your own attitude to how the faith of a believer can change at different stages in life and answer the following questions:

1   If a person is facing a challenge in their life, do you think they are more likely to turn towards their faith or to turn away from their faith?

2   Can you name anyone you know or you have heard of who you think has reached Stage 6 of their faith journey?

THE STAGES OF FAITH

19

📊 PowerPoint summary

CHAPTER 20

Synthesis: Meaning, Purpose and Relationships

SOL: 5, 6
LO: 2.10

 See also Chapter 28

LEARNING OUTCOME

Synthesise and consider the insights gained about how people with different religious beliefs and other interpretations of life respond to questions of meaning, purpose and relationships.

KEY SKILLS YOU WILL USE IN THIS CHAPTER

- Staying well
- Managing myself
- Working with others
- Being creative
- Being literate

WELLBEING INDICATORS IN THIS CHAPTER

LEARNING INTENTIONS

At the end of this chapter, I will

1 Understand the importance of questioning

2 Be able to give two examples of major tragedies that showed how people support and care for each other

3 Understand what a steward is and the importance of stewardship

4 Be able to describe the different religious festivals.

SYNTHESIS: MEANING, PURPOSE AND RELATIONSHIPS

20

195

People question things every day. This is a natural thing for people to do. What is important is what we do with the information we receive and how we respond to it. It is essential to be supportive of people and to help them in their time of need and during times of struggle.

As you work through this chapter, you will read about what happened in New York in 2001 and in Manchester in 2017. Both events were major tragedies, but they showed how people came together to support, care for and assist the most vulnerable. It also caused people to question the meaning of life.

Try to time yourself doing this activity. You have ten minutes to finish, starting now!

10 min

THINK, PAIR, SHARE

Many things have happened that have caused us to question our sense of meaning and purpose.

What do you **think** of the statement below?

'When something bad happens to us, we become stronger human beings because of it.'

Pair off with your neighbour.

Share your ideas with the larger group.

6128

3749

9264

0184

Asking Questions

By questioning what is happening around us, we are looking for meaning. Meaning refers to a sense of purpose. It helps us to make sense of the different situations we find ourselves in.

If we don't have a sense of purpose or a goal, life can seem meaningless for us. People find meaning in life by connecting with something or someone.

Humanism

Christians, Jews and Muslims believe in an all-powerful God. They look to the Bible, the Torah and the Qur'an for guidance on the nature of their God. Some people have no religious beliefs. They don't look to religion to show them how to treat others. Their faith is in humanity rather than in God. Religion is not a source of meaning in their lives, as they find meaning in the way they respect and value life. These people are called humanists.

Humanists believe that there is no God or gods and that the greatest power is to be found in human beings. They also believe that we can make sense of life itself through our own experiences.

The Humanist Association of Ireland says it is a positive, ethical philosophy. It is based on concern for humanity in general and for individuals in particular. It is a view of life that combines reason with compassion. Humanists base their understanding of life on the evidence of the natural world and its evolution and not on belief in the supernatural. Humanism is a personal life stance, not a religion. It believes we have a duty of care to all humanity, including future generations. It has been around for 2,500 years.

LITERACY LIBRARY

Ethical philosophy:
Moral, honest way of thinking about life.

Compassion:
Pity and concern for the suffering of others.

Evolution:
The process of gradually developing and changing.

Supernatural:
Events caused by some force beyond scientific understanding.

GROUP ACTIVITY

Exploration

Read the two scenarios on pages 198–200 that have caused people to question their sense of meaning and purpose.

In groups, use placemats to record your answers and statements of knowledge from the class.

Scenario 1: 11 September 2001

On a clear sunny day in September 2001, an Islamic terrorist group called Al Qaeda boarded three passenger planes and carried out co-ordinated suicide attacks against the World Trade Center in New York City and the Pentagon in Washington, DC killing everyone on board the planes and nearly 3,000 people on the ground.

A fourth plane crashed in a Pennsylvania field, killing all on board as they tried to take back control of the plane from the hijackers.

What happened that day was evil. The attacks brought on feelings of anxiety and vulnerability for many Americans, as their sense of safety was now threatened. These attacks were repeatedly condemned by Muslim leaders all over the world.

It has been almost twenty years since this terrorist attack on innocent people taking a flight or simply making their way to work that morning. Many questions have been asked and many questions remain unanswered.

New York skyline, with 9/11 anniversary lights from New Jersey.

Read the following story from a mother who lost her son on 9/11.

Phyllis Rodriguez is one mother who expresses forgiveness, not hate, towards those who killed her son on 11 September. Phyllis Rodriguez's son Greg died in the terrorist attacks on the World Trade Center. He was a computer specialist working on the 103rd floor of the north tower. She recalls how she found out that something terrible had happened that Tuesday morning: 'On our answering machine was a message from Greg, our son, that said, "There's been a terrible accident at the World Trade Center. I'm OK, call Elizabeth," our daughter-in-law.'

But Greg Rodriguez was not OK, and neither were nearly 3,000 others.

'I was just hoping, hoping that he had survived, and not allowing myself to admit the worst,' recalled Rodriguez. That came soon enough when Greg Rodriguez was declared dead. And with it came his parents' conscious decision to make a difference.

'The main thing that we realised very early the morning of the 12th is that our government, given its history, was going to do something military and violent in retaliation in the name of our son and that that wasn't going to do any good and we didn't support it.'

Wall of photos of missing persons following World Trade Center attack.

Phyllis Rodriguez and her husband Orlando released an open letter to then President George W. Bush.

'It ended up being circulated around the country and around the world. It was part of the way that helped us cope with the loss,' Rodriguez explained.

The couple wanted no part of revenge. They opposed the death penalty for the man who became known as the 20th hijacker, Zacarias Moussaoui. Phyllis befriended Zacarias's mother, Aicha el-Wafi.

'I felt that this woman has to be very, very courageous because her son is the most hated person probably at the moment and here she was standing up for her son,' said Rodriguez. 'We realised what we had in common was our common humanity. We were human beings. It is a very valuable part of my life and my healing.'

Rodriguez says she is disappointed by the way the US government has used the war on terror in her son's name.

'I feel terrible sorrow at all the losses, all the bereft families. We had the whole world in sympathy with us. We could've been leaders and working for world peace and peace in the Middle East. And what did we do? We blew it,' Rodriguez added.

Phyllis Rodriguez says she copes with the loss of her only son by opposing war and participating in human rights and forgiveness projects.'I don't think it happened for a reason, but it did happen and I feel fortunate that I had the inner resources to respond in the way that I did,' Rodriguez said.

Rodriguez says she is at peace knowing she will never see her son again, but is not at peace with the state of the world. That is why, she says, she is trying to make a difference.

Remains of the World Trade Center after the 9/11 terrorist attack.

WRITE THE ANSWERS   Enquiry

1 Name the places where the 9/11 attacks were carried out.

2 Who condemned these attacks?

3 Where did Phyllis Rodriguez's son Greg work?

4 How many people died in the World Trade Center?

5 What did Greg's parents realise on the morning of 12 September?

6 What did they hope for?

7 Who did Phyllis Rodriguez befriend? Do you think that was an easy thing for her to do?

8 Is Phyllis Rodriguez at peace? Why do you think this?

20

Scenario 2: The Manchester Bombing, 22 May 2017

Before you read the piece that follows, copy the KWL box below into your copybook and fill in the K and W columns. When you have read the full text, you can fill in the L section.

K **W** **L**

K What I know	**W** What I want to find out	**L** What I have learned

The Manchester Arena bombing was a suicide bombing attack in Manchester in May 2017. As people were leaving the arena after seeing Ariana Grande in concert, a homemade bomb was detonated by an Islamic terrorist.

This was an act of terrorism. Twenty-three people were killed that night, including the attacker. One hundred and thirty-nine were injured, many of them children. The bomber was named as Salman Ramadan Abedi, who was 22 years old and of Libyan descent.

A month after the bombing, Ariana Grande sang at the 'One Love Manchester' concert. It featured performers like Justin Bieber, Katy Perry, Miley Cyrus and Coldplay. Over 55,000 people attended. She said, 'The last thing I would ever want is for my fans to see something like that happen and think it won.' She believed the concert was important, as if she did not do something the people would have died in vain.

Ariana Grande's album *Sweetener* includes a silent tribute to the fans who died that night in Manchester at her concert. On the eve of the first anniversary of the Manchester bombing, she said, 'It's the absolute worst of humanity.'

She believes that music is supposed to be the safest thing in the world and it is because of this belief that that the events of that night weigh so heavily on her heart.

In 2018, Ariana Granda was offered a damehood in honour of the Manchester terror attack victims. She turned this down, as she believed it to be too soon for her to receive the honour as she was still grieving for those who lost their lives that night at her concert.

ONE L♥VE MANCHESTER
#WESTANDTOGETHER

WRITE THE ANSWERS Enquiry

1 What happened in Manchester in May 2017?

2 How many people died and how many were injured?

3 Ariana Grande sang at a concert one month after the attack. What was the name of this concert?

4 What other artists or pop stars were there?

5 What does Ariana Grande's album *Sweetener* include?

6 What does Ariana Grande believe music should be about?

The events of September 2001 and Manchester 2017 cause us to question the meaning and purpose of life. It is difficult to comprehend that a loved one can leave a house in the morning, go to work or a concert and not return home again. There is no finality, letting go, preparation or closure. There is anger, upset, hatred, forgiveness and utter grief left behind for their loved ones to deal with.

The events of September 2001 are remembered every year at the site where the World Trade Center once stood. Families were torn apart that day and although time has helped to heal some hurt, the once-cherished loved one is no longer amongst them. The lives of their families and friends stood still on that day.

GROUP ACTIVITY Exploration

In small groups, discuss the following:
Considering the two examples given above, how, do you think, did people begin to rebuild their lives after the event?

Meaning and Purpose in Different World Religions

Stewardship

Being a steward means looking after and protecting all creation. It calls on us to be responsible for the decisions we make about how we use the earth and its resources, such as water and wildlife. We must be aware that the choices we make about our environment will affect the generations coming after us. We must be caretakers of the earth and of each other.

As the Native American proverb says:

> 'We do not inherit the earth from our ancestors; we borrow it from our children.'

A Christian religious moral vision calls on us to be **stewards of creation** because we believe that God created the world in his own image and likeness. As a result, we are called to act as stewards to all living things and to show respect to all forms of life.

Our religious beliefs and the teachings of our Church can have a huge effect on the decisions we make about many different issues. We are all familiar with the following statement:

Reduce, Reuse, Recycle.

You may wonder what this statement about the environment has to do with religion. In order to find out, let's look at each of the five world religions and see what they have to say about this issue.

Judaism

The Jewish sacred texts tell us that God created the earth and every living thing on it. The book of Genesis contains the creation story, which explains how God created the world in seven days. In it, we see that God created the land, the water, the plants and the animals. After he had created each thing, he 'saw that it was good'.

God also created human life to live side by side with these creations, so humans are seen as a part of nature too. God tells man to work in the Garden of Eden and to watch over it. Jewish scholars have said that God's commandment to watch over the garden tells us that the land is God's property, not ours.

After his work of creation was complete, we are told that God 'rested on the seventh day after all the work had been done. God blessed the seventh day and made it holy, because on that day he rested after all his work of creating' (Genesis 2:2–3). This day of rest became the Jewish Sabbath, which allows all God's creation to take a break. No work on the land or jobs done by farm animals are allowed on this day. Furthermore, every seven years, in the Sabbath year, Jewish farmers have to let their land rest. This not only helps to restore the soil, but reminds Jewish people that the land belongs to God. The land and the people depend on each other.

Christianity

Christians share the same creation story as the Jewish people. Therefore, they see God as the one who gave us the earth. One of God's natural creations, water, plays a huge part in Christian worship, especially in the sacrament of baptism. In his parables and teachings, Jesus often spoke about nature. His life was based on the idea of living in harmony with all God's creations. In recent years, Christian leaders have spoken about our responsibility to care for God's creation. In 1998, the Catholic bishops of the Philippines published the first pastoral letter on the environment, called 'What Is Happening to Our Beautiful Land?' We can therefore see that care for the environment is a big part of Christianity's moral vision.

> 'God took the man and put him in the Garden of Eden to work it and take care of it.'
> Genesis 2:15

> 'Everything that lives and moves about will be food for you. Just as I gave you the green plants, I now give you everything.'
> Genesis 9:3

> 'The earth is the Lord's and everything in it, the world, and all who live in it.'
> Psalm 24:1

The above passages from the Bible show the main message that God wants to give us. God is the one who provides for humans and therefore we should take care of what we have received from God.

GROUP ACTIVITY   Reflection and Action

In small groups, think about the following:

1. What, do you think, are the biggest environmental threats at this time?
2. What, do you think, can we do about these threats to the environment?

Here are some ideas to help you get started:

(a) Plastics

(b) Extreme weather

(c) Quality water supply

3. When you have made your own list, focus on one idea. Make a report of your ideas for your class using PowerPoint. Discuss with your teacher the possibility of inviting someone to speak to your class on the topic.
4. What do you plan to do to ensure that planet Earth will be in a better state 100 years from now?

See also Chapter 24, p.259

LITERACY
LIBRARY

Viceroy:

A person or people who rule an area on behalf of a king or queen.

Interdependent:

Relying on each other for survival.

Universal:

Something that applies to or affects everyone in the world.

Islam

There are about 500 verses in the Islamic sacred text, the Qur'an, that deal with the natural world. It gives guidance on how Muslims should view the natural world: 'It is he who has appointed you viceroys in the earth' (6.165). Muslims see humans as having a special position as guardians of the earth. Islam has a strong sense of the goodness and purity of the earth. If water is not available for wudu (the ritual washing before prayer), then clean dust may be used. In fact, the colour green is the most blessed of all colours for Muslims. For Muslims, it symbolises nature and life. Green is used to decorate mosques and is also used in the flags of many Muslim countries.

Buddhism

According to Buddhism, all life is precious and all life is connected. Buddhists believe that all beings on the earth share the same conditions of birth, old age, suffering and death. This means that they have compassion for all living things. In fact, the Buddhist founding story features a tree. One of their leaders, the Dalai Lama, said: 'The world grows smaller and smaller, more and more interdependent … today more than ever before, life must be cha]racterised by a sense of universal responsibility, not only human to human but also human to other forms of life.' Buddhists work hard to live in harmony with their body, nature and other people.

SYNTHESIS: MEANING, PURPOSE AND RELATIONSHIPS

20

Hinduism

The Vedas, Hinduism's sacred texts, contain imagery that values the power of the natural world. This polytheistic religion has gods connected to the earth, sky and water, which means that Hindus see these things as sacred. They also have a huge respect for trees and rivers. The River Ganges plays an important role in their beliefs and worship. Their teaching of dharma places special importance on a need to act 'for the sake of the good of the world'. Mahatma Gandhi was one of the most famous Hindus. He preached about the importance of living a simple life in harmony with the earth.

We can see that all the major world religions have a similar religious moral vision when it comes to the earth. It could be said that this vision is based on the principle of **stewardship**.

WRITE THE ANSWERS — Enquiry

1   'God saw all he had made, and indeed it was very good.'
    What does this quote from the Book of Genesis tell us about how
    we should view the world?

2   What is the idea behind the Jewish Sabbath year?

3   Water is a symbol from nature that is often used in Christian worship.
    What other symbols from nature are associated with the Christian religion?

4   Why is the colour green very important for Muslims?

5   What might happen if we are not good stewards of creation?

GROUP ACTIVITY — Enquiry, Exploration

Imagine that your school is having a Green Week. Produce a booklet telling people why it is important to care for the environment. Give them ideas about how they might be good stewards of creation in school, at home and in their community.

Religious Festivals – Building Relationships

A festival is a special occasion where people come together to celebrate an important time or event. In all world religions, people gather together to celebrate something important and to build relationships with others.

THINK, PAIR, SHARE

Think about your own religion.
In **pairs**, discuss what festivals you participate in.
Share this knowledge with the class.

Festivals help us to keep connected to what we are about and what we believe to be true. Festivals help us to forget the chaos that may be in our lives and encourage us to move forward with hope and expectation.

When a festival draws near, the community feels a stronger sense of faith and feelings of hope and joy become more profound. We see this at Christmastime in the generosity of people towards the homeless and other marginalised groups in society.

Maybe in your school you could organise a special event for a marginalised group. Below are some examples:

- Capuchin Day Centre
- St Vincent de Paul
- Focus Ireland
- Team Hope Christmas Shoebox Appeal
- Peter McVerry Trust

SYNTHESIS: MEANING, PURPOSE AND RELATIONSHIPS

20

207

Tying a rakhi.

Hinduism

Festivals are very important to Hindus, as they are seen as celebrations of God's creation – of life itself. Many of their festivals are local events and hundreds of different ones take place in Indian towns and villages. Most of the festivals are joyous occasions. Their celebrations vary from colourful outdoor festivals of the hot, dry months to the quieter indoor rituals of the rainy season. Many festivals are celebrated with huge feasts.

The festival of **Raksha Bandhan** (tie/knot of protection) celebrates the love and duty between brothers and sisters. Young women tie bracelets onto the wrists of their brothers or other men, who promise to protect them in return.

Buddhism

Buddhist festivals vary from one country to another. The different forms of Buddhism celebrate different festivals. Theravada Buddhists mark the birth, enlightenment and death of the Buddha with a single festival. They also have a few set days throughout the year when laypeople join monks in fasting and meditation.

The **Poson** festival is celebrated in Sri Lanka. Monks and laypeople gather together for this festival. It celebrates the arrival of Buddhism on the island during the time of the Indian emperor Ashoka.

Buddhist devotees celebrate The Poson Festival in Sri Lanka.

SYNTHESIS: MEANING, PURPOSE AND RELATIONSHIPS

20

Judaism

There are many important religious festivals throughout the Jewish year. Some of these festivals mark events in the history of Judaism. They are celebrated not only in synagogues, but with many rituals at home. Each one is marked with a different type of food. The Sabbath (Shabbat) provides a weekly structure for the year. Each festival starts on the evening before the event and continues on into the next day. In biblical times, a day began at sunset and this marked the time.

The festival of **Hanukkah** remembers an important historical event 2,000 years ago. The Jews in ancient Jerusalem had not been allowed to practise their faith for a long time, but were then allowed to build a new temple. Hanukkah lasts for eight days. Every night of Hanukkah, the family gathers to recite blessings, light the candles and sing Hanukkah songs.

Islam

The Muslim calendar has many festivals. Some of these mark important events in the history of the faith. Others are connected with the Five Pillars of Islam.

During the month of **Ramadan**, Muslims fast between sunrise and sunset. At sunset each day, Muslims pray first and then eat. During the evening meal, special lights, such as star-shaped lanterns, may be lit. Muhammad received the first revelation of the Qur'an during the month of Ramadan, which is why it has special significance for Muslims. When the month of Ramadan comes to an end, there may be a procession. The end of Ramadan is marked by the festival of **Eid al-Fitr** (the feast of breaking the fast).

Christianity

ADVENT

The liturgical year begins with the season of Advent, which means 'the coming'. The season of Advent lasts for four weeks leading up to Christmas. Throughout Advent, Christians await the coming of Jesus Christ. During this sacred time, Christians show their love to all through their generosity and patience with others.

Advent is a time of preparation and waiting for the coming of Jesus Christ at Christmas. Christians actively prepare for the birth of Christ. They examine their lives by thinking about the past year and looking at how they could be better Christians. They want to live as Jesus lived.

Advent gives us all a chance to think about our lives. Some schools organise hampers for the less-well off families in their community. During Advent, the Advent wreath burns brightly in the church. This is a religious symbol. It is circular in shape and has evergreen branches. There are five candles, one lit each week of Advent and the final one lit on Christmas Day. By lighting the candles, Christians look forward to the coming of Jesus Christ. The three purple candles symbolise the need for people to prepare themselves for Jesus's birth. The person thinks about what he or she has done wrong and seeks forgiveness for his or her sins. The one pink candle represents joy and is usually lit on the third Sunday of Advent.

A fifth candle, which is white, is lit on Christmas Day. Christians are joyful at the birth of their saviour.

SYNTHESIS: MEANING, PURPOSE AND RELATIONSHIPS

20

CHRISTMAS

During Christmas time, Christians celebrate the birth of Jesus. Christmas Day, 25 December, is a holy day of obligation. This means that Catholics should go to Mass on that day. The word 'Christmas' means 'the Mass of Christ'. Often people go to Mass on Christmas Eve, which is called a vigil Mass. We don't know when exactly Jesus was born. The date, 25 December, was decided on by Pope Gregory I in 354 CE. We have celebrated Christmas on that date ever since. The Feast of the Epiphany, or 'Little Christmas', as it is often called, is celebrated on 6 January.

This remembers the visit of the three wise men to the baby Jesus.

WRITE THE ANSWERS   Enquiry

1. Name one festival celebrated by each world religion.
2. Why do Christians celebrate their main festival on 25 December?
3. Why are festivals important to the Hindu religion?
4. Where are festivals marked for the Jewish religion?
5. When do Muslims fast?
6. Relationships are an important aspect of all world religions. How is this shown in the festivals of the world religions?

REFLECTIVE ACTIVITY

Think about your own attitude to meaning, purpose and relationships and answer the following questions:

1. What did you like learning about in this chapter?
2. What do you understand by the proverb, 'We do not inherit the earth from our ancestors; we borrow it for our children'?
3. Describe a festival that you have attended.

 PowerPoint summary

 Weblinks

Every year Our Lady's Hospice and Care Services in Dublin organises an event called 'Light Up a Life'. Thousands of people sponsor lights on a Christmas tree in memory of friends and family.

STRAND 3
LIVING OUR VALUES

In our everyday lives, we are faced with many different kinds of choices. Some of these choices are easy to make and don't require much thought, such as deciding what you will have for breakfast.

Sometimes we are faced with more important decisions that can have an impact on our own lives or on the lives of others. This is where our values become important. Knowing what our values are and living by them can help us to decide whether we think something is right or wrong. Living by our values helps us when it comes to moral decision-making. Making moral decisions can be difficult and often requires us to think deeply about the issue or even to seek help and advice from other sources, such as religion or family.

In this strand you will explore where people's values come from and how these values can affect the decisions they make in everyday life. You will examine values such as justice, peace and care for the earth.

CHAPTER 21
Values

SOL: 5, 6, 7
LO: 3.1

LEARNING OUTCOME

Examine different sources of values and explore how the values of a person relate to their everyday life choices, their relationships and their responsibilities to others.

KEY SKILLS YOU WILL USE IN THIS CHAPTER

- Managing information and thinking
- Communicating
- Working with others

WELLBEING INDICATORS IN THIS CHAPTER

LEARNING INTENTIONS

At the end of this chapter, I will

1 Understand what a value is and be able to give some examples

2 Understand what can happen when someone does not live by their values

3 Have explored what my own personal values are

4 Have discovered how Malala Yousafzai's values affected her life and the lives of others

5 Have explored the sources of people's values.

Values

To value something means you give it great importance in your life. You appreciate it and hold it in high regard. Values reflect a person's sense of right and wrong. An example of a value someone might have is, 'People should be treated with respect and dignity.' A person's values will influence their attitudes and behaviour.

Examples of Values

How do you know what your values are? One way to examine your values is to think about what your priorities are. When the things that you do and the way you behave match your values, life is usually good and you feel content. When you go against your values or forget about them, things can feel wrong and this can cause unhappiness.

Many values are just part of us, whether we realise it or not. When you know your own values you can use them to make decisions about how to live your life.

LITERACY LIBRARY

Priority:
Something that is treated as more important than other things.

Values in Relation to Everyday Life Choices and Relationships

Read the following piece about Conor and his values.

I always knew what my values were. I've held the same values in life from a young age and I've always tried to live my life by them.

For me, my top three values are family, healthy living and helping others who are less fortunate than me. I think they are good values to live by and when I make them a priority in my life I always feel happy and fulfilled.

I only realised how important my values are to me when things changed in my life and I began to forget about my values. I was training for a marathon and got a real buzz from feeling fit and healthy. I had a steady job and while it didn't pay me a huge salary, the hours meant I could spend plenty of time with my wife, Holly, and two young daughters, Ava and Orla.

I was the president of my local St Vincent de Paul group and had worked with the organisation since my college days. I really enjoyed meeting people through the group and it felt great to know we were helping those who needed it. My favourite part was visiting elderly people in hospital who had no one else to visit them. I loved chatting with them and I often got more from the visits than they did.

What, do you think, does Conor mean when he says, 'I often got more from the visits than they did'?

The opportunity came up for a promotion in work. Holly said I should go for it if I wanted to. She has always been very supportive of me. It would mean longer hours if I got it, but my salary would almost double! I couldn't let this chance pass me by.

I was thrilled when I got the job and even happier when I got a brand new company car to drive home to Holly in. My new hours meant I had to leave the house much earlier, so I couldn't drop the girls to school anymore.

I found myself getting home from work later and later in the evening. My training for the marathon stopped as I just didn't have the time. Without my running I found myself getting cranky and snapping at Holly and the kids. I had never been sick before, but I started to get aches and pains and colds and I knew it was because I didn't have the time to look after myself anymore.

The final straw came the week before Christmas. The Saint Vincent de Paul group had been planning a party in the hospital for the elderly patients who wouldn't make it home for Christmas. Holly and the kids were coming too and the girls were going to sing a few Christmas carols. We were all looking forward to it. On the morning of the party there was a crisis in work and my boss told me I'd have to fly to England for an important meeting that afternoon. The girls were so upset when I told them and Holly was fuming. I couldn't blame them.

The following week, after the excitement of Santa and cleaning away after the Christmas dinner, Holly and I got the girls to bed and sat down. The kids had got more Christmas presents than they'd ever had before and we'd been able to get the house painted with all the extra money from my new salary. When I thought about it, though, I had been too tired from work to really enjoy the festive season. I remembered previous Christmas days when we didn't have as much but we were much happier.

Holly and I had the talk we had both been avoiding. I was going to step down from my promotion and ask to go back to my old position. It just wasn't worth it. I had lost sight of what was important to me. Family, healthy living and helping others are far more valuable to me than any company car or pay rise. I realised that I was a better father, husband and member of my community when I lived by my values.

WRITE THE ANSWERS   Enquiry

1 What values does Conor try to live his life by?

2 What things did Conor do to keep those values a priority in his life?

3 Explain what happened to make Conor forget about his values.

4 Describe how Conor's relationships with others were affected when he did not prioritise his values.

5 Do you think Conor made the right decision in the end? Explain your answer.

Personal Values and Choices

Knowing what your personal values are is very important when it comes to making choices. You can use them as a guide to make the best choice in any situation. Some of life's decisions are really about deciding and knowing what you value the most. You can rely on your values and use them as a guide to point you in the right direction.

As you move through your life, your values may change. When you are young your friends might be a top priority, but as you get older and maybe have a family, spending time with them might be something you value more than your friendships.

A good way to discover what your personal values are is to look back on your life and identify times that you felt really happy and confident that you were making good choices. Think about what you were doing, who you were with and what kind of things made you happy. Also think about times when you felt proud of yourself or when others were proud of you.

Now look at the following list of personal values. Write the ones that are important to you into your copybook and rank how important they are, with 1 being not that important and 5 being very important. Are there other values you would like to add that are not on the list? If there are, add them into your copybook.

Value	Important to me	Rank 1–5
Being liked by others		
Working in a team		
Being there for family		
Being a leader		
Being glamorous/good-looking		
Being powerful		
Standing up for what I believe in		
Being health conscious		
Fitting in with the group		
Being confident		
Learning new things		
Helping others		
Having a lot of money		
Being the best at something		
Following the rules		
Being there for friends		
Working to change society		
Having a religious faith		

THINK, PAIR, SHARE

In **pairs**, write down what your top five personal values are.

Think about one thing you do for each value that keeps it an important part of your life.

Share your answers with your partner and then with the rest of the class.

Values and Responsibilities to Others

Malala Yousafzai

The name Malala Yousafzai is known all around the world as being the youngest person to ever win the Nobel Peace Prize. She received this great honour in 2014 at the age of seventeen.

Malala was born in Pakistan to a Muslim family who valued education and women's rights. The culture in which she lived did not always value having daughters, and sons were given more attention and importance. However, Malala's father was determined to give Malala every opportunity a boy would have. He had set up his own school, as he believed education was the key to having the freedom to make choices in later life.

LITERACY LIBRARY

Extremist:
A person who holds extreme political or religious views and may use violence to uphold them.

Activism:
Carrying out actions or campaigning to bring about change in society.

Malala loved school and wanted to train to be a doctor, but everything changed when the Taliban, an extremist group, took control of her town. They banned many things, such as playing music and owning a television. But the order that girls were no longer allowed to go to school was the one that changed Malala's life forever.

Malala began to write a blog for the BBC about what her life was like under Taliban rule. It was called 'Diary of a Pakistani Schoolgirl'. In it she wrote about her hope to keep going to school and her fears for her future. Malala also spoke out about her right to an education in a Pakistani television interview in 2009. Her parents fully supported and encouraged her activism.

Malala received a humanitarian award in 2018.

VALUES 21VALUES 21

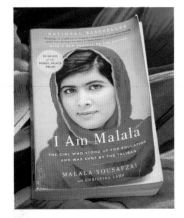

However, as people began to listen to what she had to say, concern for her safety grew. Malala refused to give up. She felt she had a responsibility to herself and other young girls in situations like hers to fight for her values of education and equality.

On 9 October 2012, Malala got on a school bus that would carry the girls and their teachers home from school. Her parents thought she would be safer travelling by bus rather than walking, as people knew who she was. Suddenly two young men stepped out into the road and stopped the bus. They boarded the vehicle and asked, 'Who is Malala?' The other students looked at Malala and immediately the sound of gunfire rang out: Malala had been shot in the head.

As Malala fought for her life in a hospital, news of the horrific attack spread. There was great anger, both at the Taliban, who carried out the attack, and at the Pakistani government, who people blamed for not doing more to protect Malala. After life-saving surgery, it became clear that Malala needed the best medical care possible. On 15 October she was flown to a hospital in Birmingham, England, where she stayed for three months. She went on to make an amazing recovery due to the quality of care she got and through her own strength and determination.

Nine months after the shooting, Malala stood up at the UN headquarters in New York and gave a speech that was shown around the world. It was her sixteenth birthday. In it she said, 'One child, one teacher, one book, one pen can change the world.' That same year she published her first book, *I Am Malala*. In 2014 she won the Nobel Peace Prize.

She is currently studying philosophy, politics and economics at Oxford University and continues to work tirelessly to promote the right to an education for girls around the world.

> What, do you think, did Malala mean when she said, 'One child, one teacher, one book, one pen can change the world'? Do you agree with her?

Malala received the Nobel Peace Prize in Oslo in 2014.

WRITE THE ANSWERS   Enquiry

1 Describe the kind of family Malala came from.

2 What happened in her town that changed everything?

3 How did people begin to know who Malala was?

4 Explain, in your own words, what happened on 9 October 2012.

5 What kind of values are important to Malala?

6 Where do you think Malala got her values from?

7 How did Malala's values affect her life choices?

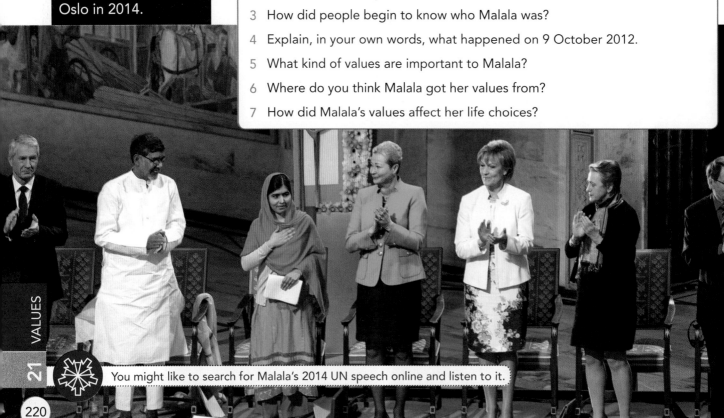

You might like to search for Malala's 2014 UN speech online and listen to it.

Sources of Values

Where do you think our values come from? Usually they come from sources that we believe in and see as being good and true. Here is an example of the source of one person's values.

Integrity:
Being honest and having strong moral principles.

Tribulations:
Great trouble or suffering.

Where do your values come from? Recently I was asked this question by a potential client and was at a loss for words for a few minutes. I'd never really thought about this before. My values have always been my values (for the most part … a few have changed).

My answer to him was: I learned my values from my family. I learned my values early in life. I grew up in a small town in Oklahoma whose population was barely a thousand people. Both sets of grandparents were farmers – dairy farmers who raised beef cattle – and most of my extended family lived in the same general area. The majority of my family still lives in the same town they had grown up in.

Growing up I learned how hard it is to make a living from the land … It is hard, hard work. It can also be very rewarding, but most times not in the financial sense. While growing up I learned what it meant to work hard, be trustworthy, be honest, have integrity and to be selfless.

As a child you never really think you are learning 'values', but you are. These values extend into your adult life and provide you with a 'compass' to navigate through the trials and tribulations life has to offer. These values may change a bit during life, but I believe the core values you learn as a child stay with you for the rest of your life.

Eric D. Brown, Technology Consultant

THINK, PAIR, SHARE

In **pairs**, **think** about three core values your family has taught you.
Share your thoughts with your partner.
As a class, discuss the most common values that people have learned from their families.

Our values come from a variety of sources. Some of these include:

1 Family
2 Peers
3 School
4 Religion
5 Media
6 Major historical events (for instance, war, recession, natural disasters)
7 Culture and society.

 GROUP ACTIVITY   Reflection and Action

You have already discussed what kind of values our families give us.

Break the class into six groups. On each placemat, write in the centre square one of the other seven sources listed above.

Each person should write in their space what kind of values their source might give to people. When everyone has finished, discuss what the group thinks are the top three values your source teaches.

REFLECTIVE ACTIVITY

Think about your own attitude to different sources of values and how a person's values relate to their everyday life. Answer the following questions:

1 Are you confident that you know what your own personal values are and where they come from?
2 Were you surprised by other values people might have that you had not thought about before?
3 If you could meet Malala Yousafzai, what three questions would you ask her and why?

 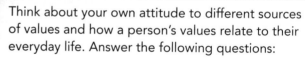 PowerPoint summary

CHAPTER 22
The Importance of Morality

SOL: 5, 11
LO: 3.2

 See also Chapter 24

LEARNING OUTCOME

Reflect upon and discuss what it means to be moral, why people living in society need to be moral and what the influences on and sources of authority are for a person's moral decision-making process.

KEY SKILLS YOU WILL USE IN THIS CHAPTER

- Staying well
- Managing myself
- Working with others
- Being creative
- Communicating
- Managing information and thinking

WELLBEING INDICATORS IN THIS CHAPTER

LEARNING INTENTIONS

At the end of this chapter, I will

1 Understand that we all make choices in life
2 Understand the importance of human relationships
3 Know what euthanasia is
4 Know the story of the Prodigal Son
5 Understand the sources of morality.

Read and reflect on the following story:

Samantha went into the shop to buy a hot chocolate on her way home from school. That morning her mum had given her €20 to pay for a school trip. She had not met the teacher that day to give the money to him, so she still had the €20 in her bag. She paid for the hot chocolate and instead of getting change for €20 she got change for €50. What should she do? What would **you** do?

THINK, PAIR, SHARE

Think about this situation.

Pair with your neighbour to discuss what you would each do.

Share with the class what you would do if you found yourself in this situation.

Choices

We all have choices to make in life. They can be the right choice or the wrong choice.

Samantha has two choices:

1 Samantha can give the change back to the shop assistant and tell her she gave her €20 and not €50, as the change indicates.

2 Samantha can say nothing, take the change and have money for her school trip as well as extra money that she can now spend on herself.

Knowing what is good behaviour and what is bad behaviour and making decisions based on this knowledge can be described as morality.

Choice is about checking the facts and looking to others for correct and sound advice. A decision can be made when all the facts have been collected. On that day Samantha decided to tell the shop assistant that she had given her €20, not €50, to pay for the hot chocolate. She therefore gave the extra money back. She would have felt guilty if she had not done this.

People can have different reasons for deciding what is moral.

When you've read and discussed the text above, fill in the KWL template below in your copybook.

K What are the reasons that I know for being moral?	W What other reasons are there for being moral?	L What have I learned today?

1 FEELING GUILTY

If we choose to do something that we feel or know is wrong, we may feel a sense of guilt. Guilt can cause us to feel bad about ourselves or our actions. We may feel that we are to blame or are responsible and regret our choice. To avoid this feeling of guilt, we might choose to do the right thing.

2 FEAR OF BEING CAUGHT

When we do something wrong, there is a chance that we will be caught. We may be caught by those in charge of us such as our parents. If we are caught, we will probably get into trouble. We don't want others to think badly of us. Therefore, this fear of being caught may make us choose the moral or right thing.

3 THE LAWS OF A COUNTRY

Every society or country has laws. The people living there must follow these laws. Laws are there to protect us and help everyone to live in peace. If we break these laws, there may be a very strict punishment. These laws can guide us in what is right or wrong.

4 THE LAWS OF A RELIGION

The laws of a religion tell us how our God wants us to act and behave. They show us what our religion sees as right and wrong. When making a moral decision, we can look at our religion's moral code. It can help us to make the right decision, as we want to follow our religion.

5 GUT INSTINCT

When we are faced with a moral decision, our gut instinct can often guide us. We may not fully understand why an action is wrong, but something inside us is telling us it is. It is often described as a sixth sense. The right or moral thing may feel natural, while the wrong or immoral thing may feel unnatural.

6 FOLLOWING THE CROWD

We all like to feel like we belong. What others think of us can influence us greatly. We often think that whatever the majority is doing must be right. However, we must be careful as this is not always the case. If we are unsure what is right or wrong, looking to the 'crowd' or other people to see what they are doing is not always a good idea.

7 OBEYING ORDERS

Sometimes we are told by others what to do. Instead of deciding for ourselves what is right or wrong, we follow the orders of others. If we are told to do something, we might think it must be the moral thing to do.

Sometimes it is not easy to follow orders. If we have a difficult moral decision to make, it might be easier to obey and do what others tell us. But we should ask ourselves if the orders we are being given are right or moral.

Often people can have a combination of these reasons for deciding what is moral.

WRITE THE ANSWERS — Enquiry

1. From the reasons above, which do you think is the most important one for helping us to decide what is moral? Explain why you chose that reason.

2. Which reason do you think is the least important? Explain why you think this.

3. Which reason or reasons would help you most in deciding what is right or moral?

4. What reason, do you think, would (a) a child (b) a teenager and (c) an adult use when making a moral decision? Explain your choices.

5. In your opinion, which of the seven listed reasons did Samantha use in the story when deciding to do the right thing?

LITERACY LIBRARY

Majority:
Most people.
Combination:
Mixture.

Society

A person's sense of right or wrong depends on many things. What one person sees as right or moral, another may see as wrong or immoral. A sense of morality is something that every person has, regardless of their age, race or religious background.

Because people live in communities their morality affects those around them, so in this way we can say that morality is both **personal** and **communal.**

When making moral decisions, people must remember that they have different kinds of relationships with others and their decisions can affect them in different ways.

Interpersonal

Interpersonal relationships are relationships we have with certain individuals, such as a parent, brother, sister or friend.

Communal

Communal relationships are relationships we have with a group of people, such as those who live in the same area as us or members of a club to which we belong.

Global

Even though we may not realise it, we have relationships with people of different nationalities and religions from all over the world. We are connected to them simply because we all live on the same planet.

Decisions made by individuals or groups of people can have a global effect, such as damaging the environment or using nuclear weapons.

Social media today has a global effect. We can find out what is happening to family and friends in Australia, America or anywhere in the world by looking at Facebook, Instagram, Twitter or any social media platform. Unfortunately, this can also be negative, as people can be cyber-bullied from anywhere in the world.

Human Relationships
Bob Geldof: Reaching the World

Read the following article about how morality can have a global effect.

📎1

This Irishman's face is recognised throughout the world. While Bob Geldof is a talented musician, he is more widely known for his work helping others. In 1984 he was moved by a BBC news item on famine-stricken Ethiopia in Africa. It made him want to reach out and do something practical to help those who were suffering.

So he called on his famous friends in the music business to help. The result was a Christmas song, 'Feed the World', which was an instant number one hit. Its popularity helped to raise both money and awareness for those in need. But the story did not end there. The following year saw one of the biggest music concerts of all time, Live Aid in Wembley Stadium, which continued the good work of raising money.

However, the problem of poverty in the developing world did not go away. So, twenty years later, in July 2005, a concert called Live 8 took place in eight cities around the world. The aim was to convince world leaders to make a choice to end poverty. By cancelling African debt and increasing the amount of aid to these countries, the politicians could make a huge change to those societies. The idea was a major success, as more than $40 billion of debt owed by the African countries was cancelled.

Bono of U2 was delighted to be part of Live 8 and described it as 'a brilliant moment'. He went on to praise the movement behind Live 8 and what it represented. According to Bono, it is the movement itself, the ordinary people who will carry the ideas forward into the next generation. It is these people who are the source and inspiration for change. He said, 'It is this movement, not rock stars, that will make it untenable to break promises to the most vulnerable people in the planet.'

LITERACY LIBRARY

Untenable:
Something that cannot be defended.

THE IMPORTANCE OF MORALITY

22

Bono was right: Live 8 *was* a brilliant moment. It was part of this brilliant movement of ordinary people. It gave the poor of society a voice. Everybody was involved, from the soccer mom to the student activist. It was the movement itself and not the pop stars that made it difficult for promises to be broken in the future.

People all over the world had been influenced by the example set by Bob Geldof. They reached out to help their fellow human beings.

 WRITE THE ANSWERS   Enquiry

In small groups and using the placemat, answer the following questions:

1   Why did Bob Geldof decide to organise Live Aid?

2   What did the song 'Feed the World' achieve?

3   Would you describe Bob Geldof as a moral person? Say why you think this.

4   How does this article show what is meant by the term 'influence'?

5   Can you think of another example where bands came together to achieve something or to send a message about something?

People make decisions in their lives every day. Sometimes these choices are straightforward, but other times can be difficult. Before making a decision, it is important for a person to think about the consequences for themselves, their loved ones and society.

Read the following debate on arguments for and against euthanasia. 'Euthanasia' means when someone who is really sick and will never get better is helped to die by another person. This is illegal in Ireland and in many European countries.

Euthanasia – The Debate

Good afternoon, chairperson and members of the audience. My name is Hannah. We are here today to debate the issue that euthanasia is a good thing. I strongly disagree with this for many reasons.

When I heard what the topic was I decided to go to my dad and ask him to explain to me what euthanasia is and what he thought about it. He explained that euthanasia is when a person who is so sick they will never get better is helped by someone else to die.

At first I didn't think this was such a bad idea, especially if the person was in pain. But then Dad reminded me of when my Aunt Lisa was sick. She was in a coma and no one thought she would survive. The doctors said she had only a few days to live. But then three days later she suddenly started to improve. It was like a miracle. Over time she got stronger and she's doing well now. Dad said people should think about cases like this and that he was strongly against euthanasia.

Next, I decided to see what people my own age thought about the issue. All my friends that I asked said they thought it was a bad idea. They made me think about things from their point of view. Some of them had very good ideas. One of them said they thought the person who helped the sick person to die would have to live with what they did for the rest of their life and would always wonder if they did the right thing. I'd never thought about it like that.

I decided to try to find out another point of view on the issue to help me to make up my mind. Our local priest, Fr William, has always been very helpful and I think he has good ideas on a lot of topics. He could help me understand what my religion has to say on the issue. Fr William reminded me about the Ten Commandments. We are told in them, 'Thou shall not kill.' For this reason, euthanasia is against our religion.

He said that humans should not try to play God. It is not up to us to make decisions about life and death. My religion has been around a long time and I think it helps us to do the right thing in a lot of situations. I think this is one more area where my religion knows best.

Finally, I looked up information on euthanasia on the internet. I discovered that it is against the law in our country and in many others. Anyone helping another person to die could end up in prison. Again, I thought that laws are there for a reason and they usually help and protect us.

Ladies and gentlemen, when I started this debate topic I wasn't fully aware of what it meant and I hadn't made up my mind on how I felt about it. But I think you can see from my points that euthanasia is not a good thing. I know I'm convinced. Thank you for listening to my speech.

THINK, PAIR, SHARE

Think about the arguments you would put forward for and against euthanasia.
Pair off with your neighbour.
Share your thoughts and ideas with the class.

WRITE THE ANSWERS   Enquiry

1. Where did Hannah go first to find out about her debate topic? How did this help her?
2. In what way did Hannah's friends help her to make up her mind about the issue?
3. What did religion have to say on the issue?
4. What do you think was the most convincing information that Hannah learned?
5. Why, do you think, did Hannah go to all these people and places to decide how she felt about the issue of euthanasia?

Sources of Morality

To **source** something is to find out exactly where it has come from. In the debate story, Hannah went to several different sources to help her make up her mind as to whether euthanasia was a good or bad thing. Our morality comes from many different sources that help to shape us into the people we are now and the people we will become.

What are these sources?

- Home and family
- Peer group
- School
- Religion
- The state.

Home and Family

The **home** and the **family** are two of the most important sources of morality. The family provides moral standards, education, religious background, love, security, customs and cultures. If we are taught good values in the home, we will learn to be respectful to others throughout life. Parents are the primary educators of their children. They instil in their children good values that will stand to them throughout life.

Often people will have the same opinion about issues as the rest of their family. This is because they have discussed these topics with those closest to them. They trust their judgement and learn a lot from them.

It is in the home that talents are nurtured and nourished. It is through the family that you learn about yourself and come to appreciate what is good. Stories are passed from one generation to the next, which helps in the formation of your character. Every family is unique and has its own identity. Family members have a responsibility to look after each other, especially in times of difficulty and distress.

Stories are passed on from one generation to the next. What stories have you been told about your family? Share this story with your neighbour or small group.

The love that members of a family show to each other is unconditional. However, no family is perfect. This is evident in Luke 15:11–31, where the father welcomes his son home after he has squandered a lot of money. Read the following parable and answer the questions that follow.

The Prodigal Son   Luke 15:11–31

A man had two sons whom he loved equally. The younger of the sons asked his father to divide the estate. When the father did this, the younger son left for a distant country, where he squandered the money on having a good time.

When all the money was spent, he didn't know what to do. Eventually, he decided to go home to see his family. Knowing that he had done wrong, he felt awful about his behaviour. As he came near his family estate, his father saw him in the distance and ran towards him. That night the father organised a big party to honour his young son.

Meanwhile, the elder son was working in the fields and heard that his younger brother had returned. Immediately he was angry that his father was holding a party for his brother. After all, he was the one who had looked after his father and worked hard on the estate when the younger brother had left.

But his father replied, 'My son, you are with me always and all I have is yours. But it was only right that we should celebrate and rejoice, because your brother here was dead and has come to life; he was lost and is found.'

 WRITE THE ANSWERS   Enquiry

1 How are the home and family an important source of morality?

2 What values have been instilled in you that you would like to pass on to others?

3 Use a placemat to discuss and record whether you think the story of the Prodigal Son is a good example of family life today?

The Peer Group

The **peer group** is another source of morality. It can be defined as a group of people the same age. Most young people want to belong to a peer group and they feel anxious and different when they are excluded from the activities of the group. Friends are important, as they help us to become better people. During adolescence, young people often make new friends because as they grow and develop, they know what type of people they want to be friends with.

Sometimes during adolescence young people become pressurised into doing things that the group decides. It is a time when they must stand on their own two feet and make decisions for themselves. Because of some of the decisions they make, they can be left out in the cold by their friends, laughed at and made to feel different. Real friends treat each other with respect and listen to and care for each other. They are supportive of one another.

Young people spend a lot of time with their friends and talk to them about all sorts of things. They can learn from each other and see things from a different point of view. Their friends may have had different experiences, so they can teach everyone about new issues or change how the group feels about others.

WRITE THE ANSWERS   Enquiry

1 What values have you learned from your friends?

2 How important are friends to adolescents?

3 Describe how the peer group can be both a positive and negative influence.

The national anti-bullying website is www.tacklebullying.ie.

The School

The **school** is a community whose members work together to help and support each other. Because you spend a lot of time in school, it is important that you work together to make it a great community for all. This means showing respect for your fellow classmates, teachers and all who work in the school community.

At school we can be influenced by other people or we can be a source of influence for others. Therefore, school is a very important place that can shape the people we become in later life.

We learn a lot about important issues in life through subjects such as Religion, CSPE and SPHE. Subjects like these can give us the knowledge to help us decide how we feel about issues. They often deal with issues of morality such as caring for the environment, social media, racism, drugs and alcohol.

When you've read and discussed the text above, fill in the KWL template below in your copybook.

What do you **know** about your school's anti-bullying policy?	**What** would you like to find out about it?	What have you **learned** that you did not know before?

Religion

Another important source of morality is **religion**. Most world religions have a **moral vision**. A moral vision is the ability to see the difference between right and wrong. For Christians the most important ideal is to follow the teachings of Jesus Christ given to us in the sacred scriptures, such as the Gospels. Members of Islam look to the Qur'an for spiritual guidance and support. Jewish people look to the Torah for their spiritual wellbeing.

For centuries Christians worldwide have been guided by the Church on moral issues, e.g. divorce, abortion. Listening to the Church's teachings and following sacred scripture can guide us in making moral decisions.

Read the following poem and answer the questions that follow.

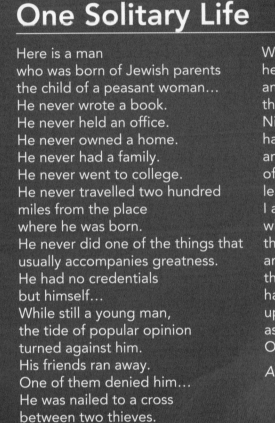

One Solitary Life

Here is a man
who was born of Jewish parents
the child of a peasant woman…
He never wrote a book.
He never held an office.
He never owned a home.
He never had a family.
He never went to college.
He never travelled two hundred
miles from the place
where he was born.
He never did one of the things that
usually accompanies greatness.
He had no credentials
but himself…
While still a young man,
the tide of popular opinion
turned against him.
His friends ran away.
One of them denied him…
He was nailed to a cross
between two thieves.
His executioners gambled for
the only piece of property
he had on earth – his coat.

When he was dead
he was taken down
and lain in a borrowed grave
through the pity of a friend.
Nineteen wide centuries
have come and gone
and today he is the centrepiece
of the human race and the
leader of the column of progress.
I am far within the mark
when I say that all the armies
that ever marched,
and all the navies
that were ever built
have not affected the life of a man
upon earth
as powerfully as has that
One Solitary Life.

Author unknown, 1926

WRITE THE ANSWERS   Enquiry

1 What do you think of the title of this poem?

2 What effect has Jesus had on our lives to date?

3 How important do you feel religion is as a source of morality today?

The State

Another source of morality for us is the **state**. In Ireland we live in what is called a democratic state. This means that every few years we elect people to represent us in parliament (Dáil Éireann). The elected government makes the laws for the country, by which each citizen must abide. The laws of the country protect its people.

One example of a law in Ireland is the penalty points system. This is to encourage safer driving on our roads. Another example is the law against drinking and driving.

WRITE THE ANSWER Enquiry

Why, do you think, are laws important to any country?

GROUP ACTIVITY Enquiry

In small groups, research how many penalty points are given when someone uses a mobile phone while driving their car or when someone speeds on a dual carriageway, through a town or on a motorway.

Read the following newspaper clip and discuss it with your class group.

More than 14,000 people have been caught on their mobile phone while driving so far this year. And they haven't been making and taking calls. Posing for selfies, updating Facebook and live streaming their every move are just some of the other things that Irish drivers have been found doing this year.

Source: TheJournal.ie

📊 PowerPoint summary

📄 Weblinks

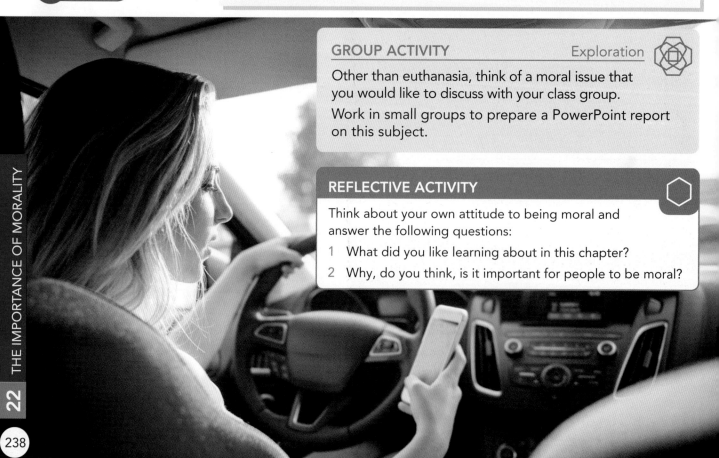

GROUP ACTIVITY Exploration

Other than euthanasia, think of a moral issue that you would like to discuss with your class group.

Work in small groups to prepare a PowerPoint report on this subject.

REFLECTIVE ACTIVITY

Think about your own attitude to being moral and answer the following questions:

1 What did you like learning about in this chapter?
2 Why, do you think, is it important for people to be moral?

CHAPTER 23
Moral Codes

SOL: 5, 11
LO: 3.5

 See also Chapter 1, Chapter 7 and Chapter 15

LEARNING OUTCOME

Examine a moral code in two of the five major world religions and discuss how each could influence moral decision-making for believers.

KEY SKILLS YOU WILL USE IN THIS CHAPTER

- Staying well
- Managing myself
- Working with others
- Being creative
- Communicating
- Managing information and thinking

WELLBEING INDICATORS IN THIS CHAPTER

LEARNING INTENTIONS

At the end of this chapter, I will

1 Understand what a code is and be able to discuss the moral code of two world religions: Judaism and Islam

2 Be able to write and discuss the Ten Commandments and understand their relevance today

3 Be able to write about and discuss the six Articles of Faith in Islam, which Muslims must believe.

A Code

When we first hear the word **'code'**, often the word **'rule'** springs to mind. Rules and codes are good things. When people follow rules, everyone is safe. Although most teenagers say they hate rules, deep down they prefer to have them in their lives than not to have them. Most groups who work together have rules. Rules point out acceptable ways to behave in different situations we may find ourselves in.

Think for a moment about the rules that are made for you:

1 At home   2 At school   3 On sports teams.

| GROUP ACTIVITY | Reflection and Action |

1 What are the rules of your school? Find out what the school's code of behaviour says. In small groups and using the placemat, take one rule from your list and discuss why it is important to your school day.

2 What rules are made for you at home? Why, do you think, are these rules made? Do you think these rules are important for the smooth running of family life? Why/why not?

3 If you play a sport, what are the rules of the game?

THE UNWRITTEN RULES

Formal and Informal Rules

There are two types of rules: formal rules and informal rules. A formal rule is written down and must be accepted by everyone. An example of this is: 'Education in Ireland is compulsory for children from the ages of six to sixteen or until students have completed three years of second-level education.'

An informal rule is not written down but is accepted by everyone.

> **THINK, PAIR, SHARE**
>
> In **pairs**, **think** of an example of an informal rule in your school.
> **Share** this with the class.

These types of rules don't become law overnight. They are developed over a certain amount of time. Formal rules become laws of the state when they serve the needs of the wider community and are upheld by the wider community.

A law is a rule that that helps or prevents certain behaviour. People must obey laws. Most laws are fair and they are designed for the common good of all. In Ireland we live in a democratic state. This means that a government is put into power by the people. The men and women we elect into government make laws on what they think is best for our country.

One example of a modern-day law is the one that forbids young people from working full time before they have reached the age of sixteen. This law is for the protection of young people under sixteen years of age.

> **GROUP ACTIVITY**   Reflection and Action
>
> In small groups, look up some of our laws in Ireland.
> 1 Do you think it is a good idea for education to be compulsory in Ireland up to Junior Cycle or sixteen years of age?
> 2 Discuss how important other laws are to our country.
> 3 Compare these laws in Ireland to laws in other countries. Are they similar or different?

MORAL CODES 23

Religion

One source of morality that is very important to people is their religion. People can be strongly influenced by the religion they have been brought up with. The sacred texts of world religions teach us about what is right and wrong. The sacred texts often guide the people. One example of this is Jews who follow the law of Moses in the Torah. The Torah shows Jews the way that God wants them to live their lives.

Moral vision is a person's view of what is right and good. It is their outlook on life and how it should be lived. Their moral vision will shape the decisions and choices they make. Our moral vision can often be influenced by our religious beliefs. Most religions have a moral vision. A moral vision is always the basis of any code or set of guidelines. For instance, the moral vision of the United Nations Convention on the Rights of the Child values the equality, dignity and freedom of all children.

WRITE THE ANSWERS   Enquiry

1   Name one source of morality that is important to people.

2   What is meant by a sacred text?

3   The sacred text often _____ the people.

4   What is a moral vision?

5   Most _____ have a moral vision.

GROUP ACTIVITY   Exploration

Find out about the work of the United Nations Convention on the Rights of the Child. In small groups, present this information to the class.

Let's now look at the moral code of two world religions:

1 The Jewish religion   2 The Islamic religion.

Development of the Jewish Tradition

See Chapter 15, pp.142–143

All religions have key or important people at the centre of their story. These people help to shape the story of the religion. One of the most important stages in the Jewish story concerns a man named Moses.

LITERACY LIBRARY

False witness:
To lie or say something untrue about another person.

Covet:
To really want something you don't have that someone else does have.

THINK, PAIR, SHARE

Think about when you studied Moses in Chapter 15. What can you remember about him?

In **pairs**, write down three things you remember about Moses.

Share what you remember with the rest of the class.

The Ten Commandments Then

1. I am the Lord your God. You should have no other gods but me.

2. You should not take the Lord your God's name in vain.

3. Remember to keep holy the Sabbath day.

4. Honour your father and mother.

5. Never kill anyone.

6. Never commit adultery.

7. Never steal from anyone.

8. Never bear false witness against your neighbour.

9. Never covet your neighbour's wife.

10. Never covet your neighbour's goods.

The Ten Commandments Today

1 God should come first in life to us.

2 Don't use bad language. Respect God's name.

3 Keep the Sabbath day special.

4 Always obey your parents.

5 Never hurt another person.

6 Never have sexual relations with someone who is married to someone else.

7 Never take something that does not belong to you.

8 Never gossip or tell lies.

9 Be careful about your thoughts about others.

10 Never be jealous of what others have or own.

REVISION ACTIVITY: MOSES

Enquiry

1 The Jewish people prepared themselves for the coming of the Messiah. If you were a Jewish person at the time, how would you prepare for his visit?

2 What did Moses see while minding his sheep?

3 What did this amazing sight turn out to be?

4 What did Moses ask the pharaoh and what was his reply?

5 What was the most terrible plague that God set on the Egyptian people?

6 What happened at the Red Sea?

7 What is the Torah?

8 Imagine that you are Moses. Write a series of diary entries. Describe the most important events of your life and how you felt at those times.

The interior of a synagogue.

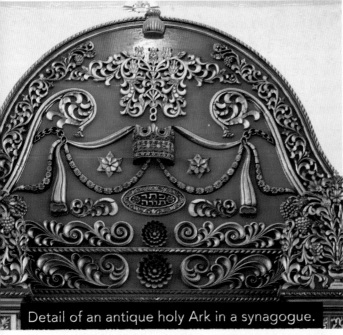

Detail of an antique holy Ark in a synagogue.

The raised platform in a synagogue is known as a bimah.

LITERACY LIBRARY

Perpetual: Something that never ends.

Place of Worship

Every religion has a place of worship and for Jews it is the synagogue. The word 'synagogue' means 'a place of meeting'. It is more than just a place for worship. It is also used for parties, meetings, office work and study.

Synagogues come in all shapes and sizes, but they have several things in common:

1 Every synagogue has a cupboard called the Ark. In it, you will find the scrolls of the Torah. The Ark is behind a curtain on the wall of the synagogue that faces in the direction of Jerusalem.

2 Above the Ark is Ner Tamid. This is the perpetual light. 'Perpetual' means that it is always lit. This is a sign of the unending covenant with God. It is also to remember the menorah, the oil lamp, which was present in the Jerusalem temple that was destroyed.

3 Above the Ark, you will also see two tablets or plaques. These represent the tablets of stone on which the Ten Commandments were given to Moses by God.

4 In the centre of the synagogue is a raised platform called the bimah. The Torah and prayers are read from there. There is also a reading desk where the scrolls are placed while being read.

GROUP ACTIVITY   Enquiry

Discuss planning a visit to a synagogue in Dublin with your teacher. If a visit is not possible, search online for synagogues in Ireland. Talk to your teacher about what steps you need to take to plan the visit. For instance:

- You will need permission from your parents
- You will need to contact the synagogue you would like to visit and check what dates suit them
- You may need to organise transport.

Before you go, find out the following information:

1 How many Jewish people worship in the synagogue regularly?

2 What day of the week do they visit?

3 Do all members of the family go?

4 Do they have to wear anything different to the synagogue?

MORAL CODES 23

245

Islamic Beliefs and How They Affect the Lives of Believers

Muslim boy reading the Qu'ran.

Every religion has core, or central, beliefs. These beliefs give the religion its identity and often affect the lives of the believers. There are Six Articles of Faith in Islam, which Muslims must believe. They are like a statement or doctrine of their faith.

They are:

1 One God
2 Angels
3 Prophets
4 Holy Scriptures
5 The Day of Judgement or the afterlife
6 God's will or fate.

These core beliefs affect how Muslims live their lives. To live a proper Muslim life, there are five practices you must perform. These practices can be compared to a house. As you can see, the house has five pillars. These pillars give it structure and hold it together.

1 SHAHADAH (CREED)

Like some other major world religions, Islam has a creed, known as the shahadah. This is a statement or declaration of faith. Before they pray, Muslims recite this creed. It says, 'There is only one God and Muhammad is his messenger.' Very holy Muslims say the creed first thing in the morning and last thing at night. These are part of the words whispered into the ear of newborn babies. The shahadah is very important for Muslims, as it is a declaration of their main belief. All their other beliefs and practices flow from it.

Muslims believe that Allah is one, worshipped alone with no other. He is seen as creator, giver and taker of life. Allah is all-powerful, all-seeing, all-hearing, all-merciful and forgiving.

2 SALAT (PRAYER)

Prayer is a way of life for Muslims. Their prayer encourages them and supports them as they try to live the kind of life that Allah wants them to lead. Muslims have to pray five times a day and it involves much preparation and planning. The different parts involved in prayer form a ritual.

Wudu: This is the washing that takes place before prayer. Muslims must make sure that the area where they perform their prayers is clean. Wudu consists of washing the hands, mouth, nostrils, face, arms up to the elbows and feet up to the ankles. It also involves passing a wet hand over the head and wiping the inside and outside of the ears with a wet finger. People also remove their shoes. As prayer involves kneeling on the ground, Muslims pray on a prayer mat, which they can bring anywhere.

A mihrab.

Face the Kaaba in Mecca: When they pray, Muslims must face in the direction of the Kaaba in Mecca in Saudi Arabia. Muslims in our part of the world must face southeast during prayer. In the mosque, the place of worship, there is a hollow in the wall call a mihrab. This is at a point nearest to Mecca and shows Muslims which way to face. If they are praying at home, their prayer mat may have a compass so they can work out the right direction to face.

Adhan: This is the call to prayer. When Muslims pray in the mosque or in a group, this call is given at the start of prayer time.

Ra'ka: Each Muslim must do a set of movements in a particular order and say verses from the Qur'an to form a ra'ka, which is like a standard unit of prayer. To begin the prayer, they raise their hands to their ears or shoulders. As the prayer continues, they bow, sit and kneel at certain stages and turn their head to the left and right at the end.

The five daily prayers are prayed at the following times:

1 **Fajr** – dawn
2 **Zuhr** – early afternoon, when the sun is about halfway before setting
3 **Asr** – late afternoon before sunset
4 **Magrib** – immediately after sunset
5 **Isha** – evening time after darkness has set in.

As you can see, the movement of the sun plays a big part in prayer times. They are used to mark the beginning and end of prayer times. Because of this, the time for prayer will change slightly depending on the time of year. For example, in Ireland the sun rises earlier in the summer months, so Fajr will be earlier than in the winter.

See also Chapter 7, pp.70–72

The call to prayer at the Umayyad Mosque in Aleppo, Syria.

MORAL CODES **23**

LITERACY LIBRARY

To purify:
To make clean.

3 ZAKAT (CHARITY)

The idea behind this pillar of Islam is to share the wealth that Allah has blessed you with. It also purifies whatever wealth you are lucky enough to have. The act of giving is a prayer in itself. Many Muslims pay the zakat during the month of Ramadan. They may give it to their local mosque, which will divide it up amongst the poor and needy. Each Muslim gives 2.5 per cent of their yearly savings as long as they reach a certain minimum. This means it is a fair system and people only give what they can afford.

4 SAWM (FASTING)

Fasting, or not eating and drinking at certain times, is part of many religions. In Islam, this fasting takes place during the month of Ramadan. This event each year is a time for Muslims to focus on their faith. Every Muslim who is well and has reached puberty is expected to take part. It is not just about food, though. It is a time for Muslims to increase their efforts to live good lives. They pray more during this time and read the Qur'an.

Because Islam follows a calendar based on the position of the sun, the time of Ramadan moves forward by eleven days every year. Muslims eat a light breakfast before dawn and then a light meal after sunset. If they miss a day of fasting for some reason, they are expected to make it up another day. Elderly people or those who are very sick and cannot fast will give a meal to a poor person instead.

Muslim pilgrims during the Hajj at Mecca, Saudi Arabia.

LITERACY LIBRARY

Pilgrimage:
A journey made by a person or pilgrim to a sacred place.

5 HAJJ (PILGRIMAGE)

The Hajj is a pilgrimage to Mecca that every Muslim should make once in their lifetime, if they are able. Muslims come from all over the world to pray to Allah and to remember their prophet, Muhammad. The Hajj takes place during the twelfth month of the Islamic calendar. It is a time when all Muslims are truly united despite their differences. Rich and poor, male and female, young and old are all seen as equals. To show this equality, all pilgrims wear a simple white garment called an ihram.

The Hajj shows how Muslims are willing to give themselves to Allah. The different stages of the Hajj pilgrimage are linked to the life of their prophet, Muhammad, and also to the time of Abraham. It remembers the time when Muhammad led his followers from Medina to Mecca and performed the Hajj himself.

WRITE THE ANSWERS   Enquiry

1 How many Articles of Faith are there in Islam? Name them.
2 Name the Five Pillars of Islam.
3 How many times a day do Muslims pray?
4 How do Muslims prepare to pray?
5 What is zakat? When is it given?
6 When does fasting take place in the Muslim religion? What does it involve?

MORAL CODES 23

Azadeh and Her Family Go on the Hajj

The following is a series of blog entries written by a fourteen-year-old Muslim girl called Azadeh. In them, she tells us about her experiences of going on the Hajj.

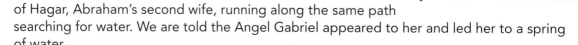

AZADEH'S BLOG

15 October

Today myself and my family finally arrived in Mecca and began to perform the Hajj. I can't believe I'm actually here with millions of other Muslims from all over the world. We started by putting on our white robes so we were all dressed the same. Then we went to the Kaaba for the welcome tawaf. This means walking seven times anticlockwise around this sacred building. I even got to touch it!

After that, we walked seven times between two hills called Safa and Marwah and drank from the Zamzam well. I had heard the story of Hagar, Abraham's second wife, running along the same path searching for water. We are told the Angel Gabriel appeared to her and led her to a spring of water.

At this stage I was very tired but we weren't finished yet! We had to travel to Mina, a village over 6 km away. Finally we set up camp. I feel so lucky to be here performing one of the pillars of Islam. It is a once-in-a-lifetime chance.

I had better go now and get some sleep. Another big day tomorrow.

16 October

We set off early and walked to the plain of Arafat. My father told me this is an important place because it faces the Mount of Mercy, where Muhammad gave his final sermon.

This part of the Hajj was very special. At noon, all the pilgrims stood and prayed. It was an amazing sight to see all those people dressed in white praying to Allah. We stayed that way until sundown. We then set off for a place called Muzdalifah, where we collected pebbles.

I am lying beneath an open sky now surrounded by my family. I had better get some sleep because we have to leave for Mina before sunrise.

17 October

Today we used the stones we collected last night to throw at the three pillars of Satan. The pillars represent the three times Abraham and his son were tempted to disobey Allah. Throwing the stones is a symbol of our own struggle against evil.

We also brought a goat we had bought to the special area for sacrifice. My mother explained that this was to remind us of the sacrifice Abraham was willing to make for Allah: his own son. We gave the meat from the animal to the poor, which I think is a nice thing to do. Did you know that at the same time, Muslims all around the world were making a sacrifice too to celebrate the festival of Eid al-Adha? I remember doing this at home last year and thinking of all those lucky enough to be on the Hajj. I'm so happy that this year I get to be here.

We returned to Mecca and circled the Kaaba again. We're going back to Mina now and will stay for two days and throw more pebbles. I hope we get to meet up with my cousins, who are on the Hajj too!

20 October

Sorry I haven't written in a few days. We were very busy at Mina, praying and talking to other pilgrims. I got to see my cousins, who are enjoying the Hajj as much as I am.

We're back in Mecca now to perform the farewell tawaf, or prayer ritual.

This has been the best experience of my life. I can't wait to go back to Ireland and tell all my friends about it. The ones who are not Muslim will never be able to see it for themselves, as non-Muslims are not allowed into Mecca. I will try my best to describe it to them and explain how it has made my faith stronger.

See Chapter 1, p.13 and Chapter 7, pp.70–72

Summary of the Hajj

1 Circle the Kaaba in Mecca seven times and pray.
2 Walk seven times between the hills of Safa and Marwah and drink from the Zamzam well.
3 Travel to Mina, camp and pray.
4 Day of standing on the plain of Arafat.
5 Collect pebbles at Muzdalifah.
6 Return to Mina and throw pebbles at the three pillars of Satan. Make a sacrifice.
7 Return to Mecca and circle the Kaaba again.
8 Return to Mina for a few days and stone the pillars again.
9 Farewell tawaf in Mecca.

WRITE THE ANSWERS   Enquiry

1 Why do Muslims go on pilgrimage to Mecca?
2 What do they wear on the Hajj and why?
3 Why do they walk between two hills and drink from a well?
4 What happens at Arafat?
5 Explain the reason behind throwing pebbles at pillars.
6 How did Azadeh feel after going on the Hajj?

REFLECTIVE ACTIVITY

Think about your own attitude to moral codes and answer the following questions:

1 What did you like learning about in this chapter?
2 Do you think the Ten Commandments are relevant to you today? Why/why not?
3 How, do you think, could the Hajj pilgrimage influence moral decision-making for believers?

 PowerPoint summary

 Weblinks

LEARNING OUTCOME

Investigate what living a morally good life means with reference to two major world religions and compare with a non-religious world view.

KEY SKILLS YOU WILL USE IN THIS CHAPTER

- Staying well
- Managing myself
- Working with others
- Being creative
- Communicating
- Managing information and thinking

WELLBEING INDICATORS IN THIS CHAPTER

LEARNING INTENTIONS

At the end of this chapter, I will

1 Know the story of Willie Bermingham

2 Understand what the terms 'moral vision' and 'religious moral vision' mean

3 Know the story of the Peter McVerry Trust

4 Understand forgiveness and reconcilation

5 Understand atonement.

⊗⊗⊗ See Chapter 22, p.253.

Moral Decision-making

Remember what morality is from Chapter 22? It is knowing what is good behaviour and what is bad behaviour and making decisions based on this. We make choices all the time based on checking facts and looking to others for advice and guidance. We often ask a parent, grandparent or older brother or sister to advise us on how best to live a morally good life.

When we say that someone is living a good life, we mean that they are a good person. They care about people and think not just of themselves, but others around them. They are selfless, kind, principled, trustworthy, considerate and loyal. We all know people who are like this. Most people strive to be all these things to themselves and to others.

THINK, PAIR, SHARE

Think about someone in your life who is like this.
Pair with your neighbour and tell them three things about this person.
Share this information with your class group.

01 Read the following story about **Willie Bermingham**. He believed that we all have a responsibility to care for those who are less well off than ourselves. He also believed that a community's worth should be based on how they treat their poorest and most helpless members.

Willie Bermingham

Willie Bermingham

Willie Bermingham was born in Inchicore in Dublin in 1942. He worked with his father, who sold coal, scrap metal and timber. He saw no real future for himself in that work, so he gave it up. He did not always see eye to eye with his dad on things, especially when he tried to give away coal to poor people, which his dad was not happy about.

He joined the Dublin Fire Brigade and was based at Tara Street Fire Station in Dublin. Through his work he experienced first hand some of the problems that faced the elderly community. Some of these were inadequate housing, a poor diet, depression often due to isolation or neglect and fear of robbery.

In 1977, he came across many situations that saddened him. He and his colleagues had to remove the bodies of elderly people from their poor living conditions who had been dead for days. He decided that he needed to take action. He had a moral vision to do something. A moral vision is seeing the difference between something that is right and something that is wrong. This is based on one's values. He believed that each of us has an obligation to care for those who are less well off than ourselves.

From this belief he set up an organisation called ALONE. This organisation was set up specifically to meet the needs of Dublin's poor and isolated elderly community.

When friendship comes knocking.

ALONE

Supporting older people to age at home

01 679 1032 alone.ie

ALONE means:

A
L ittle
O ffering
N ever
E nds

He began with a huge poster campaign to highlight the awful conditions that many elderly people lived in. Donations poured in from the public and every penny was used to provide shelter, clothing, food and support for the elderly. He lobbied ministers in government and civil servants to act quickly. He did not mind if he stepped on people's toes because he was focused on what he wanted to do to improve the lives of many elderly people.

Willie Bermingham won a People of the Year Award in 1979. He died of cancer in 1990. Today, ALONE continues to be committed to working with older people across Ireland.

WRITE THE ANSWERS   Enquiry

1   In what way did Willie Bermingham and his dad not see eye to eye?

2   What problems faced the elderly community in Dublin in the 1970s?

3   Which of these problems, do you think, is the most difficult to resolve or fix?

4   Why did Willie Bermingham found ALONE?

5   What do you understand 'moral vision' to mean?

Moral Vision

Moral vision is a person's view of what is right and good. It is their outlook on life and how it should be lived. A person's moral vision will shape the decisions and choices they make.

Our moral vision can often be influenced by our religious beliefs. Most religions have a moral vision. A moral vision is always the basis of any code or set of guidelines. For example, the moral vision underlying the United Nations Convention on the Rights of the Child values the equality, dignity and freedom of all children.

For Christians, love is a very strong theme and one that they should always live by. It is at the heart of the Christian moral vision.

CLASS DISCUSSION   Exploration

In small groups, describe what your moral vision is. Make a poster and present it to the class.

Religious Moral Vision

A person who does not shape their moral vision by religion may not seem very different from someone who does. Both may have a social conscience, a passion for justice and a love of their neighbour.

The non-religious person may be acting out of social concern. On the other hand, the religious person understands and appreciates that each of us is made in the image and likeness of God and that each of us is unique to him. Because religious people feel this way, there is a yearning to live by God's message of 'Love your neighbour as yourself'.

A person with a strong religious moral vision is Fr Peter McVerry. He continually advocates for the poor of society. Read his story below.

Peter McVerry

LITERACY LIBRARY

Advocate:
Stand up for.

Juvenile:
Young.

Peter McVerry Trust

Fr Peter McVerry grew up in Newry, Co. Down and was educated at the Abbey Christian Brothers' Grammar School in Newry. For secondary school he attended the Jesuit school at Clongowes Wood College in Co. Kildare.

In 1962, he joined the Jesuit Order and was ordained thirteen years later, in 1975. From 1974 to 1980, Peter worked in the inner city in Dublin and it was there that he met young people who were sleeping on the streets because of their home situation.

He opened a hostel for homeless boys aged 12–16 in 1979 and this then became his lifetime work. Through his work at the hostel he saw that when the boys reached 16 years and needed to leave, there were few options open to them and most ended up living back on the streets. This led him to set about providing services and accommodation for older youths.

In 1980, Peter moved to Ballymun and by the end of 1983 he had founded the Arrupe Society, a charity to challenge homelessness. This charity, now known as the Peter McVerry Trust, has developed from a three-bedroom flat in Ballymun to eleven homeless hostels, over 100 apartments, a residential drug detox centre and two drug stabilisation services.

His vision for the charity is to support all those living on the margins and to maintain their rights to full inclusion in society. In 2017, the charity worked with over 4,900 marginalised youths.

As a social activist Peter McVerry is a strong supporter of those who have no voice in society. He has written extensively on issues relating to young homeless people, such as accommodation, drugs, juvenile justice, the Garda Síochána, prisons and education. He regularly writes an article for the monthly Redemptorist magazine, *Reality*, and speaks on issues of homelessness, justice and faith to groups around the country. He criticises government policy on issues such as homelessness, drugs and criminal justice.

Peter's continuing work with and campaigning on behalf of troubled young people has made him one of the most prophetic, or visionary, voices in Ireland today.

Speaking at the fiftieth Eucharistic Congress held in Dublin in June 2013, he said, 'In a community that loves one another, there should be no one poor (unless all are poor); there should be no one homeless, no one lonely, no one sick or alone without visitors, no one in prison who has been abandoned and written off, there should be no one rejected or marginalised.'

A note on railings outside Apollo House in Dublin. Activists in the Home Sweet Home coalition took over the building in 2016 and offered accommodation to the homeless.

WRITE THE ANSWERS Enquiry

1 What is the difference between a moral vision and a religious moral vision?

2 Where did Peter McVerry go to school?

3 Search online to find out more about Clongowes Wood College. Write down five pieces of information on the school and share these with your class.

4 What religious order did Peter join in 1962?

5 What did Peter notice after he opened the hostel for young boys in the inner city of Dublin?

6 What was the Arrupe Society renamed as?

7 What is the vision of the Trust?

8 What did Peter say about homelessness at the Eucharistic Congress in 2013? Do you agree or disagree with his statement on homelessness?

Living a Moral Life

Most world religions have forgiveness as a central message. This helps people lead moral lives. Forgiveness at times can be a difficult thing for people to deal with, especially when the hurt is deep. The more innate response is to be mean or to look for revenge.

THINK, PAIR, SHARE

Think about a time when someone did something wrong on you. How did it make you feel? What did you think about?

Pair with your neighbour and tell them what happened.

Share this with your class group.

01

Greta Thunberg

'You Are Never Too Small to Make a Difference'

Prominent:
Important.

Paris Agreement:
Agreement within the United Nations on reducing emissions of greenhouse gases.

Riksdag:
Swedish parliament.

Autism:
A condition that impacts on the way that people see the world and how they interact with other people.

Influential: (p.260)
Powerful.

World Economic Forum: (p.260)
Independent international organisation committed to improving the state of the world.

LITERACY LIBRARY

Greta Thunberg was born on 3 January 2003 in Sweden. At the age of 9, she began to research climate change. Now 16 years old, she is a well-known climate activist. In the summer of 2018, she became prominent as the person who started the first school strike to raise awareness of global warming.

As a ninth-grader, Greta decided she was not attending school after the heatwaves and fires that Sweden had experienced. Her parents were not in favour of her protests and did not support the idea of school striking.

Greta demanded that the Swedish government reduce carbon emissions as per the Paris Agreement. She protested outside the Riksdag every day during school hours with a sign saying, 'School Strike for Climate'. Her idea for a school strike was inspired by protests held by high-school American students in response to the Parkland shootings in 2018, where seventeen people were killed.

She handed out flyers with a long list of facts about the climate crisis and reasons why she was striking. She also posted her ideas on Twitter and Instagram and her posts went viral.

Greta began to get attention from all over the world, which inspired other students from around the globe to take part in student strikes. School strikes took place in Belgium, Austria, the United Kingdom, the United States, Australia and many other countries. In February 2018 some Irish schools participated in protests for a better environment.

In December 2018, she travelled to the United Nations Climate Change Summit in Katowice, Poland. Over 200 nations took part in this summit to ensure the progress of the Paris Agreement. Sir David Attenborough was also there, and he said, 'The collapse of our civilisation and the extinction of much the natural world is on the horizon.' In a meeting with the UN secretary general, António Guterres, Greta Thunberg said, 'This is the biggest crisis humanity has ever faced.' She also accused world leaders of 'behaving like children', and of leaving the burden of climate change to future generations.

Greta often talks about having a mild form of autism, which she sees as helping her to focus on her cause. She says, 'I see the world a bit different, from another perspective.' She also believes that it helps that she sees things as 'black and white', because the choice for the future of the planet is very clear to her: either we stop the emissions of greenhouse gases or we don't.

On 23 January 2019, after a 32-hour train journey, Greta arrived in Davos in Switzerland to continue her climate activism at the World Economic Forum. Her journey was very different from that of many of the delegates there, who had travelled via private jets. She had no problem pointing this out to the rich and powerful group of delegates, which included Bono, Will.i.am and influential businesspeople.

In her speech, she said, 'Some people say that the climate crisis is something that we all have created, but that is not true, because if everyone is guilty then no one is to blame. And someone is to blame. Some people, some companies, some decision-makers, have known exactly what priceless values they have been sacrificing to continue making unimaginable amounts of money. And I think many of you here today belong to that group of people.'

In December 2018, *Time* magazine named Greta Thunberg one of the world's twenty-five most influential teenagers of 2018.

Greta is not the only young person who is helping spread awareness of environmental issues. A young Dublin girl called Flossie Donnelly has campaigned and fundraised for a sea bin to be installed in Dún Laoghaire. When she spoke on RTÉ News, she described the sea bin as 'really cool'. She continued, 'It has a pump which pulls in all the rubbish to make a plastic-free Irish sea.' Plastic in the water has increased over the years and this initiative will help remove some of the plastic from the water. Flossie also organises regular beach clean-ups.

WRITE THE ANSWERS   Enquiry

1   Do you think Greta Thunberg was right to organise this strike?

2   Do you think she is an inspirational young person? Why/why not?

3   What is your opinion of what she said in her speech at Davos in Switzerland?

4   Research 11-year-old Flossie Donnelly. Why do you think the sea bin so important to her?

5   There are numerous problems with our climate. What, do you think, could we do to resolve these ongoing problems?

RESEARCH   Exploration

Research other speeches that Greta Thunberg has made. Summarise your findings and report them to the class.

THINK, PAIR, SHARE

In small groups research other people of faith, for example Jennifer Garner, Natalie Portman or Juan Mata.

Think about why you chose that person.

Pair off in small groups and explain new information that you have found in the small group.

Share this information through a PowerPoint Presentation with the class.

Christianity: The Catholic Church

I want You back.

God

See Chapter 9, pp.83–86.

Sacrament of Reconciliation

When we hurt or upset someone who we really like, we feel unhappy and guilty. We think about what we have done. We long to take back the hurt we have caused. When the person forgives us unconditionally, or completely and freely, we feel better because they have not made us feel small. We are very thankful and promise ourselves not to hurt that person again.

Healing of Relationships

Reconciliation is about bringing the Christian community closer together and closer to God. Reconciliation heals any hurt that people feel and in doing so makes it easier for people to love again without any barriers.

In the Sacrament of Reconciliation, Christians are given the opportunity to meet the risen Christ. Through his forgiveness they are encouraged to move forward in harmony with themselves and their neighbours.

By doing this, God's love can be seen in the world around us. The sacrament can therefore be a healing of the relationships that one has broken. Through sin people turn away from God, but through reconciliation they can return to him.

MORAL DECISION-MAKING PROCESS

24

261

Confession

What do you think of this sacrament?

The priest who hears confession represents the community of believers. He offers forgiveness on behalf of the community. This sacrament can take place individually in a confession box where the priest hears confession privately or somewhere in the church at the reconciliation ceremony or service.

The confessor first acknowledges or admits their sinfulness. The Act of Contrition is then said, whereby the confessor thanks God for all the love he shows them and promises not to sin again.

After this the priest gives an absolution, or forgiveness, on behalf of God and the person is cleansed of their sins. Before the penitent leaves, the priest gives a penance, which normally involves a few prayers being said.

ACT OF CONTRITION OR ACT OF SORROW

Oh my God, I thank you for loving me, I am sorry for all my sins, for not loving others and not loving you. Help me to live like Jesus and not sin again, Amen.

Today many Christians worldwide attend Penitential services (Reconciliation services), where the community gathers together to pray for forgiveness. Confession is held not in a box, but in a quiet area in the church.

Reconciliation in Action

Throughout the years of Pope John Paul II's papacy, he showed reconciliation towards the Jewish faith. A Jewish rabbi said that John Paul understood Jews, not with his head, but with his heart. As a child he played with many Jewish children in his school. He prayed at the concentration camp in Auschwitz in 1979. In 2000 he prayed at the Western Wall in Jerusalem, which is a very holy place of pilgrimage for Jews. He placed in the wall a written prayer to God expressing deep sadness for all the wrongs done to Jews by the Christian community. During his 26 years as pontiff he served as a symbol of love. His reconciliation with the Jewish community is certainly a distinctive, or unique, feature of his papacy.

Reconciliation Service

A PRAYER OF CONFESSION

You are our God. We are your people.

But in today's world we can find ourselves in a place of unbelief.

We find ourselves in a world where too many people have despaired;

in a world where too many people do not know or do not care that their brother or sister, with whom they are one, is crying out for help.

Too many of us do not practise what we preach.

Too many of us are too proud to apologise.

Too many of us judge too quickly.

Too many of us forget the message that you preached so eloquently and for all ages.

My Lord and my God look at us standing before you.

You alone can see deep down into our hearts.

You know us.

We stand before you together; help us to see the truth.

Help us to understand ourselves as you understand us, so that we may forgive ourselves as you forgive us.

Judaism

The holiest day in the Jewish year is Yom Kippur. Yom Kippur means 'Day of Atonement'. The word 'atonement' means 'to make amends for the wrongs that people have done'. On this day Jews spend their time making amends to God. They ask God to forgive them for any sins they have committed:

> O Lord, you forgive the sins of your people …
> You do not stay angry forever, but you take
> pleasure in showing us your constant love.
> You will be merciful to us once again. You will
> trample our sins underfoot and send them to the
> bottom of the sea.
> Micah 7:18–19

On this day Jews fast (for the full day) and pray. They don't eat or drink anything for twenty-four hours. If you are under thirteen, pregnant, elderly or sick, you don't have to fast. Fasting helps people to focus on what is important in life. Feeling sorry for any wrongdoing and seeking God's forgiveness are important on Yom Kippur.

In the synagogue, adults pray to God for forgiveness of sins and they ask God to help them lead a better life into the future. In the synagogue, everything is covered in white during Yom Kippur. For example, the curtain on the Ark is white and the Torah scrolls are dressed in white. The rabbi who leads the service is dressed in white too. White is symbolic as it shows that people are sorry for their sins and that God will forgive them.

All the dead are remembered on this day too. The Holocaust during World War II is remembered, as many Jews lost their lives during this period in history. Special candles are lit to remember those who lost their lives during those awful times.

A prayer called the Shema is read at the end of the service. The shofar, or ram's horn, is blown for the last time. This is done to remind people to keep their promises and to do God's will in the year ahead.

WRITE THE ANSWERS   Enquiry

1 What is the holiest day of the year for Jewish people?

2 What does the word 'atonement' mean?

3 What do Jews do on that day?

4 What is Micah saying in 7:18–19? Is this message important to the Jewish people? Why do you think this?

5 Why is fasting important on this day?

6 What colour is used as a symbol around this time?

7 What happens in the synagogue?

8 Do a project on the Holocaust of World War II. Share the information that you gather with your class.

Non-religious Worldview

Remember what an atheist believes from Chapter 12. Atheists do not believe that any gods exist. They don't believe in God as a higher power who created the world and sent his son to save us. Therefore, they don't turn to religion for guidance on questions of right and wrong.

Atheists don't believe in the existence of any supernatural being that looks after their wellbeing. Therefore, there is no sin. When an atheist makes a mistake they ask for forgiveness from the person or persons they have harmed and then they move on. They believe this is better, as they 'own their mistake' and therefore it cannot be forgiven except by the person they have wronged.

Atheists don't receive forgiveness through prayer. It is therefore very important to them to behave well at all times.

GROUP ACTIVITY Enquiry

In small groups, compare the following:
- Christanity's view of sin
- Judaism's view of sin
- A non-religious worldview of mistakes.

What are the main differences?

REFLECTIVE ACTIVITY

Think about your own attitude to living a morally good life and answer the following questions:

1 What did you like learning about in this chapter?

2 Do you think it is important for people to lead a morally good life? Why/why not?

3 Give an example of a time when you made a decision to lead a morally good life.

PowerPoint summary

Weblinks

LEARNING OUTCOME

Examine how a moral decision-making process can help a person decide what is right and wrong in an everyday life situation.

KEY SKILLS YOU WILL USE IN THIS CHAPTER

- Staying well
- Managing myself
- Working with others
- Being creative
- Communicating
- Managing information and thinking

WELLBEING INDICATORS IN THIS CHAPTER

LEARNING INTENTIONS

At the end of this chapter, I will

1. Understand what it means to be a moral person.

2. Understand and discuss the stages of moral growth.

3. Understand the word 'conscience' and be able to discuss what an 'informed conscience' is.

Growing in Morality

Remember what morality is from Chapter 22? It is knowing what is good behaviour and what is bad behaviour and making decisions based on this. We make choices all the time based on checking facts and looking to others for advice and guidance. We often ask a parent or older brother or sister to help us decide about a moral issue.

Moral growth is when people learn to understand the difference between right and wrong and then decide what is the right thing to do. We learn what is right and wrong from many sources. Our family, our friends, our religions, our school and the state can help us to decide what is right.

The process of moral growth is gradual. This means it happens slowly. When we are born, we have the basic ability to know the difference between right and wrong. Over time, we learn from our own experiences and the guidance of others in our lives. Slowly we move from a process of moral immaturity to moral maturity.

THINK, PAIR, SHARE

Think about your own life. Have you been faced with a moral issue over the last few days, weeks or months?

Pair off with your neighbour and talk about the situations you may have found yourself in recently.

Share your story with the class.

Read the following story about **St Ignatius of Loyola**, who developed as a moral person over time.

St Ignatius of Loyola

Ignatius of Loyola was born into a wealthy family in Spain in 1491. When he was young he loved gambling and fighting. This continued until he was seriously injured in a battle with the French when he was thirty years old. During his convalescence he read some religious books that made him begin to question his life. Soon he began to feel at peace with himself.

When he had fully recovered he set out on a pilgrimage to the monastery at Montserrat, near Barcelona. During his stay there, he devoted himself to prayer, fasting and works of piety. Finally, he decided to devote his life to the service of God.

In his desire to serve God, he realised that he needed more education in philosophy and theology. As a result, he went back to school to learn Latin. After some time, he set up a group of priests called the Companions of Jesus and he began to call himself Ignatius.

In Rome the group was welcomed by the pope. Its members took vows of poverty, obedience and chastity and vowed to travel wherever they were needed. In 1622 Ignatius was canonised as a saint. The Jesuits, as they are called today, are involved in the education of young people all over the world.

WRITE THE ANSWERS   Enquiry

1   What is meant by 'moral growth'?

2   Who, do you think, is essential to our moral growth?

3   What sort of person was Ignatius at the start of his life?

4   What inspired him to change his ways?

5   Do you think that Ignatius grew as a person in the story? Explain your answer.

6   Find out more information on the work of the Jesuit order today.

Stages of Moral Growth

As with St Ignatius Loyola, all moral growth is gradual. As children we learn very quickly that something is either right or wrong. When we do something that is good, like putting our toys away, we are rewarded. As a reward, a child might receive a biscuit, have a story read to them or get to watch their favourite television programme.

When we do something bad, like hitting our brother or sister, we are punished. A child might be sent to the 'bold step' or the treat they were to receive might be taken from them. Children learn very quickly what happens because of good and bad behaviour. In the early days we learn a lot from our parents or guardians, as they are our primary educators. For children, rules are laid down by parents in the home and by the teacher in the school. Rules are obeyed because the parent or the teacher says so. The fact that we learn this as children influences our behaviour not only at the time, but also in later life.

Adolescence (Teenage Years)

As we move into adolescence we understand very clearly the difference between right and wrong. In many ways we have matured from the days of hitting a family member. We seek the approval of others: at school, at home and in our peer or friendship group. The peer group has a major significance in our life because its approval of what we do is fundamental to our wellbeing.

Most teenagers are anxious to fit in with their class group. They want to be the same as everyone else. When some people in the group has the latest smartphone, it is very important that the rest of the group have that phone. Often parents find it difficult to say no when their child comes home with news that everyone in the class is going on an expensive school trip in the coming months and their child will be left out if they cannot afford to let them go. Parents don't want their children to grow up too quickly, but they certainly don't want them singled out as being different from the rest of the group.

LITERACY LIBRARY

Fundamental:
Something that is very important to us.

The school and home have rules that we must obey too; if we don't obey these rules, we are punished. Staying out past our curfew often leads us into conflict with our parents because they don't know where we are. As adolescents we want to be trusted and we feel the need to assert our independence. This often spreads to the classroom, where an adolescent might daydream due to tiredness instead of doing classwork. Adolescents quickly learn what behaviour is correct and that throughout their lives rules and laws are an important influence on their behaviour.

THINK, PAIR, SHARE

Do you **think** that as a teenager you are led by what the group says or does?

In **pairs**, write down some examples of when you may have been led by others or a time when you went against the group and made your own decision.

Share your findings with the class.

Moral Maturity

Society expects people to grow morally as well as physically, emotionally and intellectually, but this does not always happen. Not everyone at thirty years of age is at the same stage of moral development as their neighbour of the same age. Sometimes a child of ten years may make a better moral decision than an adult might make. When you reach moral maturity, you move from selfishness to altruism. To be altruistic means that you think of others before yourself when deciding something.

Ireland is a country that is known for its generosity of heart and spirit. We care about other people in Ireland and abroad.

At Christmas we are reminded of those less fortunate than ourselves. The Capuchin Day Centre, which feeds many homeless and poor people, receives €450,000 annually from the government, but their running costs are €2.2 million. Without the kindness and generosity of ordinary people it would be impossible to keep this centre open. It provides 700 meals every day and over 1,500 food parcels each Wednesday to the homeless and poor of Dublin.

GROUP ACTIVITY   Reflection and Action

Organise for your class, year group or school to collect hamper items (for example, food that has a long shelf life, small toys and toiletries) for the men, women and children who visit the Capuchin Day Centre in Dublin's Bow Street.

Here is how you can do it:

1   Ask your school principal if this is something they would like the school to participate in.

2   If the principal agrees it is a good idea, ask him or her to contact parents or guardians for their support.

3   Make a list of what you would like to find in a hamper at Christmas.

4   Ask your principal and year heads if you can speak at year group assemblies about the Capuchin Day Centre and the work they do for the homeless and poor of Dublin.

5   Give a list of what you want in the hamper to all classes in the school and ask the captain or vice-captain of the class to help you organise for everyone to bring in something towards the hamper.

6   Wait and see what is collected and remind the students through the intercom system in the school, through the school website and school's social media, by texting parents from the school system and asking class captains and vice-captains to remind other students.

7   Phone the local bus company to see if they will help you to deliver the hampers.

8   Decide who from your class can go on the bus to deliver the hampers with your teacher, class tutor or year head.

9   Reflect on what you have achieved when the event is finished.

Moral maturity is very important for our society to work well. If we all stayed at the level of a small child whose behaviour is self-centred, there would be even more suffering in the world. People would want simply to satisfy their own needs and not care for anyone else.

Remember, a child's morality is often based on reward and punishment. If people continued at this level of moral maturity, they might be motivated by fear and choose to do wrong in situations where they felt that they could escape punishment. Equally, they might do wrong simply to gain the approval of others. People who are morally mature are aware of their responsibility to respect the rights of others and to think of the consequences of the decisions they make. They are less influenced by factors outside themselves.

A morally mature person would never steal anything from anyone. This is not because they are afraid of the consequences. It is because they believe that stealing is wrong and that it affects the victim too much. Credit card fraud happens a lot in Ireland and in other countries. This really affects the person who owns the credit card and the bank also. Today people need to be very careful how they use their cards online, in shops and at bank machines.

Moral Immaturity

By contrast, a morally immature person's behaviour is expressed by their desire for reward or the need for approval from society. They are affected by influences outside themselves. They obey rules because they have been told to do so. They know that if rules are obeyed, people will be happy and no punishment will be given.

Read the story below and imagine you are one of the characters in it. What would you do in this situation? Think about this question as you read the story.

The Crash

One December night, John and Patrick made plans to meet a group of friends in the park. At fifteen years old they were too young to go to the local pub, so the off-licence and park was their best alternative. It was raining, and John had been debating whether to go out at all. But with his parents at home watching television, he knew that the park was a better option. On his way out, he told his parents that he was going over to Patrick's house and would be back by 11pm. His parents liked Patrick, so they happily waved their son off.

The friends met in the park at about eight o'clock. Earlier they had sent one of the older lads into the off-licence, as he never had a problem being served. Fewer people showed up in the park that night because of the rain, so there was more drink to go around.

Very quickly Patrick got drunk and decided that he was going for a drive in a car parked at the entrance to the park. Though he had hotwired a car once before, he had never gone joyriding. At first John tried to persuade Patrick not to go joyriding as he had had too much to drink, he was under-age and he might be caught. Earlier John had heard his dad telling his sister about all the Garda checkpoints he had seen the previous night on his way home, but still Patrick could not be persuaded not to do it. As he felt sober, John decided to go with Patrick so that he could watch out for anything that might happen.

The two set off in the car and Patrick began to accelerate more and more. John asked him to slow down and to pull over. However, Patrick would not listen. He just went faster and faster, going around corners at high speed. By now John was very scared and nervous. Minutes passed and suddenly there was an eerie silence in the car. Then a thud. What had he hit? Both boys looked at each other as Patrick stopped the car. Nervously John got out first. In front of him a woman was lying very still on the road. John shouted at Patrick to get out of the car. Slowly Patrick got out and people began to gather around. All he wanted to do was run away, but he knew that it was too late as people would recognise him.

THINK, PAIR, SHARE

In **pairs**, **think** about the following questions:

1 In your opinion, did John try hard enough to prevent Patrick from driving the car? Explain your answer.
2 Why, do you think, did Patrick want to flee the scene?
3 Do you think that both boys should be punished equally?
4 What do you think happened when the Gardaí came?
5 How morally mature was John in relation to Patrick?
6 Do you think that an incident like this might lead someone to moral maturity? Explain your answer.

Share your findings with the rest of the class.

K W L : Conscience

When you've read and discussed the text above, fill in the KWL template below in your copybook.

K What do you understand and **know** about the word 'conscience'?	W What do you **want** to find out about the word 'conscience'?	L When you are finished learning about conscience, what new thing have you **learned**?

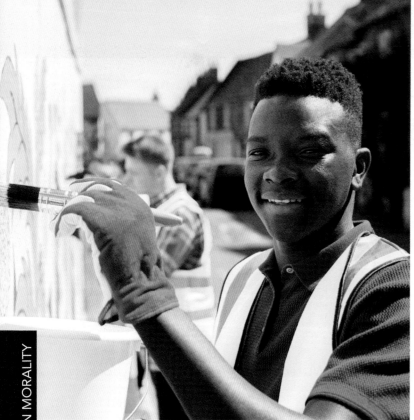

Conscience

The word **conscience** is derived from the Latin word 'to know'. Many people describe their conscience as their inner voice telling them what to do in a situation in which they find themselves. Others say 'always let your conscience be your guide', thus giving them inner peace.

One must be careful with this theory of the inner voice, as it might tell us to do something wrong, e.g. 'If he wants to spread rumours about me, I will spread rumours about him!' Conscience, therefore, needs to be more than just a voice inside us.

Having a conscience sets us apart from the animal world. Animals act by instinct, but human beings think through what the best way to behave is. Our conscience tells us what the right or wrong thing is to do.

The Catechism of the Catholic Church teaches people that conscience is a law that they must obey because it is written on their hearts by God. From this Catholics are encouraged to show love to others and to do good rather than evil. Conscience is our ability to know, using our judgement and knowledge, what is the right and wrong thing to do in a situation.

Having an informed conscience means having all the facts on the matter before a decision is made. There are different ways in which we can inform our conscience. We might decide to look to the experts and read up on the matter. We could try to talk to someone who has been in a similar situation.

A religious person would inform their conscience by reading their sacred text or by speaking to a leader from their religion. In this way they have tried to get all the information before they make their decision.

THINK, PAIR, SHARE

Think about an incident where you used your conscience when making a moral decision.

Pair with your neighbour.

Share your ideas with the rest of the class.

Decision Time

As the girls sat around eating their lunch and having a laugh, Eoghan, the captain of the hurling team, walked by. Jessica leaned closer to Chloe and Megan and whispered, 'Don't say anything to anyone, but I really like Eoghan. I'm going to ask him to be my friend on Instagram. If he ignores me, I'll be so embarrassed.' Chloe and Megan were surprised. They had no idea that Jessica liked Eoghan, but they promised not to say a word.

Later that evening Chloe was on the phone to Rebecca, another girl in their class. As they were chatting, Chloe let it slip about Jessica liking Eoghan. 'But don't tell her I told you. She'd kill me,' Chloe said.

The next day in the canteen Jessica and Chloe were on their own, as Megan was at home sick. Eoghan and his friends were sitting nearby. A group of girls walked by and one of them called loudly, 'Why aren't you sitting with Eoghan, Jessica?' Another one laughed, 'Sure they're a perfect match, the captain of the camogie team and the hurling captain.'

Eoghan looked over at the girls, confused. Jessica bent her head as her cheeks turned red with embarrassment. 'I'll kill Megan!' she muttered. 'She must have told someone. How could she do that to me?' Chloe just nodded. She and Jessica had been friends for years. They'd known Megan only since first year. Jessica just presumed that it was Megan and not Chloe who had let her secret out. Chloe was afraid to tell Jessica the truth.

As the day went on Chloe felt as if she had the weight of the world on her shoulders. A nagging voice in her head kept telling her that she'd have to come clean. It wasn't fair on Megan. She'd have to tell Jessica the truth, clear her conscience and face the music.

WRITE THE ANSWERS Enquiry

1 What does the word 'conscience' mean to you?

2 What do you think of the saying 'always let your conscience be your guide'?

Truth is an important value for most people. Everyone would like the relationships they have with others, such as family and friends, to be based on truth. People can rely or depend on those who tell the truth.

When someone lies it may get them out of a difficult situation, but it can also encourage them to repeat the behaviour at another time. Therefore, dishonesty, or telling lies, becomes part of their character or personality.

Being honest is not always easy. People who have integrity or goodness in them stick to their moral principles. They know the clear difference between right and wrong no matter what the cost is to themselves. They choose honesty even if it is not the easiest choice.

In the story 'Decision Time' it was important for Chloe to tell Jessica that it was she who told Rebecca the secret and not Megan. She felt guilty for letting her friend believe it was someone else. Truth is very important as people respect you for telling the truth.

CLASS DISCUSSION Reflection and Action

1 Do you think being truthful is an important value to have? Write down your answer in your copybook.
2 What have you learned about always being truthful to yourself and others?
3 Discuss the importance of truth with your class group.

REFLECTIVE ACTIVITY

Think about your own attitude choosing between right and wrong and answer the following questions:

1 What did you like learning about in this chapter?
2 Do you think it is important to think about things before making an important decision? Why/why not?
3 Do you think moral maturity/immaturity is related to age?

HONESTY IS THE FIRST CHAPTER IN THE BOOK OF WISDOM

---

25 GROWING IN MORALITY

PowerPoint summary

CHAPTER 26
Moral Issues

SOL: 5, 6, 7
LO: 1.1, 1.3, 3.2, 3.6

LEARNING OUTCOME

Debate a moral issue that arises in the lives of young people and consider what influences two different viewpoints on the issue.

KEY SKILLS YOU WILL USE IN THIS CHAPTER

- Working with others
- Managing information and thinking
- Being literate
- Managing myself

WELLBEING INDICATORS IN THIS CHAPTER

LEARNING INTENTIONS

At the end of this chapter, I will

1 Have explored the kinds of moral issues that affect people at different stages of their lives.

2 Have reflected on what influences people's viewpoints on a moral issue.

Moral Issues

At different stages of our lives we can be confronted with moral issues. Moral issues are actions that have the potential to help or harm others or ourselves.

As a child the moral issues we face tend to be easier to solve and are often decided for us by others, such as our parents. However, as we grow older the moral issues that arise for people are usually more complex and because we are older we need to make moral decisions for ourselves. Making moral decisions in our modern world can be confusing and difficult. At the adolescent, or teenage, stage of life there can be many temptations and influences pulling us in all directions.

LITERACY LIBRARY

Confront:
Face up to or deal with a problem or difficulty.

Potential:
Possible or capable of becoming something.

Relevant:
Something that is important or significant to a person.

THINK, PAIR, SHARE

Look at the following examples of moral issues.

In **pairs**, discuss whether you **think** they are moral issues that affect people as children, teenagers or adults. Some of them may be relevant to people at all three stages of life.

Share your answers with the rest of the class.

1 Gambling
2 Bullying
3 Abortion
4 Illegal drug use
5 Lying

6 Racism
7 Mistreating animals
8 Violence towards another person
9 Driving while using a mobile phone
10 Stealing

Different Viewpoints

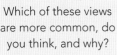

Which of these views are more common, do you think, and why?

While we might have similar moral beliefs and values to those around us, such as our family and friends, how we view moral issues or what choices we make about them are down to us as individuals.

In order to fully understand a moral issue, it is important to look at it from different viewpoints. Very few moral issues are simply black or white, right or wrong. How we view a moral issue can be influenced by many different things – those around us, what we have learned from our family, what our religion says, what kind of society we live in and our own personal experiences.

For example, take a moral issue like racism. A person may be influenced by different viewpoints on the issue. Look at the following two teenagers' views on the issue.

DAVID – AGED 15

I'm not a racist person, but I do think that people from a different race than me are just different. My brother was on his way home from school and was attacked by two guys and they were both from a different race. Most people where I live are from the same race as me and there are no problems. Maybe people should just live and go to school with people from their own race. That way everyone would be happier. My dad thinks it would stop a lot of fighting in the world and I think he might be right.

BRIAN – AGED 14

I have no problem with people from a different race. My sister's boyfriend is not the same race as our family and it's no big deal. I actually find it interesting hearing about the culture he came from. In my school there are kids from over twenty different races. We had a cultural diversity week in school last year and we got to try foods from all around the world and hear stories from students in our classes about things that are unique to their race. My family has travelled a lot so I've seen how lots of different races live and to be honest, I think people have more in common than they realise.

WRITE THE ANSWERS

Enquiry

1 Write down the differences between David's and Brian's views on racism.

2 What influenced their different viewpoints?

GROUP ACTIVITY: WALKING DEBATE   Enquiry

Make three different areas in your classroom. One area is called 'I strongly agree', another is called 'I strongly disagree' and the other one is called 'I'm not sure'.

Your teacher will call out some statements on moral issues. After each statement you must go to one of the different areas depending on how you view the issue:

- Do you strongly agree with it?
- Do you strongly disagree with it?
- Are you unsure?

Listen to people's reasons for why they have chosen a particular area. Remember, it is important to be respectful of everyone's opinion, even if it is different from your own.

As you listen, think about what may have influenced people's viewpoints on the issues. After hearing viewpoints on each statement, check if anyone wants to change the area they are standing in.

Statement 1: If a person takes drugs and becomes addicted to them, then it is their own fault.

Statement 2: It is OK to use a fake ID to get into an over-16s disco.

Statement 3: If someone is convicted of murder, they should receive the death penalty.

Statement 4: I would buy fake designer goods that have been made in a developing country.

Statement 5: People who don't recycle their waste properly should be fined.

Which of these statements do you feel most strongly about and why?

Read the following story about the moral issue of cheating in an exam.

LITERACY
LIBRARY

Qualified:
Officially trained to
perform a job.

The Test

Edel felt sick as she walked into school that morning. Everyone
knew the Leaving Cert was the biggest exam of your life. She had
her heart set on a college course that would lead her to becoming
a nurse. She felt the rest of the exams had gone fairly well, but
she wasn't sure if she had done well enough to get the points she
needed. Today was Biology, though. She had to get a good grade
on this paper if she wanted her place on that course.

She had worked so hard at her studies, but Biology was a subject
she struggled with. Everyone said she would make a great nurse
and it was the only career she could imagine herself having. She
didn't want to let her parents down after all the money they had
spent on getting her extra grinds in Biology to help her.

Her mam had told her not to worry, that if she didn't get the
grade she needed, she could always do her second choice course.
She could still be a nurse, but it would take her an extra year to be
qualified and the college was miles away, where she'd
know no one.

Edel sighed as she took a last glance over her
Biology notes before heading into the exam hall.
She tried to be positive: she had worked hard,
she deserved this.

With half an hour left in the exam, Edel looked over what she had written. She thought she'd done enough to get the grade she needed. The first few sections of the exam had gone OK, but the last section had thrown her. The question had asked her to draw a diagram, but she just couldn't remember how it was supposed to look. She glanced over at her friend Ciara, who was still scribbling away furiously. At that moment, one of Ciara's sheets of paper fell to the floor. Ciara was so busy writing she didn't even notice. Edel could clearly see it was the diagram she couldn't remember. She looked around and saw the exam superintendent was at the back of the room and hadn't noticed either.

Edel felt torn in two. All she had to do was look down and see what Ciara had written. Ciara was brilliant at Biology, so Edel knew her diagram would be right. It was risky, though. What if the examiner saw her? She might think Ciara had dropped her sheet on purpose to help Edel. If she was caught, what would her parents say? She remembered the lecture they had been given at the start of the exams. They'd been warned about what could happen if they broke the rules. She knew it could mean her whole exam being cancelled. She thought about how much she wanted a place on that nursing course, though. The question was worth fifty marks and could be the difference between getting the grade she needed or not. She wouldn't be hurting anyone if she copied Ciara's diagram and got away with it. No one would ever know. Ciara didn't even need a good grade in Biology for her course in law. It was so unfair.

Edel looked down at the page on the ground. She began to copy what she saw written there onto her own sheet of paper. As she was drawing the diagram, Ciara looked over at her, then down at the ground and saw exactly what Edel was doing.

Edel felt so guilty as she saw a look of hurt confusion on Ciara's face. Just then the examiner turned and started walking towards where the two girls were sitting.

WRITE THE ANSWERS   Enquiry

1 Explain why the biology exam was so important to Edel.

2 What evidence is there in the story to show that Edel deserved to do well in the exam?

3 What would influence Edel to decide to copy the diagram?

4 What possible consequences could there be, for Edel and for others, if Edel is caught copying Ciara's work? Are there both positive and negative consequences?

5 'Edel felt so guilty as she saw a look of hurt confusion on Ciara's face.' How do you think Ciara felt when she saw what Edel was doing?

6 What advice would you give to Edel about what she should do in this situation? Why would you give her this advice?

Debating an Issue

Debating an issue or topic allows us to consider the world around us by thinking about different arguments for or against an issue and engaging with views that might be different from our own.

In a formal debate, two teams are given a statement, or motion, relating to an idea or opinion. People who are arguing for or to support the motion are called the proposers. Those who argue against or disagree with the motion are called opposors.

Each team plans what they are going to say in advance of the debate. In order to do this, they think carefully about both sides of the motion and they do research to find out as much information as they can about the issue.

Preparing for Your Debate

As a class you are going to debate a moral issue that can arise in the life of an adolescent and you will consider what influences different viewpoints on the issue. In order to think about all the possible influences on the motion, you should consider it under the following headings:

1 What does the law say about the issue?
2 What would your parents have to say on the matter?
3 What would your peers/friends think?
4 Are there any school rules around the issue?
5 Are there any religious teachings on the issue?
6 Has this issue been spoken about in the media?
7 Is there any scientific research on the issue?
8 Does anyone have any personal experiences with that issue that they are willing to share?

The moral issue you will be debating is:

'People should have unlimited access to the internet and be free to say whatever they want to on social media.'

Split the class into two groups and decide which side will propose the motion and which side will oppose it. In smaller groups, look at the issue under the headings given on the previous page. Prepare a short speech about the issue under your heading and decide who will deliver this speech to the class on behalf of the group.

When you are ready, allow each group to share their speeches with the class. When everyone has spoken, open the motion to the floor. This means individuals can raise their hand and ask a question of the other team. Remember the following key rules:

1 Only one voice at a time.
2 Everyone should be given a chance to speak if they wish.
3 People should be respectful and open to others' ideas.
4 No one is allowed to make any personal remarks to or about anyone else.

After the Debate

Write a piece in your copybook about your experience of the debate. You should include the following:

1 Explain your role in the debate.
2 Explain the key points made by your team.
3 What points did the other team make that you thought were good?
4 What, do you think, were the two biggest/most important influences on people's viewpoints on the issue: was it the law, religious teaching, family rules, peers, school rules or something else?
5 After listening to the debate, did your opinion change or become stronger on the issue?

 PowerPoint summary

 Weblinks

WRITE THE ANSWERS
Enquiry

Pick one of the following debate motions on moral issues and write a speech for or against the motion. Use the same preparation method you used for the class debate.

1 Animal testing should be allowed if it helps to create medicines that could save people's lives.
2 The legal age for drinking alcohol should be reduced to fifteen years old in Ireland.
3 People should not be allowed to wear religious clothing in public places.

REFLECTIVE ACTIVITY

Think about your own attitude to moral issues that arise in the lives of teenagers and answer the following questions:

1 How, do you think, does having a debate about a moral issue help people to decide what they think is morally right or wrong?
2 Do you think there are any moral issues affecting teenagers today that have not been mentioned in this chapter?

CHAPTER 27
Justice, Peace and Reconciliation in Today's World

SOL: 6, 7
LO: 1.1, 1.11, 3.7

LEARNING OUTCOME

Research the understanding of compassion, justice, peace and reconciliation found in two major world religions and ways in which these understandings can be seen in action in our world today.

KEY SKILLS YOU WILL USE IN THIS CHAPTER

- Working with others
- Managing information and thinking
- Being creative
- Communicating

WELLBEING INDICATORS IN THIS CHAPTER

LEARNING INTENTIONS

At the end of this chapter, I will

1 Have an understanding of what 'compassion' means and see it in action in the Buddhist and Christian faiths

2 Have an understanding of what 'justice' means and see it in action in the Christian and Jewish faiths

3 Have an understanding of what 'peace and reconciliation' means and see it in action in the Christian and Islamic faiths.

GROUP ACTIVITY   Exploration

Split into groups of four.

The teacher will hand out six sheets of A3 paper.

Write the word 'compassion' on two pieces of paper, 'justice' on two and 'peace and reconciliation' on two.

Each person writes down in their own section of their group's sheet what they think the word on their placemat means. You can write a few different words or sentences.

Share your ideas and agree on a common understanding of your word. Write this in the centre square.

Hang the sheets on the walls and discuss them as a class.

LITERACY LIBRARY

Motivate:
To give someone a reason for doing something.

Altruistic:
Showing concern for the welfare of other people rather than yourself.

Compassion

To have compassion for someone or something means to understand another person's pain or suffering and to try to do something to ease it. You don't just pity the person who is suffering or their situation; you actively try to improve things for them. When you have compassion you are motivated to go out of your way to ease another's pain, whether that pain is physical or emotional.

Some of the qualities of compassion are patience, kindness and warmth. People who have compassion are sometimes described as being altruistic. When we show compassion, we connect with another person.

GROUP ACTIVITY   Exploration

Split into groups of four or five.

For each of the following situations, explain how a person might show compassion – what would a person of compassion say or do?

Situation 1: You are walking home from school and you see another student being bullied by a group of people from your school. The group run away and the person is left crying.

Situation 2: The week before Christmas a house in your community goes on fire. The family's home and possessions are destroyed. They are new in the area, having moved from another country, and don't know anyone.

Situation 3: You are out with your friends playing in a field that has a small stream running beside it. You hear a noise coming from the side of the stream and discover that three kittens have been dumped in a bag and left to die.

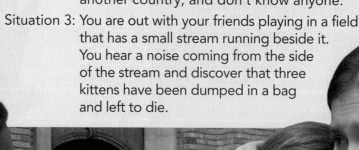

Buddhism and Compassion

01

The Dalai Lama

The Dalai Lama is a title given to spiritual leaders in Buddhism. The fourteenth and current Dalai Lama is Tenzin Gyatso. He is one of the most recognised and respected moral voices in the world today.

He once said, 'If you want others to be happy, practise compassion. If you want to be happy, practise compassion.' Buddhists believe in Four Noble Truths, the first of which is the truth of suffering, or dukkha. They believe all humans experience this throughout their lives. For Buddhists, the way to respond to this is through compassion. The goal of the Buddha, the founder of Buddhism, was to try to relieve the suffering of all living beings everywhere.

LITERACY LIBRARY

Dignity:
Being worthy of honour and respect.

RESEARCH

Use the internet to find more information about the Tzu Chi Foundation.

Design a class poster to showcase your findings.

BUDDHIST COMPASSION IN ACTION

The Tzu Chi Foundation is the world's largest Buddhist charity. It is based in Taiwan and was founded by a female monk in 1966. Tzu Chi translates as 'compassion and relief'. The organisation has thousands of volunteer staff. The idea behind it is based in compassion. It calls on Buddhists to actively engage in improving society. The volunteers work all over the world in many different ways. They distributed emergency supplies in New Orleans after Hurricane Katrina and brought aid to war-torn countries such as Afghanistan.

The foundation aims to maintain the dignity of victims of natural disasters. As well as emergency food aid, the group provides fertiliser and seed to get fresh crops planted. Tzu Chi also built thirteen new schools in China after the old ones were destroyed by an earthquake. The inspiration for their work comes from the Buddhist understanding of using compassion to help those who are suffering.

Members of the Buddhist Tzu Chi Foundation prepare decorations for their annual celebration in Taipei.

JUSTICE, PEACE AND RECONCILIATION IN TODAY'S WORLD **27**

Christianity and Compassion

In the Christian Bible, God is spoken of as the 'Father of compassion'. 2 Corinthians 1:3–7 says, 'Praise be to the God and Father of our Lord Jesus Christ, the Father of compassion and the God of all comfort, who comforts us in all our troubles, so that we can comfort those in any trouble with the comfort we ourselves received from God. For just as the sufferings of Christ flow over into our lives, so also through Christ our comfort overflows.'

For Christians, Jesus Christ lived a life of compassion when he was on earth. He challenged his followers to act compassionately towards others, particularly those in need or distress. Most importantly, he showed compassion to those who society had condemned, such as tax collectors.

CHRISTIAN COMPASSION IN ACTION

Coláiste Choilm in Tullamore, Co. Offaly has been running their India Immersion Project since 2000. Every few years a group of approximately twelve students and two teachers travel to Mumbai in India for two weeks. The roots of the project are founded in the Christian call to show compassion to others. There is a huge amount of preparation involved before the trip and the students give up their free time to do it.

While in Mumbai they work at a shelter for boys called the Don Bosco Shelter. Here they help the boys with their schoolwork and spend time getting to know them. Many of the boys in the shelter don't have parents and most come from great poverty.

Another place the students of Coláiste Choilm go to is a centre called Ashadaan, which was founded by Mother Teresa. This is a place where people who are poor, sick and dying are taken in from the streets of Mumbai to be cared for.

The Irish students show great compassion to the residents of Ashadaan by helping to care for them and spending time with them. They also give a donation of money to the centre from the fundraising they do before the trip.

LITERACY LIBRARY

Condemn:

To completely disapprove of. To say very strongly that something is bad.

Would you like to take part in a trip like the India Immersion Project and if so, why?

WRITE THE ANSWER   Enquiry

Write about how the students of Coláiste Choilm show the Christian understanding of compassion in action.

01 **RESEARCH**   Exploration

Break into groups and do some research to produce a project on either the Don Bosco Shelter or the Ashadaan Centre in Mumbai.

Justice

Justice is all about fairness and equality. It is about making sure that qualities like honesty and righteousness are enjoyed by all people. Justice cares about people's rights and righting wrongs when those rights are violated. It wants everyone to have access to the same opportunities and resources.

Over the course of history there have been many examples of injustices happening around the world. Thankfully, individuals and groups have worked for justice to be restored and to improve the lives of others.

LITERACY LIBRARY

Violate:
To show no respect for people, laws or agreements.

Injustice:
A lack of fairness and equality.

Essential:
Something that is extremely important and needed.

CLASS DISCUSSION   Reflection and Action

Can you think of any events you have heard about happening around the world where people have suffered from injustice?

Christianity and Justice

The Bible teaches that God is a God of justice. Deuteronomy 32:4 says, 'All his ways are justice.' Throughout the Bible there are stories and teachings that show that concern and care for those who experience injustice is essential. In the Old Testament the nation of Israel was commanded by God to care for society's less fortunate.

The model of such behaviour is Jesus himself, who reflected God's sense of justice by bringing the Gospel message to even the outcasts of society. The Christian understanding of justice is that followers should speak up for those who are suffering from injustice. It is looking at what's wrong in society and figuring out how to make it right.

CHRISTIAN JUSTICE IN ACTION

In Loreto schools all over Ireland, groups of students give up their free time to work for justice. JPIC stands for Justice, Peace and the Integrity of Creation. Laura, a student from Loreto College, St Stephen's Green in Dublin, tells us about her experience of being part of this group.

LITERACY LIBRARY

Ethos:
The spirit or set of beliefs of an organisation, culture or community.

I joined the JPIC group in the school as I have always been aware of social justice and I wanted to act on this. Since I was in first year the JPIC group has always been very active in school promoting justice and highlighting inequalities. We have a JPIC notice board in our school and I remember the quote they had on it from Ghandi: 'Be the change you want to see in the world.' This really motivated me to join. Why give out about inequalities when we are in a position to make a difference, no matter how small it is?

When I joined the group, which is only for senior students, I realised that the vision of the group comes from the Loreto ethos and Mary Ward, the founder of the order. It is rooted in the Gospel message: justice, peace and integrity of creation. Every Loreto school has a JPIC group. Students research issues relating to the concepts and vision of JPIC in our world today. The aim of the group is to raise awareness of these topics among students, staff and the wider community.

We are very active in highlighting our cause in the school through poster campaigns, having events outside the school to raise awareness to the general public and by organising activities in the school, such as fair-trade quizzes, teacher–student debates and a human rights week. We also attend various human rights events in the city, such as the World Peace Conference.

It is not enough to read or simply talk about justice in our world. It is important that we are all agents of social change. We can help make a difference.

RESEARCH   Exploration

Go to the Loreto Schools Network Ireland and look up information on JPIC groups in Loreto schools around the world.

Break into groups and design a PowerPoint presentation on some of the different activities you find out about to present to the rest of the school.

Judaism and Justice

Like Christianity, Judaism teaches that God wants humans to pursue justice. It is a theme that is found throughout the Hebrew Bible. Ancient rabbis have said that the Torah begins and ends with justice. Deuteronomy 16:20 states, 'Justice, justice you shall pursue.' Judaism believes that justice is to be found when people act in accordance with God's laws and imitate God's vision of justice. Jews believe they have a responsibility to strive for justice as it is their duty as followers of God. Their starting point for justice is found in the commandment to 'love your neighbour as yourself' (Leviticus 9:18). Acts of loving kindness and respect for others are central to the Jewish understanding of justice.

JEWISH JUSTICE IN ACTION

The World Jewish Relief Organisation (WJR) is inspired by Jewish values. It helps people in poverty to live with dignity and hope. They support the world's poorest Jewish communities, especially those in Eastern Europe.

They have a very interesting history, as they helped Jewish children to escape to safety during World War II. Their vision for their work comes from the belief that all Jews are responsible for one another. They also work beyond the Jewish community, inspired by the Jewish values of caring for the stranger and recognising the dignity and potential of all people.

Young Orthodox Jews at the Western Wall, Israel.

Read the following article about some of their work.

WORLD JEWISH RELIEF RESPONDS TO INDONESIAN TSUNAMI

In September 2018, a powerful earthquake and tsunami hit the island of Sulawesi in Indonesia. Aftershocks from the earthquake continued to wreak devastation on the area, with buildings collapsing and homes washing away. Subsequent mudflows added to the death rate and created serious difficulties for search and rescue missions.

After the earthquake and tsunami, more than 2,000 people were confirmed dead. Over 10,000 were injured, almost half of them seriously. More than 1,300 people are still missing. More than 70,000 houses were reported to be damaged, causing tens of thousands of people to become displaced. Many residential areas were completely wiped out by the tsunami.

World Jewish Relief joined up with a trusted local partner in Indonesia to organise emergency relief for the area. Their aim was to provide shelter kits containing blankets, mattresses, flashlights and basic tools. For the many displaced and now homeless people, emergency supplies such as nappies, clothes, sanitary products and underwear were also urgently required.

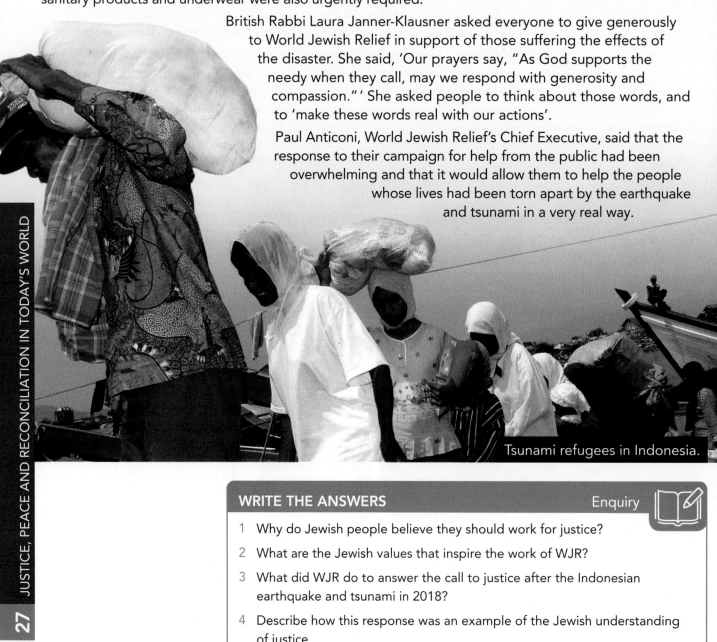

British Rabbi Laura Janner-Klausner asked everyone to give generously to World Jewish Relief in support of those suffering the effects of the disaster. She said, 'Our prayers say, "As God supports the needy when they call, may we respond with generosity and compassion."' She asked people to think about those words, and to 'make these words real with our actions'.

Paul Anticoni, World Jewish Relief's Chief Executive, said that the response to their campaign for help from the public had been overwhelming and that it would allow them to help the people whose lives had been torn apart by the earthquake and tsunami in a very real way.

Tsunami refugees in Indonesia.

WRITE THE ANSWERS   Enquiry

1 Why do Jewish people believe they should work for justice?

2 What are the Jewish values that inspire the work of WJR?

3 What did WJR do to answer the call to justice after the Indonesian earthquake and tsunami in 2018?

4 Describe how this response was an example of the Jewish understanding of justice.

Peace and Reconciliation

Peace means to be free from conflict, such as war, and freedom from fear of violence. Reconciliation is when people are brought back together again after a disagreement or after a person has been hurt by someone else. It repairs the relationship between them.

Peace and reconciliation go hand in hand and are essential for people to be able to live together in harmony. One of the most famous organisations that works to promote peace and reconciliation is the United Nations (UN), which was founded in 1945 after World War II. The UN sends peacekeepers to regions that are recovering from war. It provides a platform for dialogue between countries that are in conflict with each other. In order for peace and reconciliation to happen, there must be respect and acceptance of the differences between people.

Christianity and Peace and Reconciliation

Christians view peace in two ways. First there is the common understanding of peace that has been spoken about above. But there is also a deeper meaning of peace for followers of Christianity: 'Let the peace of Christ rule in your hearts' (Colossians 3:15). This type of peace happens when Christians open their hearts and minds to the teachings of Jesus and as a result feel safe and at peace within themselves.

One of the most well-known Christian prayers about peace comes from St Francis of Assisi.

Lord, make me an instrument of Thy peace;
Where there is hatred, let me sow love;
Where there is injury, pardon;
Where there is doubt, faith;
Where there is despair, hope;
Where there is darkness, light;
And where there is sadness, joy.
O Divine Master,

Grant that I may not so much seek to be consoled as to console;
To be understood, as to understand;
To be loved, as to love;
For it is in giving that we receive,
It is in pardoning that we are pardoned,
And it is in dying that we are born to eternal life.
Amen.

GROUP ACTIVITY   Reflection and Action

Split into groups.

Rewrite the prayer of St Francis of Assisi in your own words to explain it more clearly.

The first two sentences are done below as an example for you. When you are finished, write your prayer on a sheet of paper and stick them up around the classroom for the other groups to look at.

Example:

Lord, help me to be a person who brings your peace to others;

In places or situations where I see hate, help me to show what love means.

LITERACY LIBRARY

Tolerate:
To allow or agree to something even if you don't like it.

Sacrament:
A religious ceremony that gives believers a special blessing or grace.

Residential:
A place suitable to live in.

Chaplain:
A Christian official who is responsible for the religious needs of an organisation.

Sectarian:
Hatred of someone because of their religious beliefs.

For Christians, reconciliation is much more than the simple process of forgiving and forgetting. True reconciliation in Christianity is achieved not just by tolerating those who may have caused hurt, but by actively embracing them in love and welcoming them back into your life.

Reconciliation is the fixing of relationships. Christians are told that they cannot expect forgiveness from God unless they are willing to forgive others who may have done them wrong. One of the biggest Christian Churches, Catholicism, sees reconciliation as so important that it is one of its seven sacraments. The sacrament of reconciliation involves the believer confessing their sins to God through a priest. They say sorry for their sins, ask for forgiveness from God and promise to try not to sin again.

Christian Peace and Reconciliation in Action

CORRYMEELA

Corrymeela is Northern Ireland's oldest peace and reconciliation organisation. They run a residential centre in Ballycastle and the group is made up of full-time workers and volunteers.

Its founder, Ray Davey, was a chaplain at Queen's University in Belfast. He saw the sectarian tensions that existed in Northern Ireland in the 1960s and wanted to do something about it. He himself had been held in a prisoner of war camp during World War II and saw the damage that conflict can do. Ray and some of his students raised the money to buy a site to build an 'open village where all people of goodwill' could come together and learn to live in community.

The idea behind Corrymeela is to bring people together from different backgrounds – political, religious and social. You can read their statement of commitment below, which they say publically together once a year to remind them what their vision is.

As a community of Christians drawn from many traditions, we:

AFFIRM our faith in the reconciling power of God in Jesus Christ;

CELEBRATE the promise of life;

CONFESS our own responsibility for the destructive conflicts in our society;

BELIEVE that we have been called to seek a deeper understanding of our faith;

SURRENDER ourselves to the spirit of Jesus to overcome our own divisions and make ourselves instruments of His peace;

COMMIT ourselves to work for a society whose priorities are justice, mutual respect, the participation of all, concern for the vulnerable and the stranger, stewardship of resources and care for creation;

AGREE to pray regularly for each other, to join in the worship of the community, to give time to the life and work of the community, to care for and support each other, to live out our commitment in our daily lives, to give, according to our ability, to the funds of the community;

AND WISH through the power of the Spirit, to walk the way of the Gospel together.

RESEARCH   Exploration

Find the Corrymeela website and search for the video that tells their story.

Write a piece in your copybook explaining what you learned about Corrymeela from watching the video.

Say why you think Corrymeela is a good example of Christian peace and reconciliation in action.

JUSTICE, PEACE AND RECONCILIATION IN TODAY'S WORLD

27

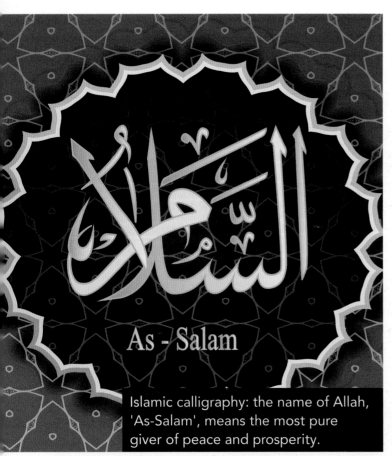

Islamic calligraphy: the name of Allah, 'As-Salam', means the most pure giver of peace and prosperity.

Islam and Peace and Reconciliation

The word 'Islam' has its roots in the word 'salam', which literally means 'peace'. One of the ninety-nine names given to Allah, the God of Islam, is Peace. Muslims believe that their prophets brought one main message to the people: to submit to one God and to work for peace.

Islam calls on its people to live in peace with God, within themselves, with others and with the environment around them. The Islamic term for reconciliation is sulh. According to Islamic law, the purpose of sulh is to end conflict and hostility among Muslims so that they can live in peace and harmony.

Allah said, 'The believers are but brethren, therefore make peace between your brethren and be careful of your duty to Allah that mercy may be had on you.' The prophet Muhammad said, 'Anyone who goes to make peace between two persons, the angels of Allah send blessings upon him until he returns and he will be given the reward of the Night of Destiny.' Therefore, we can see that peace and reconciliation is an important part of the Islamic religion.

ISLAMIC PEACE AND RECONCILIATION IN ACTION

IMPIC stands for Irish Muslim Peace and Integration Council. Their motto is 'Bridging Communities, Building Peace'. Muslims from all over Ireland are invited to join the group and they work to help Muslims integrate into the Irish community. They also try to promote the true teachings of Islam, which are based in peace and love. They encourage members to show respect and tolerance for all people, regardless of their beliefs or backgrounds, and they condemn anyone who uses violence in the name of Islam.

Their work has become even more important since some extremist Muslims have begun to use terrorism around the world. IMPIC strongly rejects any form of terrorism and are anti-extremism.

The group believes in interfaith and intrafaith dialogue. It was founded by Shaykh Dr Umar Al-Qadri, an Islamic scholar who started the Islamic Centre in Blanchardstown in Dublin. This is not related to the Islamic Cultural Centre of Ireland in Clonskeagh, Dublin, which is the largest Islamic Centre in Ireland. Shaykh Dr Umar Al-Qadri believes it is his responsibility as a Muslim to contribute to a peaceful society and to fight against extremism. To do this he works closely with Irish government organisations and gives talks in mosques and universities.

LITERACY LIBRARY

Prophet:
A messenger of God.

Hostility:
Anger and hatred.

Integrate:
To mix with and join a society.

Scholar:
A highly educated person in a particular branch of study.

PowerPoint summary

Weblinks

One very positive thing that the IMPIC has done to promote peace and reconciliation between Muslim communities in Ireland and their neighbours is to hold community Iftars. This is when the mosques are opened during Ramadan and non-Muslims are invited in to join the Muslim community in an Iftar meal. The Iftar meal is the meal Muslims have to break their fast in Ramadan.

Read the following article, which talks about an important Iftar.

IRISH MUSLIMS CONDEMN RAMADAN TERRORIST ATTACKS
28 June 2015

The Islamic Centre of Ireland has condemned the terrorist attacks that took place in Tunisia, Kuwait and France on Friday.

Shaukh Al-Qadri, founder of the Irish Muslim Peace and Integration Council in Blanchardstown, said, 'Whilst some people are doing their best to improve relations between Muslims and non-Muslims, these awful events have taken place.'

'I condemn the attacks and it is the responsibility of every Muslim leader and scholar to condemn them. Terrorists are criminals, enemies of humanity, enemies of religion, enemies of morality and the enemies of human values.'

The comments were made as part of an Iftar – a fast-breaking meal held by Muslims during Ramadan. Guest of honour at the event was renowned peace campaigner and Holocaust survivor Tomi Reichental, who said that he was 'very touched' by the warm welcome extended to him by the Muslim community.

Also speaking at the event was Lynn Jackson from the Holocaust Education Trust Ireland, who spoke about the assistance given to Jewish people by Muslims in Paris during World War II.

They were joined by Rev. Eugene Griffin, a Christian priest, and Rev. Myozan Kodo, a Buddhist monk. More than 150 guests attended the Iftar.

Source: Adapted from TheJournal.ie

Holocaust survivor Tomi Reichental speaks to students in Gorey Community School, Co. Wexford.

1

ACTIVITY
Exploration

Prepare a two-minute speech that you would give about Islam and peace and reconciliation. You may use a PowerPoint presentation if you wish and include images.

REFLECTIVE ACTIVITY

Think about your own attitude to the understanding of compassion, justice, peace and reconciliation shown in different world religions and answer the following questions:

1 Have you ever been involved in an action that promotes compassion, justice or peace and reconciliation?

2 Can you see any similarities between the different religions' understandings of these concepts?

3 Which two examples of these concepts in action did you most enjoy reading about and why?

JUSTICE, PEACE AND RECONCILIATION IN TODAY'S WORLD

27

CHAPTER 28
Caring for the Earth

SOL: 6, 7, 8, 9
LO: 2.2, 2.3, 2.7, 3.8

LEARNING OUTCOME

Explain how a Christian understanding of caring for the earth promotes the wellbeing of all people and the planet and discuss its relevance in today's world.

KEY SKILLS YOU WILL USE IN THIS CHAPTER

- Working with others
- Managing information and thinking
- Communicating
- Being creative
- Being literate

WELLBEING INDICATORS IN THIS CHAPTER

LEARNING INTENTIONS

At the end of this chapter, I will

1 Understand what the term 'stewardship' means and explore how people can be stewards of the earth in different areas of their lives

2 Explore and understand what the Christian teaching on caring for the earth is

3 Be able to explain why Christians should care for the earth

4 Understand how caring for the earth and the wellbeing of people are linked

5 Explore how the Sustainable Development Goals promote care for the earth and wellbeing of people

6 Learn about the organisation A Rocha and its work to care for the earth.

'We do not inherit the earth from our ancestors; we borrow it from our children.'

Native American proverb

LITERACY LIBRARY

Inherit:
To receive something from a previous owner.

Ancestor:
A person related to you who lived a long time ago.

Nurture:
To care for and protect something or someone while they are growing.

Maintain:
To give something what it needs to keep going.

Dwellers:
People or animals that live in a particular place.

Resources:
A source of supply, support or aid that can be used when needed.

Generations:
All the people born and living at about the same time.

Principle:
A basic idea, rule or truth.

THINK, PAIR, SHARE

Write down what you **think** the Native American proverb to the left means and how it could influence the way we live our lives.

In **pairs**, discuss your answers.

Share your ideas with the rest of the class.

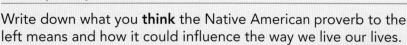

Caring for the Earth

Caring for the earth is something all humans are responsible for, whether we are religious or not. At times, we forget that the earth is a planet that is like a living, breathing being that needs to be looked after. Like a human, it needs to be nurtured and kept healthy for it to survive.

Think about it this way: if you built a house and simply walked away, leaving it empty, it would eventually begin to rot and crumble. The houses people live in must be maintained for them to be a safe place to live. The earth is like a huge house in which all the people of the world live. As dwellers of the earth, humans must make sure we tend to it and keep it safe for us to live in.

Stewardship

Being a steward means looking after and protecting all creation. It calls on us to be responsible for the decisions we make about how we use the earth and its resources, such as its water and wildlife. We must be aware that the choices we make about our environment will affect the generations coming after us. We must be caretakers of the earth and of each other.

All the major world religions have a similar religious moral vision when it comes to the earth. It could be said that this vision is based on the principle of stewardship.

GROUP ACTIVITY   Reflection and Action

Break into six groups and give each group a large sheet of paper with a placemat diagram on it.

- On two sheets write 'Care for the Earth at Home'.
- On another two sheets write 'Care for the Earth at School'.
- On the final two sheets write 'Care for the Earth in our Community'.

Each person should fill in their piece of the placemat with ways people can show care for the earth in the given place.

Discuss the ideas as a group.

Stick the sheets up around the room and let the other groups see the work each group has done.

Christian Understanding of Caring for the Earth

Do you think there is too much focus today on caring for the environment and not enough on caring for each other?

Psalm 24 begins with the words, 'The earth is the Lord's, and everything in it, the world, and all who live in it.' This sums up what Christians believe about caring for the earth. In the Book of Genesis, Christians are told that God created everything and put Adam and Eve in the Garden of Eden to work it and take care of it. Even Christians who don't take the Genesis story of creation literally can still believe the message behind it. They believe that God put humans on earth as stewards of creation.

It is important to understand that when Christians talk about caring for the earth, they don't simply mean looking after the animal and natural world. As Christians believe that God made humans too, Christianity also promotes the wellbeing of all people. Humans are part of God's creation, so looking after his creation means humans should look after each other too.

Why Should Christians Care for the Earth?

1 TO SHOW LOVE TO GOD

Christians believe that God made the world. The Book of Genesis tells them that God created human life to live side by side with the rest of his creations, so humans are seen as part of nature. After God created each thing he, 'saw that it was good'.

Throughout the Bible, Christians are reminded that God loves all his creations. Looking after these creations, which includes the earth and the humans living on it, is a way for Christians to show love to their God.

2 THE EARTH NEEDS CARE TO SURVIVE

In the Old Testament Moses was told that the Israelites were to farm the land for six years and in the seventh year, the land should be left to rest. The lesson to be learned from this is that people cannot constantly take away from God's creation. For his creation to be successful and continue to sustain us, people must be patient and wise with it. The earth must be given time and ways to rejuvenate and people must be careful how they use it.

LITERACY LIBRARY

Rejuvenate:
To breathe new life into something.

3 THE EARTH IS A GIFT THAT IS ON LOAN

Christians believe that creation belongs to its creator, God. They say we don't own the earth, but are allowed to enjoy the fruits of creation. In ancient kingdoms, stewards ran the country or land in the absence of the king. Christians believe they should be caretakers of the earth for God, like stewards were in ancient times. As the earth is the place where future generations will live, Christians believe they have a responsibility to their God to take care of his creation for those who will come after them.

4 CARING FOR THE EARTH SHOWS GOSPEL VALUES IN ACTION

Christians believe that Jesus came to earth to show people what the Kingdom of God is like. His words and actions, found in the Gospels, show his people how they should live and how they should treat others if they want to be part of his kingdom.

When he was on earth, Jesus cared for the sick, created food and calmed storms. He showed concern for all God's creations. Christians therefore believe that in order to live out the Gospel values, caring for the earth must be part of their lives.

WRITE THE ANSWER   Enquiry

Imagine God was writing a letter to his people on earth today.

Write what he would say to them about caring for the earth and why he wants them to be stewards of creation.

Pope Francis on Caring for the Earth

Pope Francis, as head of the Catholic Church, is one of the most influential leaders in today's world. In 2015, he wrote an encyclical on climate change called 'Laudato Si'. The title means 'Praise Be to You' and in it, he writes under the heading, 'On care for our common home'. It is the first official document in the history of the Catholic Church to confront the issue of caring for the environment.

We can see how Christians should view care of the earth in Chapter 2 of the encyclical when he writes, 'The creation accounts ... suggest that human life is grounded in three fundamental and closely intertwined relationships: with God, with our neighbour and with the earth itself.' What he is saying is that Christians cannot care for people without caring for the earth, as people are dependent on the earth.

He has also said, 'Nurturing and cherishing creation is a command God gives not only at the beginning of history, but to each of us. It is part of his plan; it means causing the world to grow responsibly, transforming it so that it may be a garden, a habitable place for everyone.'

LITERACY LIBRARY

Influential:
To have a great impact on someone or something.

Encyclical:
A letter sent by the pope to all the bishops in the Catholic Church.

Fundamental:
Basic; of great importance.

Intertwined:
Two things that are closely connected.

Dependent:
Needing the support of something in order to continue.

Habitable:
Suitable or good enough to live in.

GROUP ACTIVITY: RESEARCH Exploration

In groups, research what Pope Francis has said and done in relation to caring for the earth.

Report your findings to the rest of the class using a poster or a PowerPoint presentation.

Care for the Earth and Wellbeing of People

A child does her homework in a dump in Kathmandu in Nepal.

It is the world's poorest people who are most likely to suffer from environmental destruction.

LITERACY LIBRARY

Vulnerable:
Something that can be easily harmed.

THINK, PAIR, SHARE

Think about the statement to the left.

Write down how and why you think it is true to say that those living in poverty are more likely to be affected by environmental issues.

Discuss your thoughts in **pairs**. **Share** your ideas with the rest of the class.

One-quarter of the world's population lives in poverty. These people are the most vulnerable to changes caused by drought or flooding, to the failure of crops or to rising sea levels.

The way people in the richer parts of the world live can have terrible effects on the people who are already struggling to survive. Our decision to drive a big car, to fly to faraway places for short periods of time or to waste heating fuels can have a direct impact on someone who is living on the other side of the world. Environmental damage can prevent people, especially the poor, from having good and hygienic living standards.

Poor people often rely more directly on the environment than the rich for their survival, so they are more likely to be affected by environmental problems. Often, people living in these poorer parts of the world are uneducated about the harm they may be doing to the earth by cutting down trees for fuel or polluting water while using it in a harmful way just to stay alive.

The reality is that the world's resources are allocated to meet a few people's wants, not everyone's needs. Politicians and businesses often concentrate on creating wealth and growing economies in ways that ignore humanity and the environment. When money talks, the poor often have no voice. Humans have a responsibility not only to each other, but to the environment as well. Remember, the environment has sustained us for a long time but can only continue to do so if we don't destroy it.

LITERACY LIBRARY

Allocate:
To give something to someone as their share.

Sustain:
Provide conditions in which something can exist.

Eradication:
Destroyed completely.

Millennium Development Goals and the Environment

The Millennium Development Goals, now called the Sustainable Development Goals (SDGs), were created in 2015 by the United Nations. They cover issues such as the eradication of poverty, environmental protection, human rights and protection of the vulnerable.

A community meeting in the Republic of Guinea-Bissau.

CARING FOR THE EARTH

28

The aim of these goals is for developed countries to help those living in poorer parts of the world. They show once again that care for the earth and the wellbeing of all people cannot be separated.

Millennium Development Goal	Link to the Environment
1 Eradicate extreme poverty and hunger	The livelihoods and food security strategies of the poor often directly depend on the natural resources available to them (farming, fishing, etc.).
2 Achieve universal primary education	As resources become depleted, children spend more time gathering firewood and water or looking for grazing for the family livestock, meaning they have less time for school.
3 Promote gender equality and empower women	Poor women are susceptible to respiratory diseases caused by indoor air pollution. They tend to have unequal access to land and natural resources even though they are often responsible for collecting firewood and water and for tending fields.
4 Reduce child mortality	Water-related diseases affect children under the age of five in particular. Children are also susceptible to malnutrition as yields decline due to soil degradation and erosion.
5 Improve maternal health	Indoor pollution and carrying heavy loads of water and firewood over increasingly long distances have adverse effects on women's health and can lead to complications in pregnancy and childbirth.
6 Combat major diseases	One-fifth of the total disease burden in developing countries may be attributed to environmental risk. Poor urban planning and land management contribute to the spread of malaria. Declining natural resources force people to migrate and find new ways of earning a living, which can also contribute to the spread of HIV/AIDS.
7 Ensure environmental sustainability	Unless the current trends in environmental degradation and global threats such as climate change are reversed, it will not be possible to meet the Millennium Development Goals.

Do you think that, as a country, Ireland does enough to care for the earth?

Source: Irish Aid, Environment and Poverty Reduction (www.irishaid.gov.ie).

Gender:
Male or female.

Susceptible:
Likely to be influenced or affected by something.

Respiratory:
Breathing.

Malnutrition:
Poor diet or lack of food.

Degradation:
The beauty or quality of something is destroyed.

Maternal:
A mother during pregnancy or after childbirth.

Adverse:
Having a harmful effect on someone.

Attributed:
Caused by.

Sustainability:
The ability to be maintained at a certain level.

CLASS DISCUSSION　　　　Reflection and Action

Read the statements below. Discuss your opinion on them as a class. Could the Christian view of care for the earth help to address them?

'Approximately 1 billion people in the world suffer from hunger, while 1.2 billion suffer from obesity.'

'Just a few hundred millionaires now own as much wealth as the world's poorest 2.5 billion people.'

'If the developing world were to develop and consume in the same manner as the West to achieve the same living standards, we would need two additional planets to produce resources and absorb wastes.'

A woman in Tanzania harvests seaweed for soap, cosmetics and medicine.

CARING FOR THE EARTH

28

A Rocha – A Christian Environmental Group

INTERNATIONAL
ROCHA
Conservation and Hope

A Rocha is an international Christian organisation. Inspired by God's love, A Rocha carries out scientific research, environmental education and community-based conservation projects.

A Rocha began in Portugal in 1983. Its name means 'The Rock' in Portuguese. It can now be found in countries throughout Europe, Africa, the Middle East and North America. A Rocha's work includes running workshops, wildlife clubs, summer camps and education centres. In all the countries where they work, A Rocha is identified by five core commitments and to a practical outworking of each:

- Christian: Underlying all they do is their biblical faith in the living God, who made the world, loves it and entrusts it to the care of human society.

- Conservation: They carry out research for the conservation and restoration of the natural world and run environmental education programmes for people of all ages.

- Community: Through their commitment to God, each other and the wider creation, they aim to develop good relationships both within the A Rocha family and in their local communities.

- Cross-cultural: They draw on the insights and skills of people from diverse cultures, both locally and around the world.

- Co-operation: They work in partnership with a wide variety of organisations and individuals who share their concerns for a sustainable world.

LITERACY LIBRARY

Conservation:
Protection of plants, animals and natural areas from damage by humans.

GROUP ACTIVITY: RESEARCH

Enquiry

Divide the class into groups.

Go online to research the A Rocha organisation. Each group should pick a different project that A Rocha has been involved in that has shown care for the earth.

Explain in your project what A Rocha did and how it helped the earth.

Display your project on a poster or present it in a PowerPoint presentation.

REFLECTIVE ACTIVITY

Think about your own attitude to caring for the earth and answer the following questions:

1 Is care for the earth something that is important to you? Why/why not?

2 Will what you have learned in this chapter change how you live your life in any way? Explain your answer.

3 What was the most interesting thing you learned in this chapter?

4 Do you think the Christian understanding of care for the earth is a good one for people to have? Why/why not?

 PowerPoint summary

CARING FOR THE EARTH

28

CHAPTER 29
Synthesis: Informed Decision-making

SOL: 5, 11
LO: 3.9

LEARNING OUTCOME

Synthesise and consider the insights gained about the norms, values and principles that inform decision-making and actions in the lives of people.

KEY SKILLS YOU WILL USE IN THIS CHAPTER

- Staying well
- Managing myself
- Working with others
- Being creative
- Communicating
- Managing information and thinking

WELLBEING INDICATORS IN THIS CHAPTER

LEARNING INTENTIONS

At the end of this chapter, I will

1 Understand how people make decisions
2 Understand the importance of human life
3 Know the arguments put forward for and against abortion
4 Be able to tell the story of Savita Halappanaver.

Making Decisions

People make decisions all the time. Some of the decisions we make, for example what to eat for our lunch or what to wear to the shops at the weekend, are not very important.

Other decisions, such as what subjects we plan to study for our Leaving Certificate, *are* important, as they can have an influence on what we would like to do in the future.

We therefore need to put more thought into these types of decisions. We need to **stop and think** more carefully about what is best for us in the long term. It is only when we do this that we come to realise that decision-making is a complex or difficult thing to do.

Making Moral Decisions

Making moral decisions is an essential part of growing up and becoming morally mature. Some moral decisions require a lot of time and thought in order to make the right decision.

Making moral decisions can be described as a series of actions. When making a moral decision, we must consider all the sides of the decision, not just a part of it. If we look only at one part of the problem, we may not find the correct answer. As the saying goes, 'there are two sides to every story'.

There are also two parts to the moral decision-making process:

Part 1: Asking Questions	Part 2: Finding Answers
• What are my options or choices? • What might the consequences be for me? • Who will be affected by my decision? • How might they be affected by my decision?	• What does my conscience tell me? • What would my parents and friends think? • What does my religion tell me? • What does the law say about it?

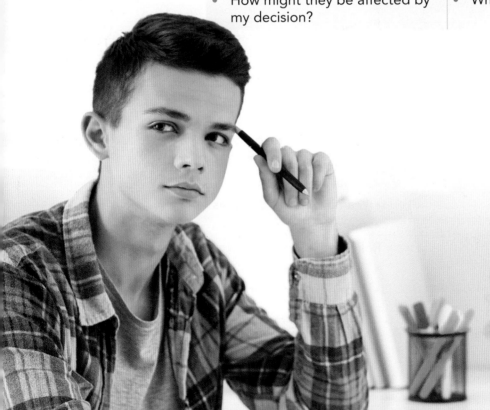

These are the questions we should ask ourselves before making any moral decisions. Some of the answers might be very clear to us, while others might take time to work through. Use the following example below to help you find the answer.

Leah: Decision-making

Fifteen-year-old Leah knew that her parents would not be happy with her new habit: smoking. It was costing her a lot of money, but that didn't worry or concern her. Everyone she knew smoked, it wasn't a big deal. The only problem was that her pocket money was never enough. On her way to school one morning she noticed her mam's purse open on the hall table. There was cash falling out of it, so she knew it wouldn't be missed.

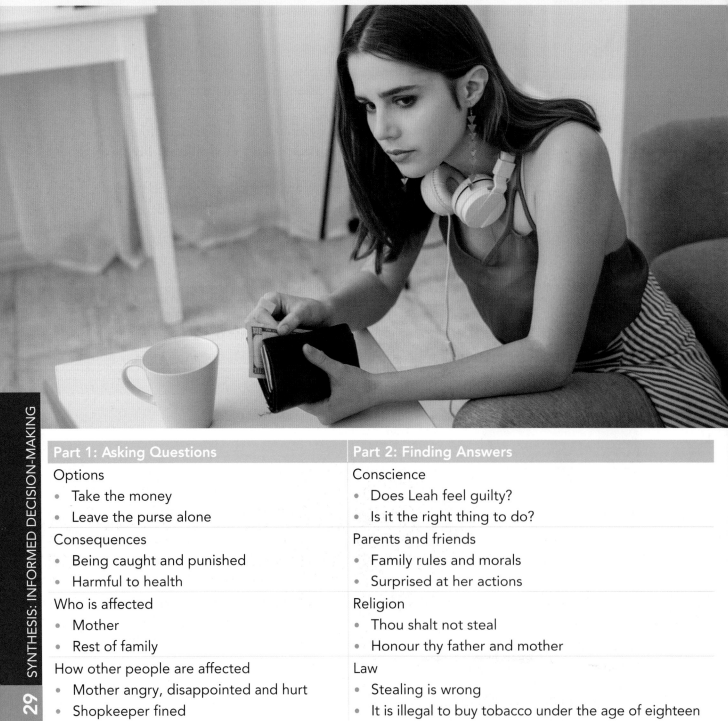

Part 1: Asking Questions	Part 2: Finding Answers
Options	Conscience
• Take the money	• Does Leah feel guilty?
• Leave the purse alone	• Is it the right thing to do?
Consequences	Parents and friends
• Being caught and punished	• Family rules and morals
• Harmful to health	• Surprised at her actions
Who is affected	Religion
• Mother	• Thou shalt not steal
• Rest of family	• Honour thy father and mother
How other people are affected	Law
• Mother angry, disappointed and hurt	• Stealing is wrong
• Shopkeeper fined	• It is illegal to buy tobacco under the age of eighteen

In small groups, apply the decision-making process to the following examples.

- Sean wants the new iPhone XS Max and sees it on the bench in the changing room of the gym he goes to. No one is around.
- Ellie's friends are drinking before the disco at the weekend. She could try to buy some alcohol at the local off-licence.
- Peter is sitting his Leaving Cert French exam. He does not know the answer to one of the questions, but he can see his friend's paper beside him.

Respect for All Life

All human life is precious and therefore should be treated with care and respect. The five major world religions teach that all human life is sacred or holy. Jews and Christians believe this because life is a gift from God. Therefore, it should be cherished and kept holy.

All human life should be treated with respect. The word 'respect' means 'having high regard for something'. Religions teach that God has a high regard for each of us. We are all made in the image and likeness of God. We are special and unique to Him. God see the value and sacredness in us all.

WRITE THE ANSWERS   Enquiry

1 Think about the people in your life who show you respect. Who are they? How do they show you respect? Give some examples.

2 Think about the people in your life who you show respect to. Give some examples of ways you show respect towards them.

3 Think of a time when someone did not show you respect. How did that make you feel? What did you learn from that situation that could make things different in the future?

All living creatures should be treated with respect. Read the short piece below about the story of two puppies who had a hard start in life.

Geraldine Gunning with Sugar and Spice.

In early 2019, the *Limerick Post* reported that two puppies had been rescued after they were found caged in a bucket and dumped in a ditch in Limerick. A woman out walking found them trapped in the bucket.

They have been called Sugar and Spice by the staff at Limerick Animal Welfare and are now recovering from their ordeal.

Treating an animal like this is not showing respect for life.

A Moral Dilemma Today: Abortion

An abortion is a procedure to end a pregnancy by removing the foetus, or unborn child, from the womb. This procedure is carried out by medical staff who use surgery or drugs to remove the foetus from the mother's womb. Abortions are legally carried out in many countries, for example Ireland and England.

In England, a foetus can be legally aborted up to the twenty-fourth week of pregnancy under certain conditions.

The big question for many when discussing abortion is: **when does life begin**? Some people believe that life begins from the moment of conception, when a separate human life begins to grow inside the woman's body. Some people believe that ending a pregnancy deliberately at this stage means causing the death of another human being.

Others believe that human life does not begin at this stage and in fact does not begin until the baby is outside the woman's body. They believe that the baby is part of the woman's body and she therefore has the right to decide what is best to do with her own body.

Although abortion may be legal in many countries, most religions teach that abortion is morally wrong.

Ireland, May 2018

On 25 May 2018, Ireland voted decisively in a referendum to reform the country's strict abortion laws, which had effectively banned all terminations. This was Ireland's sixth referendum on the issue. This referendum was based around the Eighth Amendment, which stated that 'the state acknowledges the right to life of the unborn and, with due regards to the equal right to life of the mother, guarantees in its law to respect and, as far as practicable, by its laws to defend and vindicate that right'. This amendment had been added to the Constitution in 1983 and as it gave equal rights to the foetus and the mother, abortion was effectively banned.

This was brought much into the public domain when a 31-year-old Indian woman, Savita Halappanaver, died at University Hospital Galway on 22 October 2012. She was seventeen weeks pregnant. Savita requested an abortion when it became clear that a miscarriage was inevitable. An abortion was denied to her, as the medical team did not think her life was in danger. Sepsis was then diagnosed and the doctors began to treat it, but it continued to spread, which caused a cardiac arrest and Savita's death.

Her death caused a lot of upset and controversy at the time, both nationally and internationally, which led to protests and marches against the Eighth Amendment.

The country's voters voted in favour of ending the ban on abortion. Turnout on the day was 64.51%. Of that, 66.4% voted yes and 33.6% voted no. Before the referendum day there was much debate on television, radio and online about this issue.

Taoiseach Leo Varadkar said, 'What we have seen today really is a culmination of a quiet revolution that's been taking place in Ireland for the past ten or twenty years'.

LITERACY LIBRARY

Sepsis:
When toxins spread through the body due to infection. It is a life-threatening condition.

Moral Decision-making

Think back to what we discussed earlier about moral decision-making. Making moral decisions is an essential part of growing up and becoming morally mature. Some moral decisions require a lot of time and thought in order to make the right decision. Deciding whether or not to have an abortion is probably one the most difficult decisions a person may make in their lifetime.

Remember that making a moral decision can be described as a series of actions. When making a moral decision, we must consider all the sides of the decision, not just one part of it. If we look only at one part of the problem, we may not find the correct answer.

Arguments Put Forward for Abortion

1 Every woman should be able to make her own decisions on what happens to her body.

2 If there is a high risk that the baby will be born with a fatal foetal abnormality, the woman should be allowed to decide what is best for her and should not have to travel outside her own country to receive care.

3 If a woman or young girl becomes pregnant through rape or incest, abortion may be a way of helping her through the aftermath of the ordeal.

4 Every baby that is born should be wanted by the family. No woman should be forced to carry an unwanted pregnancy.

CLASS DISCUSSION   Exploration

1 What do you think of the arguments put forward for abortion?
2 Do you think that they are fair and just arguments? Why/why not?
3 Can you think of any other arguments for abortion?

Arguments Put Forward against Abortion

1 Every foetus or baby in the early stages of life has the right to life. This is a separate human being growing inside the woman's body.

2 If a woman or young girl has been raped and a pregnancy results, she needs a lot of support around her. The foetus is still a human being. This foetus has done nothing wrong. This life is sacred and must always be protected.

3 Children are always seen as a gift from God and therefore should be treated as a blessing, never as a burden. Adoption can be an option for someone who cannot have children.

4 Doctors will always try to save the lives of both the mother and baby if complications were to occur during the pregnancy.

CLASS DISCUSSION   Exploration

1 What do you think of the arguments put forward against abortion?

2 Do you think that they are fair and just arguments? Why/why not?

3 Can you think of any other arguments you would make against abortion?

SYNTHESIS: INFORMED DECISION-MAKING

29

Dr Diarmuid Martin,
Catholic Archbishop of Dublin.

The Catholic Church

The Catholic Archbishop of Dublin, Dr Diarmuid Martin, expressed surprise at the outcome of the referendum in May 2018. He restated that his Church cannot compromise on its disapproval or opposition to abortion.

Dr Martin said that compassion is a Christian idea and that the Catholic Church must show, in the way it lives and witnesses to the Gospel, that it sincerely is compassionate. 'We have to speak with compassion even if what we speak is not acceptable' he said. He also said that he hoped, along with other bishops and the wider Church organisation, to be able to 'rebuild an image of what the church is, a reflection of the compassion of Jesus Christ'.

Catholics base their views on firm Christian teachings:

- 'So, God created mankind in his own image, in the image of God he created them; male and female he created them.' (*New International Version*, Genesis 1:27)

- Human life begins now at conception. All life must be protected from here onwards. (*Gaudium et Spes*, 1965, Document from the Second Vatican Council)

WRITE THE ANSWERS   Enquiry

1 What do you think of what Dr Diarmuid Martin said about abortion?

2 What do you think he meant when he said he wants to 'rebuild an image of what the church is, a reflection of the compassion of Jesus Christ'?

3 In small groups, look up *Gaudium et Spes*. What other interesting points does it make?

4 Do you believe this document is as relevant to society today as it was when it was written in 1965? Why/why not?

Pope John XXII on his throne in St Peter's Square in Rome during the Second Vatican Council, 1962.

Judaism and Abortion

The Jewish religion teaches that all life is blessed, as it comes from God. Every new life is a gift from God. The Talmud, the Jewish sacred text, contains significant and vital Jewish teachings on moral issues.

The Talmud states that the foetus is not a human being until it reaches the forty-first day of pregnancy. This is the day that God plants the soul in the human body.

Abortion is legal in the Jewish state of Israel. Some rabbis say that abortion is allowed in some circumstances, for example if the mother's life is at risk while pregnant or if the woman has been raped.

How to Make a Moral Decision

Deciding whether or not to have an abortion is a difficult decision for anyone to make. This decision can have an impact on a person's life for ever more. There may be feelings of guilt, anger and worry. There may be constant reminders when birthdays, anniversaries or family functions occur.

Before a decision like this is made, it is important to:

- **Stop and think** about the decision that you must make. You may be making this decision alone and therefore feel isolated in the process.
- **Think about the facts** that are before you.
- What are your **circumstances**?
- Look at all your **options.** What other choices do you have other than abortion?
- What will be the **effects** on you, those around you and the baby in the womb?
- Although you may be alone, it is important to **seek advice**. Professionals are there to help and support you.
- Think about your **religious values**. What does your **Church** say about the issue?
- When you have really thought everything through, make your decision, as it will now be an **informed decision**.

 PowerPoint summary

 Weblinks

REFLECTIVE ACTIVITY

Think about your own attitude to what helps you make a moral decision, then answer the following questions:

1 What did you like learning about in this chapter?
2 Is it important to have all the information before making a moral decision? Why/why not?

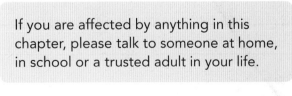

If you are affected by anything in this chapter, please talk to someone at home, in school or a trusted adult in your life.

SYNTHESIS: INFORMED DECISION-MAKING

29

Notes

Notes

Notes

Notes

Notes

Notes

Notes

Photo credits